Homer's Hero

Homer's Hero

Human Excellence in the *Iliad* and the *Odyssey*

Michelle M. Kundmueller

SUNY
PRESS

Cover art: iStock by Getty Images.

Published by State University of New York Press, Albany

© 2019 State University of New York

All rights reserved

No part of this book may be used or reproduced in any manner whatsoever without written permission. No part of this book may be stored in a retrieval system or transmitted in any form or by any means including electronic, electrostatic, magnetic tape, mechanical, photocopying, recording, or otherwise without the prior permission in writing of the publisher.

For information, contact State University of New York Press, Albany, NY
www.sunypress.edu

Library of Congress Cataloging-in-Publication Data

Names: Kundmueller, Michelle M., author.
Title: Homer's hero : human excellence in the Iliad and the Odyssey / Michelle M. Kundmueller.
Description: Albany : State University of New York Press, 2019. | Includes bibliographical references and index.
Identifiers: LCCN 2018056832 | ISBN 9781438476674 (hardcover : alk. paper) | ISBN 9781438476667 (pbk. : alk. paper) | ISBN 9781438476681 (ebook)
Subjects: LCSH: Heroes in literature. | Homer—Characters. | Homer—Criticism and interpretation.
Classification: LCC PA4037 .K83 2019 | DDC 883/.01—dc23
LC record available at https://lccn.loc.gov/2018056832

10 9 8 7 6 5 4 3 2 1

Contents

Acknowledgments — vii

Introduction: Human Excellence in Homer — 1

Part I The *Iliad*

1 Homer's Honor-Loving Heroes: Ajax and Agamemnon — 25

2 Homer's Love-Torn Heroes: Achilles and Hektor — 49

3 Homer's Pausing Hero: Odysseus at Troy — 71

Part II The *Odyssey*

4 A Hero's Story — 99

5 Remembering Home — 117

6 At the Heart of Homecoming — 133

7 The Meaning of Homecoming — 157

Conclusion: Homer's Hero — 179

Notes — 199

Bibliography — 245

Index — 255

Acknowledgments

I have neither oar nor winnowing fan to carry. My remaining labors are far more pleasant: I offer thanks to the institutions and individuals who have made my intellectual journey possible.

Many institutions have supported this book. I commenced writing it at the University of Notre Dame, eventually continuing there with the support of a postdoctoral fellowship made possible by the Jack Miller Center. I completed it at Christopher Newport University with the support of the Center for American Studies. The Intercollegiate Studies Institute supported the project during its early years, the Mercatus Center at George Mason University and the John Templeton Foundation have supported final revisions and document preparation, and the Charles Koch Foundation made possible the research assistance of several eager undergraduates. The Institute for Humane Studies, from start to finish, has provided financial assistance for which I thank it and its donors.

The book has benefited from the care and diligence of many. Thanks are due to Aimee Anderson for the correction of many an error, the clarification of many an ambiguity, and the coherence of cross-references throughout; her friendship and enthusiasm—from my days as a summer associate to the final revisions of the manuscript—have stiffened my backbone on many a difficult day. Sarah Hopkins's careful diligence ensured Homeric accuracy. Lili Samios's eye for argument (and willingness to trudge to and from the library) extended the scholarly reach. Brandon Hubbard's patience and ear aided in revisions, ensuring that the final reiterations focused the argument.

I must also thank two blind reviewers who strengthened my book. The depth of reference in classics, in particular, was largely gifted to me by a blind reviewer who took extensive pains to direct me down avenues of research of which I was unaware. A second reviewer, while offering enthusiastic support, provided many a thoughtful correction and—more importantly—solved an issue of organization with which I had grappled without success. My heartfelt thanks are extended to both of these anonymous reviewers.

From a broader perspective, the adventures that made this book possible had been given to me before my memory commences by those who shared and passed on their love of the great books. The example has ever been before me of reading as an adventure from which wealth could be won without strife. My mother and father ensured that my childhood bookshelves were overflowing with treasures destined to make reading Homer a kind of homecoming.

My peers, particularly Ashleen Menchaca-Bagnulo, Veronica Roberts Ogle, and Nathan Sawatzky, sharpened my wits with many a grand debate and served—in a manner of speaking—as prophets assuring me that eventually this project would reach this happy stage. They added greatly to the joys of the adventure. To the professors who have—at every stage of my education—torn themselves from their own labors to help me with mine, thank you. Arthur Vanden Houten, Mary Keys, and David O'Connor each contributed to my thoughts about virtue, love, and Homer in meaningful and generous ways. Michael Zuckert's playful and insightful suggestions, including the comment that I might want to read Hannah Arendt's *The Human Condition*, have kept me connected to the world after ancient Greece in productive ways.

My debt to Catherine Zuckert is deep. I am grateful for classes on Plato, conversations about Homer and manuscript organization, careful readings, and strategic advice. Catherine's gift for simultaneously communicating correction and encouragement always served as a catalyst for deeper thought and better writing. As a teacher, writer, and mentor, Catherine inspires my best efforts to be courageous, moderate, and wise.

As is customary for good reason (for custom and reason may point to the same conclusion), I save the last and deepest thanks for spouse and children. I pray that my three children look back on this experience with knowledge of their mother's gratitude and a sense of having gained—not lost—from our joint adventure. To my husband, Mark: my hope is that all our labors may be shared, so that our greatest affinity to Odysseus and Penelope may be that echo of their epic longing that is felt by all loving spouses, the desire for daily reunion.

Introduction

Human Excellence in Homer

There are many questions about politics that Homer does not answer. At the end of his epics, he has not set forth a comprehensive theory of justice, nor does he purport to have offered a satisfactory basis for justice. Life, liberty, and property are not buried within his stories; much less are positive human rights hiding in plain sight at the origins of Western civilization. Nonetheless, Homer continues to resonate with readers and to elicit scholarly study. Although he provides no blueprint for politics, justice, or rights, his epics continue to captivate our imaginations and enrich our knowledge of the human experience because he offers us an enduring portrait of human excellence that is no less instructive than it is beautiful.

To understand the portrait of human excellence found in the *Iliad* and the *Odyssey* requires reading each epic in light of the other. Through the heroes, who differ from one another in both degree and kind of excellence, Homer provides a portrait of different kinds, degrees, and mixtures of excellence. But over the course of his epics—through the development of individual heroes and through their interactions with one another—his narrative reveals how different human desires cause the growth of some virtues and undermine others. He thus provides exemplars of the quality of human excellence and through his narratives illustrates why individuals differ in their degrees and kinds of virtue. Homer's account of human virtue, embedded as it is within epic stories of war and of homecoming, ultimately reveals the consequences of desire and excellence for happiness and for the prospects for a stable, just politics. Rather than a plan for a satisfactory polis, Homer offers an illustration of two divergent paths toward human happiness and politics.

In his poetic narrative Homer illustrates how two distinct desires—the desire for public honor and the desire to preserve and be with that which is one's own—result in differing sets of virtues. As the brilliant battlefield exploits of the *Iliad* show, love of public honor—or glory—produces courage but is also associated with failures in both moderation and intellect. Homer juxtaposes the passionate pursuit of honor with the preference for that which is one's own—survival and physical comforts but also family, intimate friends, and the private household. As the *Iliad* hints and the *Odyssey* confirms, devotion to that which is one's own produces courage but also nurtures intelligence and moderation. Moderation and intelligence prove to be prerequisites to the restraint of one's impulses, to deliberate choice, and to the use of speech rather than violence to resolve conflict. From the outset of the *Iliad*, the Achaian hero least likely to rush forward in pursuit of glory proves preeminent in moderation and intelligence. By the end of the *Odyssey*, having overcome his intermittent love of glory and learned to be more wary of threats to his self-restraint, Odysseus emerges as a man who demonstrably prefers that which is his own—his own wife, family, home, dog, and even his own bed. Through the virtue that they exhibit and the friendship that they maintain, Odysseus and Penelope ultimately emerge as Homer's highest and best—if flawed—heroes.

The desires of Homer's heroes and their corresponding excellence remain relevant because the loves and virtues at the heart of Homer's story remain central to the human experience. Homer's characters thereby retain their political salience, and his epics are rightfully the subject of more than mere literary or historic interest. Two of the reigning interpretations of human excellence in Homer, to the contrary, argue that disjunctions between Homeric culture and modern life preclude application of the hero's excellence to contemporary life.[1] The usual reading of heroic excellence, most famously articulated by Alasdair MacIntyre's *After Virtue*, collapses the hero's social role and his virtue.[2] Within this reading Homeric virtue equates to success in a culturally and historically specific social role.[3] Hence, for example, the warrior-king's virtue depends on his success as warrior-king.[4] Because the king holds the social role most useful to the society as a whole, the qualities of a successful warrior-king—physical prowess, courage, and intelligence—are the highest virtues.[5] In this account any hero's virtue is synonymous with the successful performance of social function, whether the hero be king, warrior, wife, or slave. But if successful completion of one's specific social role amounts to nothing less than human excellence within Homer's epics, then the excellence of his heroes died with their culture—before even the Attic Greeks came to admire and emulate them. By this account Achilles, Odysseus, and even Penelope display virtue, but they cannot speak to modern choices, help us to understand the excellence possible within modern life, or illuminate contemporary relationships between desire and politics.

Another of the twentieth century's most influential interpretations of heroic culture, put forth by Hannah Arendt in *The Human Condition*, has also concluded that a rift in understanding between ancient Greek and modern understanding prevents contemporary access to the excellence of Homer's heroes.[6] Arendt argues that moderns have lost any conception of the true character of politics and public action and thereby lost the ability to understand the meaning of ancient Greek excellence. Both Arendt and MacIntyre argue that the excellence of Homeric heroes has no bearing on contemporary life, and MacIntyre effectively relegates Homer to history. Arendt urges instead that Homer offers us something exemplary that we should—but do not—aspire to emulate. Unlike MacIntyre, she bemoans the loss of Homeric excellence, and she urges us to adopt her understanding of it as our own vision of human excellence.

Contending that Homeric excellence remains admirable, Arendt argues that our changed understanding of politics—or rather, our loss of the political in exchange for the social—has cut us off from the opportunity to exhibit the excellence of the Homeric heroes. Arendt paints in vivid colors a world in which pursuit of public honor is esteemed as the exclusive path to human excellence and private life is altogether contemptible. The result of this reading of the ancient Greeks is twofold: she dismisses more than half the excellence in Homer—the excellence linked to private life—and simultaneously contends that the remaining excellence of the ancient Greek world is all but unobtainable to modern readers. The details in her brilliant landscape of the honor-loving polis are harsh indeed, but they thereby reveal what is ultimately at stake in the debate over the cause, content, and consequences of human excellence—the meaning of human life. Because she argues that we ought to import her understanding of Homeric excellence into our own lives and politics, Arendt's misreading of Homer is more dangerous than MacIntyre's and thus requires more extensive attention.

Arendt: Human Excellence in Public Pursuit of Honor

At the heart of Arendt's analysis lies a particular reading of Aristotle that she rapidly identifies with the sum total of ancient Greek thought. This reading results in a division of mankind, a portion of which Arendt claims the ancient Greeks denied consideration as human due to their confinement to private life. Arendt argues that private life and the labor taking place within the private sphere were not "considered to possess sufficient dignity to constitute a *bios* at all, an autonomous and authentically human life; since they served and produced what was necessary and useful, they could not be free, independent of human needs and wants."[7] Political—and therefore public—life offered the only route to individuality and excellence "due to the Greek understanding of *polis* life, which to them denoted a very special and freely chosen form of political organization and by no means just any form of action necessary to keep men together in an orderly fashion."[8]

According to Arendt the ancient Greeks believed that the distinction between a private life dominated by labor and a public, political life corresponded to the distinction between the purely animal and the divine aspects of the human condition. In their political and public aspect human beings joined the ranks of the gods: "By their capacity for the immortal deed, by their ability to leave non-perishable traces behind, men, their individual mortality notwithstanding, attain an immortality of their own and prove themselves to be of a 'divine' nature."[9] But human beings teeter between the world of gods and the world of animals, Arendt asserts: only the godlike portion—thus denoted by winning a perpetuation of the memory of their names and deeds that extends beyond animal existence—deserves the title of human. By this logic only those who perform in the public arena can possess *human* excellence. Thus, Arendt claims that "only the best (*aristoi*), who constantly prove themselves to be the best (*aristeuein*) . . . and who 'prefer immortal fame to mortal things,' are really human."[10]

The godlike, human side of existence occurs in public where honor can be won, but the animal side is hidden in a private life that is neither human nor, therefore, capable of human excellence. Arendt contends that the ancient Greeks viewed the "natural, merely social companionship of the human species" that takes place in private as "a limitation imposed by the needs of biological life, which are the same for the human animal as for other forms of life."[11] Any aspect of existence common to human and animal life, including the perpetuation of the species, care for the body, and domestic relationships, for the very reason of that commonality with animal life, "could not be fundamentally human."[12] Hence, everything that ties people firmly to their families and is often hidden in the *oikos*, or household, is subhuman. Body, children, marriage, family, home, household, and the entire domestic sphere cannot be worthy objects of love. Drawing on the *Odyssey*, Arendt quotes Odysseus's slave Eumaios, who states that a man loses half his virtue on the day of his enslavement, as evidence that "a slave lost excellence because he lost admission to the public realm where excellence can show."[13]

Ultimately, private life is futile. Lacking the conditions for both excellence and permanence, there is nothing within the household that is worthy of love. That which remains private, however difficult, can be neither heroic nor worthy of praise or love: "The daily fight in which the human body is engaged to keep the world clean and prevent its decay bears little resemblance to heroic deeds; the endurance it needs to repair every day anew the waste of yesterday is not courage, and what makes the effort painful is not danger but its relentless repetition."[14] The promise of family and fertility, of children, and of one's children's children dooms human beings to existence without permanence. Indeed, as Arendt describes private life, the best that can be hoped for within it is escape from pain, and true escape is only possible by abandoning this subhuman existence for the sake of action in the public and therefore potentially permanent stage of humanity.[15]

However one chooses to denote that which is one's own and the private realm that surrounds it, by Arendt's account only a dog, a fool, or a madman could bear any love for it. This bifurcation of life between public and private results, of course, in the banishment of slaves and women not only from all political consequence but also from excellence, individuality, and humanity.[16] There is no avenue for satisfying the love of honor in private because it has by definition no witness, no reality, no action, and hence no memory. In the end, the private realm functions to hide from view "the biological life processes of the family" and to permit men to emerge into public reality.[17]

Arendt distinguishes a public, political realm of action in contrast to the private, necessary realm of labor.[18] This distinction correlates with the distinction "between what is one's own (*idion*) and what is common (*koinon*)."[19] Within the common realm exist the "action" and "speech" that by definition are only possible in public, political life.[20] Within the realm of the subhuman, "labor" exists in the private, necessary life.[21] The polis, she argues, was ruled with persuasive speech, but the household was ruled despotically with raw power and thus was antithetical to politics.[22] Private life enslaved men and women in the domestic labors necessary for survival.[23] But public life, which by definition could not be entered because of the demands of necessity, was associated with courage because embarking on "glorious enterprise and later simply to devote one's life to the affairs of the city" required the willingness to risk one's life.[24] Courage became the "political virtue par excellence," and those men admitted to the public fellowship with which it was associated thereby transcended into a world where action, speech, excellence, and even godlike immortality made possible by the memory of one's action constituted the human experience.[25]

The risks inherent in politics were worth the gamble to the ancient Greeks because they made space for "individuality" and provided "the only place where men could show who they really and inexchangeably were."[26] According to Arendt, showing oneself in comparison to others permits the individuality requisite for human excellence and is likewise a necessary condition of human "action."[27] Action requires public viewing because it is linked to the possibility of being remembered past the lifespan of an individual man. The public view that permits memory explains the link between the public, political life that Arendt describes and the love of honor: "It is the publicity of the public realm which can absorb and make shine through the centuries whatever men may want to save from the natural ruin of time."[28] According to Arendt, what human beings want to save from natural ruin is the memory of the names and actions with which they are associated. The love of honor—of the glory given one's name by peers in the public sphere—is the desire for a degree of immortality or permanence.[29]

Through word and deed human beings express their individuality in the sight of other humans on the public stage and hence qualify in the competition for a place in memory that will outlive their biological selves. Speech in particular, Arendt argues, has a special association with the public realm in which individuality, humanity, and excellence become possible.[30] Through speech and action individuals driven by their love of honor "reveal" themselves to one another.[31] The result can be immortality because this can produce stories that will be preserved.[32] When heroes step into the public arena, they step into the story in which they have earned a place by virtue of their courage.

Ultimately, only public view can translate—through speech—into story, which for Arendt is linked to the fulfillment of love of honor. Thus the existence of the public sphere is not just important because it excludes the household and domestic matters: a person who is alone and a person surrounded by family are both equally "isolated" because they are equally excluded from view, excellence, and memory.[33] No story, she argues, is possible for either one. "Human essence," she explains, "can come into being only when life departs, leaving behind nothing but a story."[34] The paradigmatic example of the fulfillment of love of honor and embodiment of human essence is Achilles. In conjunction with Achilles's life and story, his death ensures that his continued animal existence cannot undermine the excellence of his death and therefore the meaning of his life.

However human and brilliant, Achilles cannot emerge independently. He is dependent on those who share his public arena and on Homer for the fulfillment of the meaning of his life and death.[35] Achilles's passion for honor and the resulting story give rise to politics but only because those who followed him, according to Arendt, were not content with Achilles's dependence on the poet. They sought a different vehicle for immortality: "the *polis* was supposed to multiply the occasions to win 'immortal fame.'"[36] Love of honor thus resulted in politics and ultimately freed men from dependence upon the poet for the memory of their excellence. Despite the development of the polis, Achilles remained the "paradigmatic" case of human excellence for ancient Greeks. Achilles "became the prototype of action for Greek antiquity and influential in the form of the so-called agonal spirit, the passionate drive to show one's self in measuring up against others that underlies the concept of politics prevalent in the city-states."[37]

Arendt argues that modern human beings have lost the desire to emulate Achilles's excellence and, no longer desiring public honor, do not partake in significant public lives. Hence, Arendt describes what she perceives as the "disappearance of the gulf that ancients had to cross daily to transcend the narrow realm of the household and 'rise' into the realm of politics."[38] Especially since it is contrary to contemporary ways of considering the choice of how to devote one's life, it is necessary to underscore that Arendt is arguing for a distinction between types of lives that are not only mutually exclusive but also have incommensurate values. More than a matter of individual taste, capacity, or even (as the United States Supreme Court might describe such a choice) personal pursuit of happiness, the distinction between public and private life distinguishes human from animal and excellence from subservience. As Arendt describes it, the courageous, political life was "'good' to the extent that by having mastered the necessities of sheer life, by being freed from labor and work, by overcoming the innate urge of all living creatures for their own survival, it was no longer bound to the biological life processes."[39] Politics thus understood does not serve mere survival or private life. Rather, the domestic, private world of caring for and perpetuating individual and family life exists to make the excellence of politics possible.[40]

The difficulty of understanding the dichotomy thus embedded in ancient Greek thought is further heightened by subsequent developments in the perception of the value of private life.[41] We cannot grasp the full idiocy of private life to ancient Greeks, Arendt argues, because our lives are spent in *social* rather than *political* venues: "The decisive historical fact is that modern privacy in its most relevant function, to shelter the intimate, was discovered as the opposite not of the political sphere but of the social, to which it is therefore more closely and authentically related."[42] Arendt links Rousseau's "discovery"—as she terms it—of intimacy (and the social world from which intimacy needs protection) to the rise of the novel and the decline of "public art."[43] "Society" has transformed politics into a large household.[44] According to Arendt, moderns live in a world in which society and the retreat from society into our intimate lives precludes the "possibility of action, which formerly was excluded from the household."[45]

This dramatic shift in the estimation of private life, coupled with an understanding of public life as the exclusive realm of human action, individuality, and excellence, bar the modern approach to ancient Greece and Homer. Arendt describes an ancient Greece in which human beings relied on private life for survival but could not praise either desire for private life or private life itself. No being could conceive of behavior hidden in the home or occurring alone as human, let alone excellent. By her account, the private realm was subhuman, incompatible with excellence, and valuable only insofar as it remained necessary to enable the fathers and sons of households to emerge into the public and political world where honor could be won. Whether taking place at home caring for one's family or alone striving for survival, the private life was worthy of neither human desire nor individual account because it altogether failed to register as human or individual.

Arendt is not the first or the only influential political philosopher to focus on the political significance of the distinction between the private and the public, although many contemporary scholars point instead to the advent of liberalism as the source of this bifurcation.[46] Even if the distinction between public and private is not novel, however, Arendt's claim that the private is *subhuman* remains startling. Some have argued that her conclusions about ancient Greece rest on a distortion of history and historical theory.[47] Salkever and Swanson have both contributed detailed readings of Aristotle demonstrating the existence of private humanity, excellence, and friendship within his texts.[48] Notwithstanding these critiques of Arendt's portrait of ancient Greece, her conclusions continue to carry significant weight. Perhaps this is because, as Salkever seems to concede, scholars refuting Arendt's position have often portrayed their own arguments as merely underscoring a minority view in opposition to Arendt's otherwise accurate claims about the ancient Greek perspective.[49]

Whatever the reason, the sharpness of her distinction has remained attractive, with consequences for policy debate and study of ancient texts. In scholarly policy debate, Arendt's conclusions about the requisite nature of public life for human life and excellence have provided a standard by which to make normative arguments for contemporary policy.[50] In scholarship on the ancient world, Arendt's definitions are reimported as analytical tools for the study of the very texts in which she grounded their meaning and consequences. Particularly clear examples have occurred in the debate over whether Homer's epics occur in a "prepolitical" period. For example, relying on Arendt's framework, Hammer finds politics in Homer insofar as decisions and relationships conducted in public space take a prominent place in the *Iliad*.[51] This approach is circular, adjudicating the existence of Homeric politics based on a definition of politics derived—by Arendt—from her reading of Homer. The conclusions of Hammer and others who rely on Arendt for their analysis of ancient texts on the human condition are ultimately dependent on the accuracy of her underlying reading.

Socrates: Human Excellence in the Preference for Private Life

Taken as the sum total of ancient Greek thought about private life (give or take a philosopher or two), Arendt's conclusions obscure contemporary access to and application of all ancient Greek accounts of human excellence. She rejects the existence of ancient Greek private excellence and finds modern existence incapable—or all but incapable—of exhibiting public excellence. Indeed, finding esteem for private life altogether absent in the ancient Greeks, Arendt goes so far as to accuse Christianity of being the original source of the view that "everybody should mind his own business and that political responsibility constituted first of all a burden."[52]

Aside from Aristotle, Arendt overlooks at least one important, pre-Christian articulation of this viewpoint. On the very last page of Plato's *Republic*, at the conclusion of a work that has gone to great lengths to describe and praise a life devoid of all private attachment for the guardians of the best city in speech, Socrates concludes by praising the preference for private life over the pursuit of honor. Within his Myth of Er, Socrates describes the process by which souls of the deceased choose their next lives. Among the souls described, Odysseus appears to make the best choice. Facing an overwhelming range of possibilities and having recovered "from memory of its former labors" from "the love of honor," Odysseus's soul "went around for a long time looking for the life of a private man who minds his own business."[53] Once he finds and chooses this life, Odysseus expresses pleasure at his choice: could he have had any life he wished, the life of a private man who minds his own business is the one he would most have preferred.

Within the myth as a whole, both Socrates's explanation of the best manner of choosing one's next life and his narration of other individual choices reinforce the excellence and in particular the *human* excellence of Odysseus's choice. In the afterlife described in the Myth of Er, the souls of deceased humans and animals make a thousand-year journey (pleasant for those who have lived justly and painful for those who have lived unjustly) and then must choose their next lives. Power, health, beauty, various skills, and variations in degree and duration of each quality are intermixed in different proportions in the lives waiting to be selected. Lots determine the order in which souls select their new lives so that some will have a much greater range of possibilities than others. Not everyone will be able to find his or her first choice, but the range of lives is so great that there will be a reasonably good choice available to each. In his description of the souls' manner of choosing, Socrates emphasizes that the most urgent matter in human life is to be able to make well this choice for one's next life. One's ability to choose well results from a combination of factors, including the past life, labors, and loves of the chooser and the resulting deliberation exercised by the chooser. To be clear, a good choice requires being able to discern the outcome in terms of justice of the different combinations of qualities in the various lives, and—because this calculation is complex—the choice requires that great care and self-restraint be exercised in the choosing.

Of the five Homeric characters that Socrates includes in the Myth of Er, only Odysseus takes the time to select his life carefully, and only Odysseus selects the life of a human man. Epeius, an obscure Greek warrior who built the wooden horse, chooses the life of an artisan woman, but the more prominent Homeric characters make evidently subhuman choices. Ajax, receiving an early lot but still suffering from anger over losing a contest for public honor, specifically shuns human life and selects life as a lion. Agamemnon, choosing next, also hates "humankind because of his sufferings" and determines to become an eagle.[54] Achilles, perhaps because of his close connection to the gods, remains conspicuously absent.[55] Choosing nearly last, "the buffoon Thersites" decides to become an ape.[56]

Of the named non-Homeric characters described by Socrates, two select human lives. Both of these choices are, by Socrates's own standards, noticeably marred by the failure to exercise the self-restraint and deliberation that the decision demands. The poor soul who receives the first lot, having known neither philosophy nor labor in his prior life, rushes forward to claim the life of a man who appears to enjoy every felicity—the life of a tyrant. Upon examination, however, he discovers that his life will include great unhappiness, including eating his own children. After the tyrant, Atlanta makes the next-least deliberate choice. Spying the life of a male athlete, she cannot pass up the opportunity to pursue honor and chooses without further thought.

Odysseus's choice, a deliberate and painstaking determination to live as a private human man who minds his own business, is clearly superior to most of the choices depicted. On the basis of its humanity alone, it surpasses the choices of his fellow Homeric leaders (Ajax and Agamemnon) and all save the few named figures who choose human lives—the tyrant, Epeius, and Atlanta. The tyrant's choice, both for its lack of deliberation and its substance, proves the worst. Epeius's selection of life as an artisan woman, perhaps the most ambiguous of the selections described, is suspect—at least considering cultural context—on the grounds of both gender and occupation. Atlanta's determination to pursue honor as a male athlete appears more promising, but her method of choosing reflects poorly on her choice by the standards that Socrates has described. Thus, Odysseus's deliberate choice of private life emerges as the most unambiguously positive of the choices portrayed.[57] More to the point, Odysseus's choice is clearly superior to the choices of the Homeric leaders with whom Socrates juxtaposes his decision.

This elevation—as it seems it must be—of Odysseus over Ajax and Agamemnon contrasts starkly with Socrates's description of the lives and motivating passions in the best city in speech proposed in the *Republic*. As Socrates has discussed at length, the guardians in the best city have no individual families and, like Ajax and Agamemnon, are motivated to courageous acts in war through the love of honor. Nonetheless, within the Myth of Er, Socrates describes Odysseus as specifically overcoming the love of honor in favor of private life, and within Homer's epics Odysseus is the most notoriously devoted of the Achaians to his private life. Within the *Republic*'s plans for the city in speech, notwithstanding the elimination of private life, Socrates describes minding one's own business as benefiting the city's virtue as much as wisdom, moderation, and courage combined. Thus, not only the Myth of Er but rather the *Republic* taken as a whole underscores the tension between the love of honor and the desire to lead a private life of minding one's own business. By bringing this tension to the fore and dramatically emphasizing its importance to individuals and politics alike with Homeric characters, Socrates implicitly refers his audience to Homer's epics and more specifically to the loves of three characters: Odysseus, Ajax, and Agamemnon.

Socrates uses Odysseus as an example of the preference for private life, specifically explaining that this is made possible by overcoming the love of honor and exercising self-restraint in deliberation. For Arendt, if Odysseus is thus understood, he cannot be fully human or excellent. In Socrates's account, of all the choices for reincarnation, Odysseus makes the only choice—barring Atlanta and the tyrant—to be a human man. Agamemnon and Ajax are examples, in Arendt's terms, of human excellence that few save Achilles can rival. But in Socrates's myth, both having experienced "human" life devoted to the search for honor, they opt instead for animal existence. The contrast between the Myth of Er and Arendt's understanding could hardly be clearer.

Perceiving the entirety of Homer, to say nothing of ancient Greece, as driven by love of public honor, Arendt cannot account for the existence or the relevance of the preference for private life that sometimes drives and sometimes divides Homeric characters. Much less can she trace the effect of this love in their actions, in the virtues they display, in the friendships they enjoy, and in the effect that it has on their potential for justice. Nor can Arendt see the critique of the pursuit of honor to be found within the *Iliad* and the *Odyssey*. Yet it must be admitted that, by pointing to the connection between desire and human excellence, Arendt's portrait of ancient Greece does underscore one essential dynamic of Homer's portrait of the hero. To say that Arendt has not captured the sum total of human excellence as presented by Homer is thus not the same as accusing her of failing altogether to capture any genuine Homeric element.

MacIntyre's focus on successful completion of social functions provides a theoretical basis for appreciating much of what Arendt overlooks in Homer: the potential for excellence within private life. Insofar as women are successful in their roles as defenders of the home, within his reading women are excellent—although less excellent because less useful to society as a whole.[58] In other words, where Arendt has no room for the possibility of virtue within the private sphere, MacIntyre thinks that Homer presents faithful Penelope and Andromache as excellent women insofar as they display the virtue appropriate to their social role, namely, fidelity. Hence, MacIntyre argues that Penelope and Odysseus are friends—surely unthinkable from within Arendt's framework—insofar as Penelope successfully exemplifies the excellence of a noble wife through her fidelity to Odysseus.[59] Although Odysseus and Penelope, placed in different social roles, have different kinds and different degrees of excellence, they are each excellent relative to their functions and hence stand in relation to one another as friends.

And yet MacIntyre altogether rejects what Arendt captures so clearly—the importance of desire. MacIntyre argues that the intentions and emotions of Homeric characters are irrelevant to considerations of virtue: the only consideration is success.[60] MacIntyre is not shy on this point: "moral and social structure are in fact one and the same in heroic society."[61] Thus, a dead hero is not excellent; a victorious hero—because he has successfully fulfilled his social function—is the pinnacle of virtue. Penelope's virtue depends not on her desire for Odysseus or her decision to attempt to keep the suitors at bay but solely on her success in remaining unmarried until Odysseus returns. Homeric virtue, according to this account, is not only relative to one's social role but also dependent on success and divorced from the desires of the individual.

Both approaches—Arendt's and MacIntyre's—reach conclusions that run contrary to the implications of the Myth of Er. Within his story Socrates indicates through his description of Odysseus's choice for reincarnation that *both private life and desire* are linked to the potential for a good human life, but Arendt dismisses private life and MacIntyre dismisses desire.

Homeric Excellence

The Myth of Er, although presented as a story of the soul's selection for reincarnation, speaks to every individual's need to select among the possible lives available. It speaks to the pursuit of happiness and the qualities that are necessary to make wise choices in pursuit of an excellent human life. Homer's *Iliad* and *Odyssey*, the foundation of Greek literature and the richest literary resources of the Attic Greeks, contain complex portraits of various selections for how to live one's life. As Socrates indicates and a close reading of Homer confirms, the excellence of a life is closely linked to that which an individual desires or loves. Given Socrates's parting reference to Odysseus's preference for private life, it is not surprising that Homer does prove illuminating on the subject of the individual and the political consequences of the love of honor and the desire for a private life.

Consistent with Socrates's indication, Odysseus's character proves the exemplar of the highest virtue in Homer's epics. Through Odysseus's development, his virtues, and his friendship with his virtuous wife, Penelope, Homer reveals that pursuit of virtue and excellence within private life have a salutary effect on the prospects for happiness and stable politics precisely because they escape the relentless competitiveness (and resulting lack of moderation) inculcated by the public sphere. Within a private life dominated by the love of that housed within the private sphere, competition does not determine excellence. Excellence within this realm relates to how well matched the individuals at the heart of the family are and to how well they are able to inculcate virtue in one another, in their offspring, and in those around them. In Odysseus's words, "sweet agreement in all things" between husband and wife is the greatest of goods, "for nothing is better than this, more steadfast than when two people, a man and his wife, keep a harmonious household" (6.181–84).[62]

Although Arendt and many others have been understandably impressed by the degree of nigh-immortal honor won by Achilles, in their praise of his accomplishment, they have failed to note that Achilles himself was not finally or primarily motivated by love of honor. Thus, despite the fact that he won perhaps the greatest honors ever accorded within our cultural memory and serves as arguably the best "how-to" model for achieving honor, he is not the best exemplar for the study of the effects of the *love* of honor. Conflicted and ever-changing Achilles—who takes no part in the Myth of Er but otherwise looms large among those devoted to Homer—instead illustrates disillusionment with the life of honor and the power of grief over the loss of a particular friend.

In contrast to Achilles, Ajax and Agamemnon provide examples of public action driven by love of honor—examples of that which Arendt extols in *The Human Condition* and Socrates questions in the Myth of Er. Pursuing public honor with little or no heed to private attachments, they reveal politically problematic flaws of this passion that Arendt does not prepare her readers to find in the context of ancient Greece's greatest war poem. Agamemnon and Ajax are, if not villains, heroes whose single-minded love of honor limits their potential for virtue and justice.

By asking why Socrates elevates Odysseus in contrast to his honor-loving peers, this Plato-inspired reading offers a new understanding of the Homeric hero that directly engages with the dominant understanding of human excellence articulated by Arendt and MacIntyre. No less, this reading engages with the often-quiet conclusion that Odysseus is the hero of mediocrity and of petty bourgeois preferences for comfort and life over excellence and truth. A bourgeois Odysseus, sellout to the potential for human excellence, lurks in Ahrensdorf's recent interpretation of Odysseus as narrowly self-interested and friendless, lacking "the lion heart, the single-minded passion and courage of Achilles."[63] In *Dialectic of Enlightenment*, Horkheimer and Adorno similarly present Odysseus as a traitor to truth and human desire who "survives only at the cost of his own dream, which he forfeits by disintegrating his own magic."[64] I argue that, far from presenting private life as unworthy of desire and obtainable only at the cost of renouncing excellence, truth, and humanity, Homer elevates private life as the locus of true friendship and excellence—as the object of Odysseus's ultimate desire and the source of his unique excellence.

Although four recent books turn specifically to Odysseus with related questions about his strongest desires and their consequences, they have neither reached a consensus on Odysseus's preference for private life nor focused on the ramifications for the relationship between private life and politics. Seth Benardete's *The Bow and the Lyre* finds in Odysseus a proto-Socrates: Benardete argues that, far from coming to prefer private life, Odysseus ultimately ascends from love of honor to desire for knowledge.[65] Patrick Deneen's *The Odyssey of Political Theory*, which has points of commonality with Benardete's interpretation, presents Odysseus as fundamentally and perpetually torn between private life and longing for transcendence.[66] Both Benardete's and Deneen's readings, however, discount Odysseus's passionate desire for his homecoming, overlook extensive textual evidence illustrating both the excellence of Odysseus's home and the hero's happiness in his private relationships, and fail to take into account Odysseus's own dismay at the need to leave Ithaka at the end of the *Odyssey*.

Unlike Benardete and Deneen, Jacob Howland's *The Republic: The Odyssey of Philosophy* and Jenny Strauss Clay's *The Wrath of Athena* conclude that Odysseus does ultimately come to prefer that which is his own.[67] Although Howland and Clay therefore conclude that Odysseus finds happiness in his homecoming, they largely omit the *Iliad* and leave the political ramifications of Odysseus's preference for his own mostly unexplored. Howland and Clay focus on Odysseus's journey home, concluding that Odysseus comes to prefer that which is his own as a result of his harrowing adventures. In the following study I show that, on the contrary, in the *Iliad* Homer presents an Odysseus who already differs meaningfully from his honor-loving peers. Within the *Odyssey*, moreover, Odysseus initially makes nearly superhuman efforts to arrive home after departing from Troy, almost giving up on life itself when his homecoming is snatched from him for the second time in the early months after sailing for Ithaka. Accordingly, the development of Odysseus's desires and virtues is far more subtle than either Howland or Clay allow, and Odysseus's character demands more attention during both the Trojan War and after his arrival home during the twelve books in which Homer's hero faces the difficulties of securing and rejoining his home. Only in the second half of the *Odyssey*, after the "adventures" are over, does Homer reveal that Odysseus's love of his private life and his friendship with his like-minded wife lead to the hero's greatest happiness and point to the necessity of politics. Private happiness needs protection, requiring emergence into the political.

Odysseus and Penelope, along with their household, emerge as the admittedly flawed heroes of this rereading of the *Odyssey* and the *Iliad*. Their marriage is the locus of friendship and excellence, and politics reemerges at the end of the epic of homecoming as necessary to protect the value of that which private life nurtures. The politics, like the virtues resulting from the preference for one's own, is flawed by an inadequate understanding of justice and corresponding failure to respect the value of the private lives of others. But Odysseus and Penelope exhibit virtues indicating that their capacity to serve as the foundation of a just, speech-based politics is at least superior to that of honor-motivated heroes. Unlike the honor-driven heroes, they have no inherent desire for conflict and violence. Also unlike honor-dominated heroes, Odysseus "like Zeus in counsel" and "circumspect" Penelope display wily intelligence, self-restraint, and a resulting skill in the use of persuasive speech that bode well for their ability to engage successfully in politics.

In part the importance of this study of Homer results from the finding that, contrary to Arendt's assertions, the virtues of women play a central role in human happiness and excellence. Homer recognizes and indeed celebrates virtue in female form, as demonstrated by the like-mindedness of the heroes at the heart of the happiest moment in his epics. More generally, Homer's portrait of human excellence and happiness reveals the connection between private life and politics: private life ultimately nurtures the growth of virtues—courage, intelligence, and moderation—necessary for development toward a just politics, and private life remains dependent on politics for the protection of the excellence and friendship found in private.

Reading "Homer's" Texts: The *Iliad* and the *Odyssey*

Homer's epics have been studied for many reasons. Some have used the epics as a lens with which to look backward in time—seeking to discern through or behind the texts—to the history, mythology, and society they are thought to reflect. As Donlan characterized the poet's value to the search for history, Homer is our "sole 'native informant'" of his day.[68] Taking this facet of the epics into account, it is far from surprising that much careful scholarship has centered on determining the historical accuracy and implications of the *Iliad* and the *Odyssey*.[69] Such research is inextricably bound to two related questions: Homer's identity and the method of composition. On these questions much ink has been spilled, and no end is in sight.[70]

For the subset of scholars focused on the epics as a source of knowledge about oral poetry and mythmaking, the meaning of the *Iliad* and the *Odyssey* themselves is different from the meaning employed in this book. Students of oral tradition and mythmaking use the names of the written poems to refer to something larger and more amorphous than the texts themselves. In their usage "Iliad" and "Odyssey" refer to the oral tradition of which the written poems are the single best—but not the only—piece of evidence. From this perspective, the texts that we refer to as the *Iliad* and the *Odyssey* captured in written form the final (but not necessarily the most authoritative) step in a formerly fluid process—a process through which a set of tales surrounding the Trojan War were told in many ways by many poets over generations.[71]

In contrast to the usage of students of the oral tradition, within this book the *Iliad* and the *Odyssey* refer to the text of the two written poems. Plato and Aristotle read these poems, referring to their author as Homer, and it is in part a clearer comprehension of these Attic Greeks' ubiquitous references to Homer that motivates this reading. A literary approach, nonetheless, need not mean an approach blind to the assistance offered by scholars of history or oral composition. Conceding that their objects are often different, the various methods of studying the *Iliad* and the *Odyssey* have much to offer one another. As Redfield notes, Homer's art was constructed in light of a tradition of which he became the master.[72] The brilliance of Homer's art—regardless of whether an individual with such a name existed, how many "Homers" there were, and his degree of innovation relative to the preexisting tradition—made use of the poetic techniques available with artistry that continues to provoke comparisons to Mozart and an acknowledgment that the texts themselves are polished literary masterpieces.[73] This artistry can perhaps best be observed in the subject of this book—Homer's individual characters. Although sometimes called uniform, flat, and unchanging, recent scholarship supports the individuality of Homer's characters.[74]

In common with one another, these characters claim pride of place as the original heroes of the Greco-Roman tradition and thus as the literary departure point for many an enduring question. The particular question driving this reading of Homer relates to the excellence of these characters and to the potential for friendship and justice among them. Amid the action, the desire, and the suspense, where does Homer reveal human excellence—that excellence that is worthy of admiration and emulation? Or, to phrase the question more directly, why are his characters heroes, and do they have any virtues? Do female characters ever exhibit the heroic virtues? How does the excellence of Homer's characters enhance or inhibit their capacity for friendship and justice?

The complexity of the epics defies simple answers to these questions. No less than in his weaving together of differing points in time and space, Homer's epics weave together several virtues (and failings of virtue) in differing degrees of strength in each important character. Indeed, it may be helpful to imagine Homer's epics as a pair of tapestries intended to be displayed in the same room. Attempt to discern any one virtue as emblematic of the "hero" and you may successfully trace the virtue's appearances throughout both epics, like someone who has identified all the thread of one color in the two tapestries. But the virtue thus traced will not reveal the essence of the excellence of a "hero" any more than a pile of string pulled from its place could communicate meaningfully about the tapestries of which it had once been a part.

Just as Homer does not hold up one supreme virtue as emblematic of the hero, he likewise declines to provide one supreme individual as an unflawed model of human excellence. No one character—not even Achilles—stands atop an apex of virtue against which the others can be judged based on their similarity to the crowned champion of virtue. Rather, Homer offers a host of characters different in both kind and quantity of virtue. One hero excels in intelligence, one in courage, and yet another in moderation: but comparison—let alone ranking—still proves problematic because each character is a mixture of multiple virtues in varying degrees of strength (rather than simply a representation of one virtue). Homer's use of epithets, which are shared by the heroes but allocated to specific characters in differing proportions, provides one preliminary indication of this quality.[75] Another layer of complexity arises from the differences in circumstances of various characters: some are old and others young, some male and others female, some free and others enslaved. But virtue and its absence—although sometimes manifesting differently because of differences in context—can be located within all these circumstances and, thus, adds another dimension to the analysis required to grasp the meaning of human virtue within the Homeric landscape.

To conceptualize the excellence of the heroes found in Homer's tapestry-like epics, it is necessary to start with the loves or desires. Two loves—the love of public honor and of private life—are woven through the two epics like distinct but complementary color schemes. Love of honor, as many have observed, provides the dominant color scheme of the *Iliad*. The desire for private life functions within the *Iliad* to provide contrast, casting the love of honor into sharper definition than would otherwise be possible. Conversely, the desire for private life dominates the *Odyssey* and is ultimately celebrated therein. Within the poem of homecoming, in contrast to the poem of war, love of honor ultimately recedes into the backdrop. Once this thematic contrast between the love of honor and the desire for private life is brought to light, it is possible to observe its consequences in the lives of individual characters and the plot of each epic. Some characters are driven by one love, some by the other, and yet others do not fit neatly into either category, but—more importantly—the object and strength of Homer's characters' loves shape their lives. Their distinct passions produce distinct tendencies in their virtues, thus solving and creating different political problems. For those who seek to understand why, whether, and how Homer's characters are exemplars of human excellence, grasping the relationship of their excellence to their loves is paramount. Similarly, connecting their excellence to their potential for justice and friendship requires grasping the desires that produce their different combinations of virtues.

As the forgoing has doubtless made clear, this argument encompasses Homeric virtue as presented in both epics. Yet it must of necessity start at a particular point and with a specific character or set of characters. The point of departure in part 1 is the *Iliad* and, within the *Iliad*, chapter 1 commences with the love of honor exhibited by two of Homer's most unequivocally honor-driven heroes, Ajax and Agamemnon. Unlike Achilles, whose predominant passion—whether for a particular friend, honor, or private life—vacillates, Ajax and Agamemnon remain steadfast (except for Agamemnon's moments of cowardice) in pursuit of honor. Chapter 2 turns to two characters whose loves exhibit a complexity incompatible with Arendt's reading: Achilles and Hektor. Both suffering and ultimately dying in the Trojan War, Achilles and Hektor share Ajax and Agamemnon's desire for honor, but they also love particular individuals and express the desire to lead private lives focused on spending time with their particular friends. When that which is their own is destroyed by the Trojan War, Homer's description of grief and loss reveals the humanity and the excellence possible in private life. Concluding analysis of the *Iliad*, chapter 3 provides a view of the man of many turns, pausing and pondering Odysseus. Odysseus is gifted in speech and surpasses his peers in self-restraint. He is a capable hero who wants honor but is willing to risk less for it than his peers.

Part 2, like the *Odyssey*, is evenly divided between Odysseus's voyage and his time in Ithaka. Chapters 4 and 5 detail how a man who desires his homecoming can take ten years to find it, and they chronicle the development of Odysseus's desires and virtues over the course of his voyage. Odysseus's relationship with Penelope is the focus of chapter 6. Homer portrays mutual love between Odysseus and Penelope, and he elevates their private life by showing that Penelope's virtues make her worthy of love. The friendship shared by these heroes demonstrates the excellence nurtured by love of one's own. Chapter 7 turns to Odysseus's relationship with his household and kingdom, exploring why he has returned, what he desires, and the moderation that he must command to reclaim that which is his own. At the end of the poem of homecoming, Odysseus expresses the most joy in reestablishing his familial relationships and the most grief and fear at the prospect of their loss. Odysseus is happy insofar as he is permitted to lead a private life of minding his own business.

Part I

The *Iliad*

1

Homer's Honor-Loving Heroes

Ajax and Agamemnon

Ajax and Agamemnon reveal the power of the passion that MacIntyre discounts, demonstrating that the strength of their passion is—as Arendt might have predicted—linked to the strength of their considerable excellence in courage. Each performs incredible feats for the sake of the honor that can be won in the Trojan War. Ajax is fearless on the battlefield—protecting, encouraging, and leading the Achaian forces in their direst moments. Agamemnon too pursues glory courageously on the battlefield, but the leader of the Achaian army understands that his greatest honors will result from winning the war as a whole. With his heart and mind fixed on winning the Trojan War, Agamemnon's decisions as general and political leader are dominated by the potential for victory.

Revisiting the loves and virtues of Ajax and Agamemnon does not merely confirm the power of the love of honor. Contrary to what Arendt would lead one to expect, Homer reveals the limitations of the love of honor—a dark side that is linked to the failings in excellence of both heroes. Within Socrates's myth, Ajax and Agamemnon each had the opportunity—well ahead of Odysseus, while there were still more lives remaining for selection—to choose his next life, but each made explicitly nonhuman choices by becoming animals.[1] Ultimately, close study of Ajax and Agamemnon reveals what Socrates left implicit about the cause of their failings in excellence and their subsequent rejections of humanity. Necessary though love of honor might be to win the battles of the Trojan War, this passion develops into a threat to necessary alliances between allies and ultimately becomes the motivation perpetuating the war itself.

Ajax, Wall of the Achaians

Achilles and Ajax, the two Achaian leaders who beach their ships at the ends of the Achaian fleet on the Trojan shore because they are "sure of the strength of their hands and their courage," stand apart from all of their companions for their battlefield excellence and resulting strategic importance (VIII.225–26; XI.7–9). Indeed, although Ajax is frequently described as "far the best . . . while Achilleus stayed angry" (II.768–69), the Achaian victory would not have been possible without both of them. Had it not been for Ajax's steadfast pursuit of honor and resulting leadership during Achilles's absence from the war, there would have been no Achaian force left for furious Achilles to lead back into battle. Ajax's devotion to honor—from which he is never distracted by thoughts of a particular friend, home, family, or the pleasures of a long life—drives him to be unfalteringly courageous in battle. Not simply a powerful individual warrior, in his enthusiasm for achievement on the battlefield, Ajax cooperates seamlessly with his fellow warriors and inspires them to fight more effectively and more courageously than they would or could without his leadership.[2] Through simple Ajax, rather than through the complex Achilles, the promise of love of honor to the political alliance of which Ajax is a crucial element most clearly emerges.

Because he leads only twelve ships, it is clear that Ajax's status does not stem from the size of the army he commands (II.557–58).[3] Instead, Ajax's preeminence stems from individual merit: Homer often places emphasis on this by describing Ajax as the warrior who "for his beauty and the work of his hands surpassed all other Danaans, after the blameless [Achilles]" (XVII.279–80).[4] Ajax's performance supports at least this much praise. Homer most frequently uses the epithet "wall" (or "bulwark") for Ajax, tallest of the warriors of the Trojan War.[5] When he accepts Hektor's challenge to single combat, Ajax's appearance—before the fight even begins—is enough to set both the Trojan troops and Hektor trembling (VII.208–25). Even in a rare moment of retreat, the Trojan blows against Ajax are likened to the blows of children (XI.556–62). Ajax's obvious physical advantages are complemented by consistently superlative skill and tireless courage. Whether in retreat or on the offensive, Ajax is nearly always wherever the battle is most critical and most dangerous, and he invariably comes when called to a point of particular weakness or to defend a wounded companion.[6] Agamemnon confirms this observation, noting Ajax's willingness to enter the first clash between the armies and honoring him for stepping into the most dangerous portion of the battle (IV.284–91).

What motivates Ajax to put his outstanding physical advantages and battle skills to work in the Trojan War? Why does he push forward in the most dire situations and take on the greatest challenges with a smile? In short, Ajax loves public honor, and the Trojan War provides an opportunity to win such honor. This motivation can be discerned in his bearing, emotions, and speeches. Moreover, once Ajax's love of honor is observed, the strength and single-mindedness of that love of honor likewise becomes apparent. If he fights for glory, then the extremity of the danger that he is willing—happy even—to face demonstrates the strength of his love.

A hero of relatively few words, Ajax's speeches are infrequent and short. Because they are so few, one of his terse comments indicates more about his desires than a dozen speeches from Achilles or indeed many of Homer's main characters—nearly all of whom are more verbose than Ajax. A few speeches, therefore, must serve to establish his motivation. Yet, because his behavior is completely consistent with his speech and neither his speech nor his behavior so much as hint at any conflicting desire or even distracting thoughts, the case for Ajax's dedication to honor is strong.

Ajax's desire to win glory—not merely his ability to do so—begins to show itself as he prepares to face Hektor in single combat. Ajax does not immediately volunteer to accept Hektor's challenge,[7] but once his lot is chosen, his words and manner exhibit great joy at the prospect of winning the glory that would accompany defeating Hektor.

> [H]e saw his mark on the lot, and knew it, and his heart
>   was gladdened.
> He threw it down on the ground beside his foot, and spoke
>   to them:
> "See, friends, the lot is mine, and I myself am made happy
> in my heart, since I think I can win over brilliant Hektor."
>   (VII.189–92)

In the ensuing combat, which Ajax joins with a (literal) smile on his face, he knocks Hektor from his feet, but he does not kill Hektor before the combatants agree (at Hektor's request) to stop for darkness (VII.212, 248–82). As Hektor returns to Troy, happy to have escaped with his life, Ajax reaps the honor accorded his courage. First, the Achaian army honors him: "the strong-greaved Achaians led Aias, happy in his victory, to great Agamemnon" (VII.311–12). Then Agamemnon honors Ajax prominently in the feast that follows by giving him "in honour the long cuts of the chine's portion" (VII.321–22).

Although generally a warrior of few words, when Ajax encourages his fellow Achaians in battle he articulates his understanding of the honor that is at stake. He makes explicit that they risk their lives for the sake of the honor to be won (and the shame to be avoided).

> Dear friends, be men; let shame be in your hearts, and
>   discipline,
> and have consideration for each other in the strong encounters,
> since more come through alive when men consider each
>   other,
> and there is no glory when they give way, nor warcraft either.
>   (XV.561–64)

> Friends and fighting men of the Danaans, henchman of Ares,
> be men now, dear friends, remember your furious valour.
>   (XV.733–34)

> Friends, there is no glory for us if we go back again
> to our hollow ships, but here and now let the black earth
>   open
> gaping for all; this would soon be far better for us.
>   (XVII.415–19)

As Ajax continues to fight, he reminds his comrades of the necessity of putting themselves wholeheartedly into this fight—even though death may result. Glory is on one hand and shame on the other. Their reputations as men are on the line, and they must risk their lives in full battle fury if they are to retain them.

Ajax lives by his own words, consistently remaining in the most dangerous place in battle and thus demonstrating that he has earned the honor that Agamemnon meticulously affords him.[8] This is most evident in Ajax's defense of the ships during the near defeat of the Achaians before Patroklos enters the battle—one of the most impressive and most dangerous feats of the *Iliad*. While Achilles remains withdrawn, torn between his competing desires, Ajax proves vital to Achaian survival as he first defends their ramparts, then protects the ships, and finally fights fire from the decks. During this portion of the battle, Ajax demonstrates repeatedly that but for his courage and skill the war would have then been lost.[9] Even when he finally retreats, Homer makes it clear that Ajax's retreat reflects the sheer force of the enemy and not cowardice: "Their volleys were too much for Aias, who could hold no longer his place, but had to give back a little, expecting to die there" (XV.727–28).[10] In retreat, Ajax's importance becomes yet clearer: only when he gives way can the Trojans finally set the first ship afire.

Ajax is most obviously perceived as "Ajax the wall," defending those who are behind him and putting himself into the most dangerous positions as he pursues the honor that Agamemnon and indeed his companions of all ranks lavish on him. The text is replete with evidence of this quality, from his unfailing willingness to face the greatest place of danger in battle to his choice for the beaching of his own ships in the most vulnerable position on one extreme of the Achaian flank. In the brilliance of this courage and individual prowess, however, it is easy to overlook the skill with which he cooperates with his fellow warriors and inspires them to pursue glory with him. Despite his superiority in size and battle skill, it may be this teamwork—if such a modern term can be forgiven—in which he most surpasses his peers. This quality is most obviously evident in Ajax's willingness to move about a battle to wherever his companions tell him he is needed. When Patroklos falls, Ajax works with Menelaus and others to assure the defense of Patroklos's body (XVII.113–236).[11] When Odysseus is injured and Menelaus calls for Ajax's aid, Ajax steps forward to fight beside Menelaus (XI.472–87). When the Achaians are driven to their ramparts, Ajax responds to his fellow warriors' call to come to the most vulnerable portion of the defenses (XII.329–69).

Less obvious than Ajax's unfailing compliance when called to protect a vulnerable warrior or point in the Achaian line is the skill with which he commands and executes intricate tactical teamwork. While it is not unusual in the *Iliad* for warriors to cooperate by defending the wounded, managing horses or a chariot, assisting with armament, retreating from the field, or calling encouragement to one another, Ajax does more than this. Consider the intricate, offensive teamwork with which he cooperates with his illegitimate brother, Teukros.

> [A]nd ninth came Teukros, bending into position the
>   curved bow,
> and took his place in the shelter of Telamonian Aias'
> shield, as Aias lifted the shield to take him. The hero
> would watch, whenever in the throng he had struck some
>   man with an arrow,
> and as the man dropped and died where he was stricken,
>   the archer
> would run back again, like a child to the arms of his mother,
> to Aias, who would hide him in the glittering shield's
>   protection. (VIII.266–72)

Teukros continues, striking down eight Trojans in rapid succession and then proceeding to hit another handful in an attempt to kill Hektor. When Hektor finally wounds Teukros—having found a weak moment in Teukros's timing with Ajax—Ajax moves smoothly from providing the shield necessary for his half brother's attacks to ensuring that Teukros lives to fight another day.

>   Aias
> was not forgetful of his fallen brother, but running
> stood bestriding him and covered him under the great
>   shield. . . .
> [T]wo staunch companions, stooping beneath it, caught up
>   Teukros
> and carried him, groaning heavily, to the hollow vessels.
>   (VIII.330–34)

Later, while defending the Achaian ramparts, Ajax and Teukros nearly defeat Zeus's son Sarpedon using the same tactic (XII.400–405; see also XV.437–83).

Although this intricate coordination far outstrips the teamwork of the *Iliad*'s most prominent Achaian brothers (Menelaus and Agamemnon), one might wonder whether their teamwork arises from their relationship as half brothers.[12] This explanation seems unlikely because Ajax's particular ability to coordinate his actions with others manifests with many companions with whom he has no family relationship, including Menelaus, Lesser Ajax, and a host of warriors of lesser prominence. Ajax appears to have no particular friend; instead, he regards every Achaian with whom he fights as a brother or friend. For example, when Ajax and Lesser Ajax fight side by side, Homer compares their cooperation to that of a pair of oxen (XIII.703–8).[13] Books later, the Ajaxes work seamlessly together again, this time to defend Patroklos's body. Ajax commands his peers, coordinates their actions in the midst of chaos, and—perhaps most importantly—inspires intricate cooperation in the heat of battle.

> All you have said, Menelaos, is fair and orderly.
> But come: you and Meriones stoop and shoulder the body
> at once, and carry it out of the hard fighting. Behind you
> we two shall fight off the Trojans and glorious Hektor,
> we, who have the same name, the same spirit, and who in times past
> have stood fast beside each other in the face of the bitter war god. (XVII.716–21)

As the scene continues, the Ajaxes fight a rearguard action together, protecting those returning the body to Achilles (XVII.722–61).

Ajax also works closely with less prominent soldiers, those who are unnamed or named only once in the *Iliad*. Wounded and retreating leaders are often helped off the front by soldiers of lesser fame, but Ajax—in contrast to his peers—works with them rather than merely treating them as servants or orderlies. For example, in book XI, Eurypylos[14] comes to the retreating Ajax's aid and then calls others to help defend Ajax (XI.575–76). When wounded himself, Eurypylos must retreat into the ranks of Achaians, but he shows concern for Ajax before leaving, calling his comrades to "turn again and stand and beat off the pitiless death-day from Aias, who is being overpowered" (XI.587–89). In response to this call, a group of soldiers forms a defensive wall of shields around Ajax. Ajax, still in need of assistance, does not flee but fights from behind this wall of shields.[15]

When the Achaians are forced to defend from the most desperate position (their fortifications and then their ships), Ajax works ever more closely with the men he leads. At one moment he urges them forward (XV.500–513; XV.560–64; XV.733–41), the next he fights savagely himself, and then, winded, he takes respite behind those he leads.[16] Rather than merely calling out encouragement, as Agamemnon or Nestor might do, Ajax gives tactical directions: "Aias ranged their whole extent with his numerous orders, and would not let any man give back from the body, nor let one go out and fight by himself far in front" (XVII.356–58). Ajax works tirelessly to make the Achaians "stand hard and fast about him and fight at close quarters" so that, although the ground runs red with blood, far fewer of his men perish because "they ever remembered always to stand massed and beat sudden death from each other" (XVII.359–65).

Of all the Achaians, Ajax is the most unfailing in his courage, in his commitment to his fellow soldiers and the Achaian cause as a whole, and in his enthusiasm for honor and desire to avoid shame. In contrast to Ajax's pursuit of honor through battlefield excellence, there is very little to say about his private life. Indeed, the epics provide no evidence that Ajax has a private life or is even aware that such a phenomenon exists. Ajax never mentions any family at home—not even his father. Much less does he speak of a wife or sons (let alone daughters).[17] He never speaks of—let alone expresses a desire for—his homeland or the possibility of a long life. And while he works closely with his half brother Teukros, because he works superlatively with so many soldiers, it is hard to attribute this primarily to any family bond. Rather, it is as if Ajax treats all his fellow warriors as his brothers and friends. The silence of Ajax and of Homer about Ajax's homeland and family points to the conclusion that his commitment to public honor is coupled with indifference to private life.

Nor is there any evidence that Ajax feels so much as a strong attachment to any specific woman, even the captured woman whom he was awarded during the war (I.137–39). He places some value on (attractive) women yet expresses lack of understanding of attachment to any particular woman. When urging Achilles to accept Agamemnon's offer of women in exchange for Achilles's return to the war, Ajax reasons that Achilles's wrath is out of proportion with the value of "one single girl"—especially when "now we offer you seven, surpassingly lovely, and much beside these" (IX.636–39). To Ajax one woman is as good as any other (provided she is attractive). Beyond this comment to Achilles, Ajax never refers to his own captured prize woman or to the incentive of capturing the women of Troy. Indeed, he seems—if not indifferent—at least relatively unmoved by the thought of capturing women as prizes. As his comment to Achilles indicates, to the extent that such prizes are desirable in his eyes, they are fungible honors rather than individuals.

Throughout the *Iliad* Ajax's heart is undivided in its pursuit of honor, and the text is replete with examples of how his passion and consequent courage—through his own feats and the courageous feats that he inspires and coordinates—proved necessary to the Achaian survival during Achilles's absence. In the *Odyssey* Homer offers a final glimpse of Ajax, a glimpse that confirms the perpetuation of Ajax's love of honor through the end of the war and into the afterlife. But, as told by Odysseus, Ajax's love of honor drives more than his battlefield courage and excellence. Ajax's love of honor is also the cause of his only quarrel with a fellow Achaian. After Achilles was slain during the Trojan War, Thetis offered Achilles's armor as a "prize, and the sons of the Trojans, with Pallas Athene, judged" a competition between Odysseus and Ajax for the honor of Achilles's divinely made armor (11.546–47). When Odysseus bested Ajax and won the armor, Ajax became consumed with anger (11.542–46). Later, when the two competitors for the arms of Achilles meet in Hades, Ajax remains angry over the honor that he lost, refusing even to speak with Odysseus (11.543–67).[18] The *Odyssey* thus provides a final piece of evidence of Ajax's love of honor—the continuation of his anger at the loss of honor to Odysseus. At least in this one instance, Ajax's love of honor undermines his otherwise uninterrupted harmony with his fellow warriors. In Socrates's Myth of Er, this loss is the formative event that shapes Ajax's choice to be reincarnated as a lion: he "shunned becoming a human being, remembering the judgment of the arms" (620b1–3).

Agamemnon, Lord of Men

Like Ajax, Agamemnon derives honor from individual prowess and the prizes that he accumulates through it. But unlike Ajax, this is not the most important source of his honor. Even more than individual performance, Agamemnon's honor depends on being the leader of the victorious army in the Trojan War. Thus, although he evinces concern for individual honor on occasion—indeed, at one point he puts his whole enterprise at Troy at risk for this—ultimately he is most dedicated to the honor associated with leading his army to victory in war. Accordingly, when Agamemnon appears to humble himself, he invariably does so in pursuit of the even greater honor of leading his army to victory. Yet Agamemnon's devotion to honor is not less powerful for this difference from that of Ajax.

While the *Iliad* is replete with references to Agamemnon's love of honor and the consequences thereof, the relative strengths of Agamemnon's various private attachments and love of public honor play out most obviously in the first book of the *Iliad*. Indeed, although the opening lines of the epic draw attention to the wrath of Achilles, Achilles is not initially responsible for the crisis in the Achaian camp. Rather, Agamemnon's refusal to give up a captured woman is the immediate problem. Agamemnon has refused to ransom Chryseis—the prize allotted to him after an earlier battle—to her father Chryses.[19] Because the woman's father, a priest of Apollo, prayed to the archer god, the Achaian army has suffered from a plague of divine arrows. On the tenth day of this rain of arrows, which kept the corpse fires burning around the clock, Achilles called an assembly and brought forward the prophet Kalchas to explain Apollo's assault (I.52–67). To end the attack, Chryseis must be returned to her father (without any ransom) and sacrifices made to Apollo (I.94–100).

Agamemnon responds to the call to return Chryseis with wrath "raging, the heart within filled black to the brim with anger from beneath, but his two eyes showed like fire in their blazing" (I.103–4). Agamemnon's words explain how highly he values Chryseis by comparing her favorably to the wife he has left at home.

> [I]ndeed, I wish greatly to have her
> in my own house; since I like her better than Klytaimestra
> my own wife, for in truth she is in no way inferior,
> neither in build nor stature nor wit, not in accomplish-
>   ment. (1.112–15)

If necessary for the safety of his army, however, Agamemnon will return Chryseis: "Still I am willing to give her back, if such is the best way" (I.116–17). His willingness to return Chryseis, the woman he values more highly than his wife, is conditional. He will return her only if his own honor is satisfied by replacing her with "some prize that shall be my own, lest I only among the Argives go without, since that were unfitting" (I.118–19).[20]

This scene clarifies much about Agamemnon's relative love of family and honor. First and most evidently, Agamemnon does not love, like, or even publicly honor his own wife. Klytaimestra holds no special place in the eyes of Agamemnon.[21] Second, he is somewhat motivated by the desire to share his bed with a pretty woman and even with a particular pretty woman valued for her particular characteristics. Unlike Achilles's speech about Briseis, Agamemnon's speech about Chryseis provides no indication of tenderness; yet, Agamemnon also shows us something about his estimation of women through his adamant preference for this specific woman. He may be willing to give her up to protect his army (and thus retain the ability to win the war), but he admits—as Ajax would not— that the exchange of this one woman for another may be some kind of loss. Third, Agamemnon's speech reveals that while he values Chryseis more than his wife, he loves honor yet more. The bottom line—though he does not wish to relinquish Chryseis—is that he will do so as long as his estimation of his own honor is satisfied.[22]

This first scene is a good indicator of how Agamemnon operates throughout the *Iliad*: his love of honor dominates his other, lesser loves. His desire for honor prompts him to alienate Achilles by taking Briseis when Chryseis must be relinquished. His desire for honor pushes him to distinguish himself on the battlefield, and when he wishes to flee (to save his own life, not for the sake of returning to his homeland) appeals to honor persuade him to continue the war. Moreover, his leadership methods presume a similar preoccupation with honor on the part of the men who follow him. Even when he is forced to abandon some of his arrogant demeanor, he attempts to protect his honor with a (seemingly transparent) claim of temporary madness. With the possible, partial exception of affection for his brother Menelaus, considerations of honor are always foremost for Agamemnon. Even in death he bemoans from Hades the inglorious nature of his death and congratulates Achilles on the glory of his battlefield death. Complications arise only when Agamemnon's honor as an individual and as commander of the Achaian forces come into conflict with one another.

The first, the most famous, and perhaps the most indisputable evidence of Agamemnon's devotion to his own honor is his willingness to jeopardize his chance of victory in the Trojan War for the sake of maintaining his personal honor before the army. It is not blind fury that motivates him to take Briseis from Achilles. By his own admission he would take someone's prize—regardless of their role in his loss of Chryseis—in order to satisfy his own honor: "If they will not give me one I myself shall take her, your own prize, or that of Aias, or that of Odysseus, going myself in person; and he whom I visit will be bitter" (I.137–39). Nor is Agamemnon ignorant or even temporarily blinded to the dangerous result of his insult to Achilles. Far from it—he dares Achilles to sail home and explains in inflammatory terms that he takes Briseis precisely to demonstrate superiority over Achilles.

> [B]ut I shall take the fair-cheeked Briseis,
> your prize, I myself going to your shelter, that you may learn well
> how much greater I am than you, and another man may shrink back
> from likening himself to me and contending against me.
> (I.184–87)

When Nestor tries to calm him and stop the feud, Agamemnon admits the wisdom of Nestor's words. Still, Agamemnon is unable to moderate his anger and cannot yield to Achilles (I.286–91). Even though he knows his decision will prove dangerous for Achaian prospects in the war, Agamemnon's love of honor demands that he take the prize of Achilles.

This example underscores a second way in which Agamemnon's love of honor differs from that of Ajax. Until his dispute with Odysseus, Ajax's love of honor benefits the political unit of which he is a part: he is spurred on to ever more courageous feats in war for the sake of honor, and this attitude inspires greater love of honor, coordination among, and courage in the warriors with whom he fights. By contrast, Agamemnon's love of honor brings the Achaian army its greatest moment of danger and threatens its leader's decision-making ability.[23] The anger that takes hold of Agamemnon, his resulting loss of the ability to moderate his impulses, and the rift that this causes with his most valuable warrior nearly cost the Achaians their lives and the war. Ajax's love of honor and his resulting courage may prove essential to the survival of the Achaian army during Achilles's absence from the fight, but Agamemnon's love of honor and his resulting inability to moderate his own impulses place the Achaian forces close to total defeat—causing Ajax's abilities to be so desperately needed.

Agamemnon, the Lion

Fortunately for the Achaians, Agamemnon's pursuit of honor also has some positive effects. Contrary to Achilles's accusation of cowardice (I.225–28), Agamemnon is brave and effective in battle. At times he proves himself willing to be a risk-taking warrior, particularly before he is wounded in battle in book XI. In the initial battle scene in the *Iliad*, by virtue of his courage and skill, he has an evident place—if not the supreme place—among the most elite warriors (IV.223–25; V.37–42; V.533–40; VI.33).[24] When Hektor proposes single combat, Agamemnon volunteers and then places his lot with the others for a chance to face the most feared of the Trojan warriors (VII.92–93, 176). Later, in his greatest scene of battlefield accomplishment, he pushes the Trojans back from the Achaian ships, "always slaying" as he "urged on the rest of the Argives" (XI.153–54). In nearly three hundred consecutive lines (roughly half a book) of battlefield supremacy, Agamemnon forces their enemies backward almost to Troy. As Homer describes him, he advances like a lion or a spreading fire (XI.113–247).

Perhaps more importantly for the purposes of understanding his driving motivation, Agamemnon's eventual retreat from the field after he is wounded does not end his pursuit of honor. For while one method of winning honor lies in personal achievement on the battlefield, Agamemnon knows that victory in the Trojan War would win him more honor than any personal exploit could. Agamemnon provides a sense of this in some of his speeches, but Diomedes describes Agamemnon's situation the most concisely: "This will be his [Agamemnon's] glory to come, if ever the Achaians cut down the men of Troy and capture sacred Ilion. If the Achaians are slain, then his will be the great sorrow" (IV.415–17). Agamemnon's knowledge that victory in war can bring him great honor—and his desire to win honor through such victory—surfaces most clearly when he suggests accepting defeat and sailing home. On both these occasions Agamemnon associates flight and defeat with disgrace, and a reminder of the glory that he would gain through victory persuades him to stay.[25]

The first scene in which Agamemnon suggests discontinuing the war occurs at the end of the day in which the Achaians are pushed back to their fortifications for the first time in the *Iliad*. Agamemnon, "shedding tears, like a spring dark-running," proposes fleeing in their ships (IX.14–16). Although he attempts to use divinely inspired madness as a justification, he also calls Zeus's workings a "vile deception" and bemoans the "dishonour" that he associates with loss of the war (IX.17–22). Diomedes then adds cowardice to the charge of dishonor and madness that Agamemnon has made against himself (IX.32–44). In response to Diomedes's insult, Agamemnon agrees to follow Nestor's recommendation to ask Achilles for help. When this fails, Diomedes proposes a new battle plan for the next day, promising his commander the potential for glory and urging his leader to "yourself be ready to fight in the foremost" (IX.693–709). Agamemnon responds to this appeal with courage and his best battlefield performance the next day.

The next time the Achaians are driven back, Agamemnon has a similar exchange with his lords. As the wounded leaders—now including Agamemnon, Nestor, Diomedes, and Odysseus—discuss their options, Agamemnon once again proposes flight as the only viable option (XIV.48).

> [T]hen such is the way it must be pleasing to Zeus, who is
>   too strong,
> that the Achaians must die here forgotten and far from
>   Argos. . . .
> and I know it now, when he glorifies [the Trojans] as if they
> were blessed gods, and has hobbled our warcraft and our
>   hands' strength.
> Come then, do as I say, let us all be won over; let us
> take all those ships. . . .
> There is no shame in running, even by night, from disaster.
> The man does better who runs from disaster than he who
>   is caught by it. (XIV.69–81)

Before this idea can gain momentum, Odysseus responds with a dark look and biting words (XIV.82). In part, Odysseus's response speaks to the impracticality of Agamemnon's plan, but he also appeals to his leader's sense of shame at the glory that flight would grant to the Trojans.

> Now I utterly despise your heart for the thing you have spoken;
> you who in the very closing of clamorous battle
> tell us to haul our strong-benched ships to the sea, so that even
> more glory may befall the Trojans, who beat us already.
> (XIV.95–98)

Agamemnon backs down (XIV.103). Once again, Diomedes follows up with a plan: the wounded leaders will return to the battle, not to fight, but to spur others to the front (XIV.109–32). Agamemnon, shamed into continuing the war, assents without further deliberation (XIV.133–34, 379–81).

Although his concern with his public honor is usually foremost, there are moments when Agamemnon seems to set aside his love of honor and humble himself, particularly vis-à-vis Achilles. Contrary to initial appearances, however, these moments are consistent with Agamemnon's ultimate prioritization of winning the honor—the highest honor—associated with leading the entire Achaian force to victory. Accordingly, Agamemnon's humbling of himself in exchange for Achilles's return to the war is consistent with his desire for honor, because he believes that the greatest honor would be winning the Trojan War. By sacrificing some honor—publicly admitting a mistake, returning Briseis, and offering Achilles opulent gifts—he increases his chance of acquiring the greater honor that would accompany victory in the war.

The very manner in which Agamemnon ultimately makes his pleas for Achilles to return demonstrates Agamemnon's continued commitment to honor. First, he repeatedly blames his behavior in the quarrel with Achilles on divinely inspired madness (IX.115–16; XIX.86–94). Thus Agamemnon attempts to mitigate any loss of honor entailed in admitting both that he had been wrong to take Briseis and that the Achaians need Achilles's help. Second, both in books IX and XIX, as Agamemnon finishes explaining his madness, he transitions immediately to asserting supremacy over Achilles. In book XIX this is implicit as he commences giving military commands to Achilles: "Rise up, then, to the fighting and rouse the rest of the people" (XIX.139). In book IX, rather than speaking directly to Achilles, Agamemnon speaks to the messengers that he is about to send to Achilles. Without Achilles present, Agamemnon asserts himself more overtly, making a bold claim of supremacy for one so desperately needing help: "Let him give way. . . . And let him yield place to me, inasmuch as I am the kinglier and inasmuch as I can call myself born the elder" (IX.158–61). Even while honoring Achilles in an attempt to entice him to return, Agamemnon continues to claim the place of supreme public honor.

One additional aspect of Agamemnon's character seems at first to point toward prioritization of something other than his desire for honor. As much as Agamemnon lacks regard for his wife, there are moments when he seems to share an important friendship with his brother Menelaus. Do not his repeated displays of concern for Menelaus's safety denote a powerful love for his brother? For instance, Agamemnon convinces Menelaus not to face Hektor in single combat (VII.104–19). Later, he fears that his brother may be chosen to go on the night raid with Diomedes (X.241). Earlier, during the evening of the night raid, when an uneasy Agamemnon first sees his brother approaching, Agamemnon welcomes Menelaus to join him in his unhappy ponderings (X.35).

The concern and affection displayed in these encounters pale in comparison to Agamemnon's reaction when Menelaus is slightly wounded in book IV. At first, it seems that Agamemnon panics for his brother out of genuine affection: he shudders and groans, takes his brother by the hand, calls him "dear brother," and sends for a healer (IV.148–91). But his subsequent speech, after these initial signs of brotherly concern, betrays a different source of anxiety.[26] As he repeatedly articulates, Agamemnon is concerned for the life of his brother because of the eventual consequences for himself.

> But I shall suffer terrible grief for you, Menelaos,
> if you die and fill out the destiny of your lifetime.
> And I must return a thing of reproach to Argos the thirsty,
> for now at once the Achaians will remember the land of
>   their fathers;
> and thus we would leave to Priam and to the Trojans Helen
> of Argos, to glory over, while the bones of you rot in the
>   ploughland
> as you lie dead in Troy, on a venture that went
>   unaccomplished. (IV.169–82)

Faced with the possibility of his brother's death, Agamemnon thinks primarily of the shame that this would ultimately bring on himself.

Agamemnon believes that he will not be able to hold the campaign together if Menelaus dies. He would be forced to return to Argos, empty-handed and thus disgraced. Admittedly, part of Agamemnon's disgrace would be due to the deceased brother moldering on the Trojan plains, but Agamemnon ultimately seems most concerned with the Trojans gloating over his own flight.

Agamemnon, Shepherd of the People

It should come as no surprise that Agamemnon, motivated as he is by the war's promises of honor and threats of shame, uses the same incentives in his efforts to motivate soldiers to risk themselves in battle. Thus, Agamemnon's love of honor can be observed in the way he manages both his ranking commanders and ordinary soldiers. It is here, as he urges both his elite warriors and his troops forward, that Agamemnon's speeches and actions provide the most explicit view of his understanding of the power of honor to motivate men to risk their lives in combat—in short, to produce courage. He motivates his men through various appeals to their love of honor: one moment he fans their desire for glory and reputation, then he points directly to the immediate and material rewards allotted to honor glorious combat performance, next he reminds them of the shame of defeat. Through these appeals, Homer reveals not only how the Achaian army is motivated to act courageously throughout the Trojan War, but he also gives us insight into Agamemnon's own understanding of what men (including himself) desire.

Examples of how Agamemnon manages and motivates those under him are scattered throughout the *Iliad*, but their consistent logic becomes unmistakable when they are examined in relationship to one another. The "carrots" in Agamemnon's motivational arsenal consist of (1) the food and wine that he provides to his men and (2) the spoils of war that they have captured and anticipate capturing.[27] These material carrots are mixed with an immaterial incentive—the implication and sometimes the promise of the honor that accompanies them. The "sticks" that Agamemnon wields are the shame and disgrace of defeat, cowardice, and the loss of the memory of one's name. Consistent with his own desires, Agamemnon only once mentions to his men as a motivating force the ability to go home to their families. And he does this when he does not genuinely wish his army to be persuaded—in his disingenuous "test" in book II.

In the *Iliad*'s first battle, as Agamemnon drives his men forward, rebuking some and praising others, he reminds them of the food and drink that he has provided and the corresponding distinction with which they were treated at his feasts. He couples this reminder of past honors with a reminder of the resulting obligation to fight on the front line of the coming battle. Consider his urgings to Idomeneus.

> I honour you, Idomeneus, beyond the fast-mounted
> Danaans whether in battle, or in any action whatever,
> whether it be at the feast, when the great men of the
>   Argives
> blend in the mixing bowl the gleaming wine of the princes.
> Even though all the rest of the flowing-haired Achaians
> drink out their portion, still your cup stands filled forever
> even as mine, for you to drink when the pleasure takes you.
> Rise up then to battle, be such as you claimed in the past.
>   (IV.257–64)

When, a few lines later, Agamemnon finds Odysseus and others hanging back from the front lines, he makes a similar appeal, albeit in a rougher tone (IV.340–48). Later, in book VIII, Agamemnon taunts his followers with accusations of shame and disgrace for hanging back in fear of Hektor, reminding them of the meat and wine that he has provided in the past (VIII.228–41).

Agamemnon is also quick to offer a distinction or prize for exceptional courage or ability, as when he honors Ajax with the best cut of meat after his combat with Hektor.[28] More famously, when he must try to win Achilles back, Agamemnon offers "gifts in abundance" for Achilles's assistance (IX.120–57).[29] By repeatedly listing these gifts publicly, Agamemnon calls attention to the fact that he intends to honor Achilles before the Achaians. Agamemnon and Achilles's alliance had been broken when Agamemnon publicly failed to honor Achilles sufficiently; now, Agamemnon tries to buy this alliance back by publicly offering unparalleled honors.

Time and time again, Agamemnon makes explicit the link between what he gives those who follow him (food, drink, special treatment during a feast, gold, women, one of his own daughters, and other plunder) and the degree of honor he thus bestows. The degree of honor that he awards them—via his gifts and public feasting—then corresponds to the courage he expects them to exhibit on the battlefield. To perform less excellently than the degree of honor he has paid them is—as surely as Agamemnon bothers to honor them in the first place—a disgrace.[30]

One aspect of Agamemnon's motivational arsenal is noteworthy through its absence. Though he frequently refers to the desire for honor (and the fear of disgrace), Agamemnon only once refers to the families waiting at home. And this one mention lacks reference to love of or desire for those families. Instead, he refers to the "wives and young children" who "are sitting within our halls and *wait for us*" (II.136–37, emphasis added). This is the one and only time in the *Iliad* that Agamemnon mentions wives and children with speech that could even arguably be interpreted as tenderness. Yet, rather than conveying desire for those who wait at home, Agamemnon emphasizes the need (and vulnerability) of those at home waiting. Most tellingly, Agamemnon only uses the families waiting at home as an incentive in this one instance in which he is testing his men. He appeals to the families waiting at home when he hopes that his army will *reject* what he says and insist on staying to fight the war to its conclusion.

The only additional mention that Agamemnon makes of his own family (aside from his insults to Klytaimestra in book I) is a passing mention of Orestes and his three daughters in the context of offering Achilles his pick of a wife from among his daughters (IX.141–47). In other words, Agamemnon is only interested in his own family and the families of those who follow him insofar as they enhance or interfere with his ability to win the war (and thus enhance his honor). Agamemnon simply does not perceive love of family as a strong force, either for himself or for the men who follow him.

As with his assessment of the value of Chryseis, Briseis, and his daughters—all of whom he esteems primarily as indicators of his or someone else's honor, Agamemnon thinks of the Trojan women in terms of their impact on his honor. In his many mentions of Trojan women and children to the Achaians, Agamemnon focuses on the wives they will carry off and the children they will kill. As he told Teukros and promised Achilles, the captured women will be used as prizes to honor those who have performed well. Moreover, as a corollary to this, Agamemnon understands the harm that he will inflict upon both the women and the children of Troy as bringing dishonor to his enemy (and thus, relative to those he has defeated, more honor to himself).

Agamemnon repeatedly describes the fate of his enemies' families in terms of the extent of the shame that he wishes to bring to the men against whom he fights. When Menelaus is lightly wounded, Agamemnon promises him that the Trojans "must pay a great penalty, with their own heads, and with their women, and with their children" (IV.161–62). Later in the same book, as he urges his army on, he promises the vengeance that they will take upon the Trojans: "Vultures will feed upon the delicate skin of their bodies, while we lead away their beloved wives and innocent children, in our ships" (IV.237–39). Two books later, as he stops Menelaus from taking a prisoner, Agamemnon insists on the death of the captive: he explains that no one will escape, not even any baby boy "that the mother carries still in her body, not even he, but let all of Ilion's people perish, utterly blotted out and unmourned for" (VI.58–60). Suffice it to say that Agamemnon seems more concerned with the families to be destroyed in Troy than a return of his men or himself to the families left behind in Achaia.

The Shade of Agamemnon

Victory in the Trojan War is Agamemnon's ultimate goal because he believes that it will bring him the greatest honor. There are other goals and perhaps even people that he cares about. There is no reason to doubt that brotherly affection and friendship may explain a portion of the concern that he has for Menelaus's life. And his own personal honor—in the quarrel with Achilles, in his attachment to Chryseis, and based on his personal battlefield accomplishments—has importance to him and causes him temporarily to risk the greater honor that is at stake in the war. His desire for personal honor is not always foremost—as when he reminds Menelaus not to be haughty to the great leaders[31]—but there is no reason to conclude that it diminishes over the course of the poem.[32]

Even after death Agamemnon continues in his love of honor. This is made clear by Agamemnon's speech to Odysseus in Hades. Having been killed (together with Kassandra) by Aigisthos and Klytaimestra upon his homecoming, he bemoans this "pitiful death" (11.412).[33] Agamemnon explains to Odysseus how his own death—even compared to all the deaths they had seen in battle—would have wrenched Odysseus's heart (11.416–18). Agamemnon expresses some longing for his own son, Orestes, regretting that Klytaimestra "never even let me feed my eyes with the sight of my own son" before his death (11.452–53). But Odysseus can tell Agamemnon nothing in response to his inquiries about Orestes, and so we learn little about how his love for his family (or at least his son) may have been affected by death (11.457–61). What is evident, however, is that Agamemnon spends far more of his conversation with Odysseus focused on his own disgraceful death (and warning Odysseus of the potential for a similar fate) than he does yearning for or pondering the fate of any member of his own family.

In Agamemnon's final appearance, in the last book of the *Odyssey*, he has a conversation in Hades with Achilles in which the two compare their deaths. Achilles, speaking first, comments that it is a pity that Agamemnon could not have died in glory at Troy.

> How I wish that, enjoying that high place of your power,
> you could have met death and destiny in the land of the Trojans.
> So all the Achaians would have made a mound to cover you,
> and you would have won great glory for your son hereafter.
> In truth you were ordained to die a death most pitiful.
> (24.30–34)

In response to this commiseration from Achilles, Agamemnon proceeds to detail the honor that Achilles was accorded by the army and Thetis upon his death (24.35–94). In closing this speech, the longest speech given from Hades in the *Odyssey*, Agamemnon congratulates Achilles on this honor and bemoans again the circumstances of his own death. This time Agamemnon altogether fails to mention his family beyond the horrible death brought to him by his wife.

> You were very dear to the gods. So
> even now you have died, you have not lost your name, but always
> in the sight of all mankind your fame shall be great, Achilleus;
> but what pleasure was there for me when I had wound up the fighting?
> In my homecoming Zeus devised my dismal destruction,
> to be killed by the hands of my cursed wife, and Aigisthos.
> (24.92–97)

In death, as in life, Agamemnon's love of honor—of glory, of an immortal name, of the praise of his fellow men—remains his strongest love.

Conclusion

That two of the most prominent warriors of the Trojan War, as portrayed in the *Iliad*, should be dominated by love of honor and exhibit little love for their own private lives is hardly surprising.[34] Ajax and Agamemnon exhibit a single-minded passion for honor that Arendt ascribed to all Homeric heroes. Nor does Homer provide any basis on which to conclude that Ajax and Agamemnon ever diminish in their devotion to honor and the courageous pursuit of public accomplishment. To the contrary, they persevere in love of honor while developing, through their hardships, a tendency toward strife with those of their companions with whom their love of honor pits them in competition. The more closely one examines them, the more sense their portrayal in the Myth of Er makes. Their choices of reincarnation as animals—powerful, warlike, regal animals[35]—follow from their loves and their experiences within their lifetimes. Homer's portrayal of the brilliance of their courage is thus balanced by a persistent, if underemphasized, revelation of a more troubling aspect of the love of honor.

Within the drama of the *Iliad*, the love of honor of both Ajax and Agamemnon proves to be a problematic, if powerful, motivating force. Although Homer provides few details about the consequences of Ajax's anger at Odysseus, Ajax's brilliant battlefield courage combined with his quarrel with Odysseus suggest that rewarding outstanding public accomplishment with public honor may have powerful but volatile political ramifications. Agamemnon's love of honor, though strong enough to motivate him to courage in battle, pits him against his own soldiers, causes him to quarrel bitterly with his most important warrior, and thus endangers his whole campaign against the Trojans. Indeed, the drama of the *Iliad* arises from the faction among the Achaians created by Agamemnon's love of honor. The love of honor instigates competition among those who should work together and undermines the moderation necessary for stable cooperation and political alliance.[36] Ultimately, the love of honor produces qualities antithetical to fulfilling the role of warrior king with excellence. Homer thus foreshadows the position that Salkever finds in Aristotle and Plato, challenging the belief that "the virtues of the best human life are most clearly displayed in the practice of war and the pursuit of undying glory."[37]

Even more clearly than for Ajax, Agamemnon's love of honor undermines his potential to act with self-restraint and in accord with deliberation.[38] In his anger at Achilles and in his two decisions to continue the war rather than flee for home, desire for honor rather than reason or deliberation determines Agamemnon's course of action as the leader of the entire Achaian army. This renders Agamemnon a weak leader and an easy target for manipulation by Diomedes and Odysseus—hardly an exemplar of excellence. Furthermore, Agamemnon's failings in self-moderation demonstrate that the war itself—with all the suffering that it inflicts on Trojan and Achaian alike—continues because of the love of honor. By the end of the *Iliad*, the passion that is a necessary tool for successful prosecution of the war has become—if it was not such already—the reason for its continuation.

Rounding out the character portrait of these exemplars of the love of honor, it is noteworthy that neither Ajax nor Agamemnon provides any reason to believe that he excels in cerebral virtues such as intelligence or cunning. Due to his superlative physical gifts, Ajax perhaps has little incentive to employ intelligence, but Agamemnon's failure in this regard subjects him to manipulation and weakens his ability to command his own army. In the *Odyssey* Agamemnon's death results from falling into one of literary history's most infamous traps.

Proceeding from two heroes whose love of honor is dominant to heroes whose love of honor is mixed with other desires, the next chapter turns to Achilles and Hektor. Both characters are in transition or at least torn between the love of honor (to which Ajax and Agamemnon are devoted) and the love of their own private life (of which Ajax and Agamemnon are ignorant). As a result, these characters are more complex than Ajax and Agamemnon, and tracing the connection between their loves and their virtues proves correspondingly difficult. Nonetheless, both are valuable in the search for understanding human excellence in Homer because through the characters of Achilles and Hektor Homer demonstrates that love of honor is not always dominant in the greatest battlefield heroes.

2

Homer's Love-Torn Heroes
Achilles and Hektor

Arendt presents Achilles as the "paradigmatic" case of human excellence in ancient Greece. According to her reading, the height of Achilles's public, immortal achievement is one of the essential moments exemplifying and causing the ancient Greek understanding of the love of honor. Presenting him as the pinnacle of ancient Greek excellence, Arendt claims that both Achilles's strongest passion and the source of his excellence are public honor: Achilles "became the prototype of action for Greek antiquity and influential in the form of the so-called agonal spirit, the passionate drive to show one's self in measuring up against others that underlies the concept of politics prevalent in the city-states."[1]

Arendt and Homer agree that the love of honor bears on the meaning of human excellence, but Arendt's monochrome portrait of Homeric heroes overlooks their complexity and development and thereby misidentifies their loves and the sources of their virtues. By reading the Homeric hero, especially Achilles, as driven solely by the love of honor, she distorts the hero and his virtues. Hence, this chapter is devoted to demonstrating that two of the *Iliad*'s most brilliant heroes, far from exhibiting an unequivocally dominant desire for honor, are complex and changing, cognizant of the value of private life, and only partially devoted to honor. Both men love their own families and have especially close relationships with specific individuals: Achilles suffers greatly because of the death of his dearest Patroklos, and Hektor's greatest fear is that his wife Andromache will be dragged into captivity at the end of the war. In their complexity—in the multiplicity of their loves—Achilles and Hektor struggle with competing desires and thereby illustrate the inadequacy of Arendt's analysis of Homeric excellence.

Were this book devoted to the question of how to win honor or to the effects of great honor once won, then admittedly Achilles would be the central figure in this work, as he is in so much scholarship on Homer. But the subject at hand is the effect and value of the love of honor. Most brilliant though he may be of the Homeric heroes, in this category Achilles lags behind both Ajax and Agamemnon. This is not to say that Achilles has no interest in or even love of honor. His famous wrath, the subject of the opening lines of the *Iliad*, occurs as the result of an affront to his honor and proceeds to shape much of the *Iliad*. Yet, at least after his initial outrage, honor is never Achilles's foremost desire. Instead of public honor, his particular friend Patroklos proves to be Achilles's greatest love, the cause of his most unrestrained wrath, and the motivation behind his most courageous battlefield exploits. In the case of Hektor, the love of honor competes with the desire to prioritize that which is his own—his own life, his son, and his wife. The ongoing competition in Hektor's heart, regardless of which love proves dominant, demonstrates that love of honor alone does not drive this Homeric hero.

As clearly as both Achilles and Hektor—the greatest of the Achaian warriors and the greatest of the Trojan warriors—demonstrate that Arendt misidentified the loves of Homeric heroes, these two characters provide limited insight on the connection between desire and specific virtues. Because both heroes have multiple loves and then die in the Trojan War, it is difficult to draw clear connections between their desires and their excellence.[2] We are never able to assess them as conclusively as Ajax and Agamemnon, not only because of their fascinating relative complexity but also because they do not outlive the war. Achilles and Hektor both die navigating the consequences—in their lives and in their hearts—of the war prolonged by Agamemnon's desire for honor.

Still, a close reading of Achilles and Hektor yields more than a poetic refutation of the honor-dominated human that Arendt sees in all Greek warriors. Through these two characters Homer depicts friendship and family as an important part of the human experience and reveals private suffering as a high price of the Trojan War. The extent to which Homer's warriors are windows to the private destruction caused by war has been overlooked by many, but it has also been highlighted by a noteworthy minority.[3] In the wake of World War II, Simone Weil argues that the dehumanizing nature of force is the central subject of the *Iliad*. Inverting Arendt's conclusion, she argues that the price of war in the

Iliad is the loss of humanity: "it changes the human being into stone."[4] Alice Oswald's interpretive poem, *Memorial*, likewise directs the reader's attention to the graphic loss of life that is the subject of so many of the *Iliad*'s lines. Oswald's poem refocuses the reader's attention on Homer's choice to emphasize the connection between battlefield death and the suffering of families at home.[5] Accordingly, Achilles's story cannot be told fully without reference to his grief over the death of his friend Patroklos, and Hektor's fate is poetically intertwined with the story of Andromache's grief. Homer's attention to these aspects of his heroes' narratives underscores their centrality to the human experience.

Brilliant Achilles

More than at any other point in the epic, Achilles appears to be Arendt's paradigmatic lover of honor in his opening quarrel with Agamemnon. In this quarrel Agamemnon publicly insults Achilles by taking his battle prize for the explicit purpose of demonstrating Agamemnon's own superiority. Achilles's initial wrath, which drives him to abstain from the war and the potential glory to be won in it, occurs as a result of this affront to his honor. Arendt's characterization of Achilles thus appears most credible in the first book of the *Iliad*.

In his initial wrath, Achilles is clearly furious, but even in this moment he is not single-mindedly focused on the blow to his public honor. Rather, Achilles's attention is divided between bitter thoughts of the dishonor that Agamemnon has inflicted on him by taking his prize-woman Briseis *and* his desire for Briseis herself. Accordingly, Achilles complains of this undeserved dishonor (I.171, 241, 352–56), but Homer emphasizes Achilles's sense of Agamemnon's injustice and Achilles's longing for Briseis, his "dear" prize (I.168).[6] In his last appearance in book I, Homer shows us Achilles "sorrowing in his heart for the sake of the fair-girdled woman whom they were taking by force against his will" (I.428–30). As the epic continues, Achilles continues to distance himself from honor, focusing instead on the pleasures of private life and private attachments. Indeed, until the moment of Patroklos's return to battle, Achilles indicates that he places no value on honor and instead exclusively plans a private life.[7]

After Homer leaves him sorrowing over the loss of Briseis, Achilles next appears when the Achaians come to plead for his return to the war. On the eve of what appears likely to be complete defeat by the Trojans,

Agamemnon has sent Odysseus, Phoinix, and Ajax to offer Briseis's return (and a long list of rich gifts) in exchange for Achilles's return to battle. After making this offer on Agamemnon's behalf, Odysseus adds the enticement that the army will honor Achilles "as a god" (IX.303). But Achilles explicitly refuses honor at the price of a short life, arguing that honor means nothing because all men are "held in a single honor, the brave with the weaklings. A man dies still if he has done nothing, as one who has done much" (IX.319–20). Rather than yearning for either the honors promised by Agamemnon or those that could be won directly on the battlefield, Achilles speaks tenderly of Briseis and plans a long and happy life in his homeland. He tells Odysseus that "any who is a good man, and careful, loves her who is his own and cares for her, even as I now loved [Briseis] from my heart, though it was my spear that won her" (IX.341–43). Intending to return to his homeland to enjoy a long and wealthy life of domestic happiness, Achilles explains that "the great desire in my heart drives me rather in that place to take a wedded wife in marriage, the bride of my fancy, to enjoy with her the possessions won" by Peleus (Achilles's father) (IX. 398–400).[8] Based on his mother's prophecy, which foretold that he would either win everlasting glory and die in the war *or* return home to a long life, he specifically chooses to forgo honor (IX.410–20).

In contrast to Odysseus's plea, Ajax's speech, which occurs at the end of this scene, is based on friendship between fellow warriors at least as much as on honor (IX.626–42). As one who knows Ajax's character might expect, Ajax does not make his plea to Achilles on behalf of their particular friendship. Rather, Ajax appeals to Achilles based on guest friendship and on friendship with Odysseus, Phoinix, and himself as a group: "Respect your own house: see, we are under the same roof with you, from the multitude of the Danaans, we who desire beyond all others to have your honour and love" (IX.640–42). Indeed, just prior to this statement, Ajax had explained to Achilles that he thought it only reasonable to accept Agamemnon's offer of gifts because, in Ajax's estimation, one person may be exchanged for another without loss: "And yet a man takes from his brother's slayer the blood price, or the price for a child who was killed, and the guilty one, when he has largely repaid, stays still in the country, and the injured man's heart is curbed, and his pride, and his anger when he has taken the price" (IX.632–36). Achilles softens more in response to this argument than in response to Odysseus's offer of honor, but he is not persuaded. Achilles concurs with Ajax in his mind, but his heart's anger still overpowers his feeling for Ajax and the army (IX.643–55).

As Achilles's story develops, his susceptibility to friendship becomes increasingly evident. Initially, it is Achilles's own interest in the fate of a specific wounded Achaian friend that starts the chain of events that eventually pulls him back into the war and toward his own death. Watching from his ships, Achilles sees a wounded man pulled from the battle and, thinking it may be a friend, he sends Patroklos to ascertain the man's identity (XI.597–616).[9] This raises a dilemma: why is Achilles concerned enough to take action over the wound of one friend—the identity of whom he is not even sure—when he remains unmoved by the fact that an entire army of friends are in the process of fighting and dying? Or, to put it another way, why does one potentially wounded friend cause him to send Patroklos to investigate while Ajax's friendship-based appeal leaves him resolute in his decision to stay out of the war?

The answer to this question, as well as insight into Achilles's response to Patroklos's eventual death, lies in distinguishing between Ajax's and Achilles's experiences of friendship. For Ajax friendship is general, shared among a large group of men who are as close as brothers. For Ajax, however, even the life of a brother may be purchased. Notwithstanding the fact that he would risk dying in their defense on the battlefield, Ajax views friends (like family members and women) as fungible. For Achilles, friendship is particular, and accordingly the life of a friend is literally without price. Hence his most dearly loved friend may convince Achilles to do that which all his other friends combined cannot persuade him to do.

When Achilles's dearest friend, Patroklos, returns from investigating the identity of the wounded soldier, he has learned the grim position faced by all their Achaian friends. Patroklos—now weeping—makes his particular and fateful plea for Achilles's return to the war or, barring this, permission to use Achilles's armor. Patroklos's heartfelt plea elicits a multifaceted response from Achilles, revealing the many desires that Achilles now feels. First, Achilles pities his friend even as he mocks him for shedding tears that would be more appropriate for the death of a father (XVI.1–19). Then Achilles expresses—in equal degree—desire for honor, for Briseis, for the ability to return home, and for wealth (XVI.80–86). When he finally agrees to let Patroklos use his armor, Achilles's instructions balance the concern that Patroklos's glory not surpass his own and "fear [that] some one of the everlasting gods on Olympos might crush" Patroklos (XVI.87–94). Similarly, in both his parting words hurrying Patroklos into battle and his subsequent prayer to Zeus, Achilles articulates his desires for homecoming, for glory for Patroklos, and for the "unwounded" return of his friend (XVI.125–29, 233–48).

Entering the battle, Patroklos at first succeeds in driving back the Trojans but soon is killed by Hektor. Once this happens, Achilles's desires narrow to one thought. It becomes evident that Achilles's love for this friend is—at least now—his dominant passion. Almost immediately (and then repeatedly) Achilles emphasizes acceptance of an early death and the loss of his return to his homeland (XVIII.78–93, 101–3, 330–32). In other words, he renounces the desires that had been foremost while his friend still lived and it seemed feasible to live a long, pleasant life at home with Patroklos.[10] This being no longer possible, Achilles tells his companions, "There is nothing worse than this I could suffer, not even if I were to hear of the death of my father . . . or the death of my dear son" (XIX.321–26). In the absence of the desire to continue living, the need to kill Hektor becomes the only barrier to Achilles's suicide: "the spirit within does not drive me to go on living and be among men, except on condition that Hektor first be beaten down under my spear, lose his life and pay the price for stripping Patroklos" (XVIII.78–93). Achilles's primary goal is now to kill the man who slew Patroklos (XVIII.115, 334–37).[11]

As a prerequisite to rejoining the war, Achilles reconciles with Agamemnon. Achilles's indifference to the amends made by Agamemnon is particularly noteworthy because Agamemnon publicly returns precisely that over which Achilles had been so enraged in the opening book: his "dear" prize Briseis and (through opulent gifts and public repentance) his public honor. Yet during the public speeches necessary to bring about this reconciliation, the glory-fated hero shows neither concern for strategy nor pleasure at the material and verbal honors that Agamemnon lavishes on him. His primary—perhaps even sole—desire is for battle to begin (XVIII.145–53, 199–208, 275). Achilles hesitates once only, reluctant to neglect Patroklos's corpse, but Thetis's promise to protect his friend's body releases Achilles to proceed to battle (XVIII.16, 21–27). Only once in his many speeches after Patroklos's death and before entering battle does Achilles so much as mention glory (XVIII.121).

When battle does recommence, Achilles, now "insatiate of battle," searches for Hektor with "anger . . . driving him" (XX.2, 75–77). A spare handful of references indicates that Achilles is at least not insensible to the love of honor.[12] Over the course of the three books of battle, he is described as "straining to win glory" (XX.502–3), then as "violent after his glory" (XXI.543–44); finally, he signals to his fellow Achaians not to throw their spears at Hektor for fear they will take his preeminence in glory (XXII.205–7). Achilles himself mentions glory just once—when he reproaches Apollo for rescuing one of the god's favorites and thereby depriving him of glory (XXII.18). But, as in the scenes before the battle, references indicating Achilles's desire for glory are scant in comparison to the copious references to Achilles's preoccupation with the loss of Patroklos, his resulting fury, and his desire to either kill Hektor or die himself.

Indeed, the most prominent theme in the three books describing this battle is Achilles's "fury," which garners six mentions by the narrator in book XX alone (XX.75–77, 386, 400, 442, 467–68, 490). Achilles directs this fury, clearly caused by Patroklos's death, against Hektor. "Anger" is "driving him" to seek and confront Hektor in the battle (XX.75–77). When he confronts Hektor, Achilles proclaims, "Here is the man who beyond all others has troubled my anger, who slaughtered my beloved companion" (XX.425–27). Achilles repeatedly explains that he wishes either to kill Hektor or to die (XXI.224–26, 273). Even slaughtering the less prominent Trojans who oppose him—warriors he would once have captured and ransomed—relates to the loss of his friend: he claims that they too must "pay" for Patroklos's death (XXI.100–15, 122–35).

Another indication of Achilles's relative disinterest in honor lies in his disregard for his own burial. Although he has repeatedly conceded that Hektor may prevail and despite the importance of burial as an indicator of honor, he refuses to exchange promises with Hektor that the victor will return the body of the loser to his companions (XXII.260–72). Nor, once Hektor lies dying, does Achilles revel in pleasant thoughts of the honor won by his defeat of the most feared of the Trojan warriors. Where a glory-driven warrior would rejoice in thoughts of the future remembrance of his own name and the glorious burial that would someday be given him for this accomplishment, Achilles remains focused on his anger and his loss. He wishes that his fury would permit him to eat Hektor raw (XXII.345), and he plans the burial that he will bestow on his friend and that he will deny Hektor (XXII.331–36). Achilles notes once to his companions in passing, "we have won great fame" (XXII.393), but his combined speeches and actions demonstrate that his interest in this glory pales beside his devotion to the burial, honoring, and mourning of Patroklos (XXII.364, 378–90).

This distinction—between Achilles's awareness of the glory he has won and his passionate devotion to his deceased friend—is discernable in Achilles's speeches during battle and immediately after Patroklos's death, but the distinction becomes overwhelmingly evident between Hektor's death and the end of the *Iliad*. Achilles's focus turns almost wholly to mourning and burying Patroklos (XXIII.6–11, 19–23, 43–53, 59–64, 245–50; XXIV.3–8).[13] His primary distraction from grieving and overseeing the funeral arrangements for Patroklos occurs when he pauses to abuse Hektor's body (XXIII.19–22, 24, 183–84; XXIV.14–18), but otherwise Achilles appears without interest other than "beloved" Patroklos who "was his true friend" (XXIII.144–45). The only evidence that he contemplates his own future indicates a lack of interest in the glory that will be associated with the name of Hektor's slayer. Instead, Achilles is more cognizant of accepting the fact that he will never return to his homeland (XXIII.144–51) and arranging for his own bones eventually to be buried with those of Patroklos (XXII.245–50). When, at the gods' insistence, Achilles returns Hektor's body to King Priam, the resulting encounter with Hektor's father provides a final window on the living Achilles's desires: he mourns his friend (XXIV.511–12, 592–95), thinks of the home that he will not see again, and begins to mourn for the father who waits in vain for him (XXIV.507–12).[14]

The *Odyssey* includes two postmortem glimpses of Achilles, one of which is pertinent here.[15] In a brief encounter with Odysseus (which Odysseus later recounts), Achilles bemoans his own death: he would prefer existence as a living slave over lordship in Hades (11.487–91). Having renounced glory, Achilles next asks about his son and father and wishes that he were able to protect his aged father (11.491–503). Upon learning that his son, Neoptolemos, is alive and famous, Achilles walks away "happy" from his short conversation with Odysseus (11.538–40). Whether Achilles's happiness results from his son's survival or his son's fame remains a mystery, both because of ambiguity in Odysseus's wording and because of the absence of further dialogue between these heroes. Nonetheless, important conclusions can be drawn about Achilles's desires in life and after his death. Even if he is happy for his son's fame, Achilles's preference for existence as a living slave indicates that he does not believe glory to be the highest good.[16]

More importantly, before his death—while he is in the process of winning the glory that will shine through the ages—Achilles himself does not desire honor above all else. Over the course of the *Iliad*, his desires change, and—at least after the outrage that he suffers in the opening book—honor is never his foremost desire. Indeed, although he is at first highly (but not solely) concerned with honor, by the middle of the epic he ranks honor as unimportant next to the possibility of taking a wife of his own choosing and living a long, wealthy life in his father's house. Later, as he helps Patroklos prepare for battle and then prepares to kill Hektor himself, Achilles is cognizant of honor and ranks it as something positive to be won, but neither his own speeches nor Homer's descriptions indicate that Achilles's love of honor comes close to rivaling his desire to kill Patroklos's killer. Once he has returned from the battle in which he kills Hektor, Achilles never mentions honor again. In other words, after Patroklos dies, Achilles's greatest love cannot be honor because it is most demonstrably his friendship for Patroklos. Love for his friend unleashes Achilles's greatest courage and a correspondingly epic loss of moderation.

Hektor, Breaker of Horses

Although Arendt does not mention him specifically, Hektor, as the most highly esteemed Trojan hero, seems the most likely of the Trojans to exhibit the dominant love that she ascribed to all ancient Greek heroes. Among the Trojans, Hektor is nearly always the chief warrior and leader, although occasionally he is temporarily eclipsed by Sarpedon or Aineias. Hence, for example, Hektor takes the lead in negotiating the terms of the duel between Alexandros and Menelaus; he leads the Trojans and their allies into battle more often than anyone else; and when battlefield decisions must be made, Hektor consults with his allies, brothers, and lords and then determines their joint course of action.[17] Among the Achaians, it is evident from the outset that Hektor is the most feared of the Trojans and Trojan-allied warriors. In the opening scene, when Achilles predicts that Agamemnon will regret losing his help in battle, Achilles warns that the Achaians will "drop and die" before "man-slaughtering Hektor" (I.242–43; see also V.467; VI.7–79).

Like Achilles, Hektor is ultimately in an impossible situation: Zeus, willing the greatest glory to Achilles, has decreed that Hektor will be given glory and then die at Achilles's hands (XV.592–614). Yet, unlike Achilles, Hektor does not know (although he suspects) that his situation is impossible. Hektor only knows that his own life, the lives of the members of his family, and the lives of all the Trojans likely depend on his performance in the war. Indeed, Hektor does not even have the comfort of knowing that a glorious death would improve the chance of Troy's victory. His own survival and continued leadership may well be more critical to Troy's defense than any courageous battlefield exploit. Because Hektor lacks the knowledge that Achilles enjoys about the implications of his actions, Hektor's alternatives have a complexity unlike Achilles's stark alternative between life and honor. Hektor may live, or he may die. In either event, he may have glory or shame, and in either case his family and people may flourish or be killed and enslaved. Viewed in light of the many uncertainties that he faces, Hektor's choices appear nothing if not human.

Accordingly, when Hektor ultimately falls in battle, it is not necessarily the result of his preference and choice for either public honor or private life. He might have chosen death in battle as a means to protect his family, or he might have chosen death in battle (having despaired of victory in the war and the glory accompanying victory) as the most glorious option available to him. Indeed, Hektor's position as the defender of a city—a city that he must defend if his own life is to continue and the lives of his wife and son are to be preserved—complicates matters yet further.[18] For Hektor, the best possible outcome is a combination of glory and protection of his private life: if he were to win the war, he would be publicly honored for having successfully defended Troy, and he would also thereby secure the possibility of enjoying a long life with his wife and son. Thus Hektor's actions do not sufficiently indicate his desires, and it is necessary to listen to his words and observe his emotions as he acts in order to understand what Hektor loves.

But Hektor, in this regard like Achilles and unlike Agamemnon and Ajax, suffers from shifting and sometimes conflicting desires. He references glory, shame, personal safety, and the safety and well-being of his city and his family.[19] No specific desire clearly dominates. Unlike Achilles, however, Hektor does not so much develop as alternate. Hektor seems at a loss to maintain a clear first priority from one scene to the next, equivocating repeatedly between preferring private life and glory. Through his character portrait as a whole, Homer shows that Hektor pays a great price for loving honor, but the poet likewise reveals both that

Hektor's first choice has never been to die leaving behind an immortal name and that Hektor loves his family.

The distinction between Hektor's prominence on the battlefield and in Trojan political leadership is critical to understanding that Hektor continues to lead his city's war efforts while opposing the decision to be at war. Although prominent among the Trojan warriors, he does not enjoy a political preeminence on par with his battlefield prominence. Numerous scenes clarify that, were the choice Hektor's, Helen and her possessions would be returned and the war ended. Indeed, Hektor states repeatedly that he would prefer the death of the brother who started the war to the war's continuation. In their first conversation Hektor tells Alexandros that it would have been better had Alexandros "never been born, or killed unwedded" (III.40).[20] The city is to be blamed for its support of Alexandros: "The Trojans are cowards in truth, else long before this you had worn a mantle of flying stones for the wrong you did us" (III.56–57). Hektor wishes that his brother had not brought this war to his city because his brother brings "shame, for others to sneer at" and "to your father a big sorrow, and your city, and all your people" (III.42–51). Seeing only shame and sorrow without the possibility of any gain from the war, Hektor is "happy" when his brother offers to try to end the war by challenging Menelaus to single combat.

Hektor later reiterates these sentiments to his mother, Hekabe, repeating his wish that Alexandros would die and prevent the sorrow that he brings to the "Trojans, and high-hearted Priam, and all of his children" (VI.280–83). If Alexandros were dead, the war would end and then, Hektor tells Hekabe, "I could say my heart had forgotten its joyless affliction" (VI.285). When Hektor subsequently visits his brother's house, he continues to blame Alexandros for the war and the death of their people: "The people are dying around the city and around the steep wall as they fight hard; and it is for you that this war with its clamour has flared up about our city" (VI.327–29).

Despite his wishes, the war continues. There is only one scene in the *Iliad* in which the city's political leaders deliberate about the continuation of the war and how much they would be willing to give up to persuade the Achaians to sail home. In this one scene Priam consults with his allies, lords, and sons and decides to offer the Achaians the return of Helen's possessions but—because of Alexandros's refusal—not Helen herself (VII.345–80). The audience knows, if not because he wishes his brother dead as a means to end the war then because Hektor has already agreed to return Helen, that Hektor would have argued for the return of Helen to end the war. Yet Hektor is inexplicably absent (or at least silent) during the political deliberation. Priam's determination to let Alexandros drag the city into war stands.

Hektor's stance toward the war, as a necessary evil that he will endure, contrasts starkly with Agamemnon's. Agamemnon, when faced with the death of a brother on the battlefield, wishes for Menelaus to survive so that the war will not end. Agamemnon wants the war to continue to reap glory, so he desires the well-being of the brother who must survive for the war to continue. Hektor, when faced with the prospect of a war that shows no sign of ending, wishes for the death of his brother as a means of ending the war. Unlike Agamemnon, Hektor does not relish the war as an opportunity to win glory. This observation does not establish why Hektor wishes the war to end—whether to avoid shame, protect the people, avoid death, or protect his family—but it does distinguish Hektor from Agamemnon insofar as Hektor does not desire the context in which glory is most likely to be won. Glory is not Hektor's first choice.

Ultimately, Homer leaves Hektor's second choice ambiguous. Hektor articulates to his wife the desire to win public honor; yet he explains to his fellow warriors the importance of the wives and children that their efforts protect. Hektor's speeches and actions bear out the continuation of this tension in the unhappy hero's desires. Homer reveals the range of Hektor's complex set of desires most clearly as he describes the Trojan general's interactions in his network of relationships with family, fellow Trojans, and political allies.

Far more than the Achaians, Hektor and the Trojan warriors are integrated into their families. This is only to be expected, given the nature of their position as defenders of Troy, and yet it is striking—after the absence of this aspect of life in the Achaian army—to hear the protection of and even partnership with their wives (and other nonwarrior family members) referred to by the Trojans. In several instances during battle, Hektor refers to protecting the Trojan wives and children (VIII.164–66; XVI.830–32; XVII.223–24). He explains, as he encourages his army, that a man has "no dishonour when he dies defending his country, for then his wife shall be saved and children afterwards" (XV.496–97). Similarly, when Sarpedon rebukes Hektor and wishes to incite him to greater courage in battle, Sarpedon refers to their families. Sarpedon, his own wife and infant son far away, argues that because Hektor and his fellow

Trojans "fight in defence of their own wives," this responsibility "should lie night and day" on Hektor's mind and cause him to inspire his army to "unwearying" fighting (V.480–92). These words work: they "bit into the heart of Hektor," who springs straightaway into the battle to lead the Trojans and fight himself (V.493–98).[21]

But Hektor does not just fight on behalf of the wives of Troy. He also fights in partnership with them. Or, if this claim is too strong, at the very least he views their actions as potentially contributing to or detracting from the successful defense of Troy, and he therefore coordinates their efforts with those of the warriors. This is perhaps most dramatically demonstrated when Hektor follows the counsel of his brother Helenos ("best by far of the augurs" [VI.75]) to instruct the Trojan women in supplication to Athena. Rather than stay on the front lines and attempt to turn back an Achaian attack with his warriors, Hektor returns to Troy to instruct his mother and the women of Troy to supplicate Athena for help (VI.74–101).

The implication that Hektor values the contribution of the Trojan women, even within the otherwise masculine (within the *Iliad*) world of war, is further supported when Hektor later credits Andromache with the critical care of his war horses and assigns the wives of Troy a role in its defense. Speaking to his horses during battle, he explains the care that Andromache had given to them: "Now repay me for all that loving care in abundance Andromache . . . gave you: the sweet-hearted wheat before all others and mixed wine with it for you to drink, when her heart inclined to it, as for me, who am proud that I am her young husband" (VIII.184–90). Later, deciding that the Trojans shall spend the night camped upon their field but fearful lest the Achaians attack the city, Hektor gives orders for the Trojan wives to participate in keeping watch over the city: "And as for the women, have our wives, each one in her own house, kindle a great fire; let there be a watch kept steadily lest a sudden attack get into the town when the fighters have left it" (VIII.517–22).

Nor is Hektor's relationship with the women of his city limited to employing them in its defense. During Hektor's return to Troy to instruct Hekabe to supplicate Athena, Hektor demonstrates his attachment to his own private life though his affection for his wife and child. Once his defense-related duties have been fulfilled by speaking with his mother and by urging Alexandros back to the front line, Hektor speeds to see his wife and son. As he explains to Helen, Hektor desires to visit "my own people, my beloved wife and my son, who is little, since I do not know if ever again I shall come back this way, or whether the gods will strike me down at the hands of the Achaians" (VI.365–68). Hektor leaves Alexandros and Helen to search for his "perfect" (as he calls her) wife (VI.370–80). Arriving at their home, Hektor learns that Andromache did not go with the other Trojan women to Athena's temple to propitiate the goddess. Rather, upon hearing that the Trojans were losing, she went to the city wall "like a woman gone mad" (VI.380–89). Homer's preface to the couple's only meeting in the *Iliad* thus stresses Andromache's public and Hektor's private aspects: the warrior eagerly seeks his wife within their home, and the wife observes the war from the best vantage point a woman can reach.[22]

When he finds his wife and son on the ramparts, Hektor smiles to see his baby boy (VI.391–403).[23] Andromache clings tearfully to her husband as she explains her fears: "Dearest, your own great strength will be your death, and you have no pity on your little son, nor on me, ill-starred, who soon must be your widow" (VI.404–8). Andromache, an orphan of the war, emphasizes her own vulnerability: "Hector, thus you are father to me, and my honoured mother, you are my brother, and you it is who are my husband. Please take pity upon me" (VI.429–30).[24] But Andromache does not just plead for pity. She presents Hektor with a new battle strategy, explaining to her husband how he can defend the city without putting himself in personal danger. Andromache points to a weak spot on the city walls and describes how the Achaean champions have repeatedly attacked it (VI.431–39).

Hektor responds to his wife's appeal and strategic advice by indicating that he too has given thought to these considerations. But Hektor refuses to assent to his wife's strategy, explaining that he cannot bear the shame of failing to fight in the foremost ranks for glory (VI.440–46). Then Hektor proceeds to share his own fears with Andromache. He believes that Troy will fall—a fact that Andromache, in her concern for Hektor's importance to her son and herself, had not noted. He describes her future life working in captivity, demonstrating that even as she has given thought to how to run a battle, he has given thought to how his enslaved wife would be forced to labor through her grief and pain (VI.447–65). Hektor's vision of a fallen Troy troubles him both because of his concern for the grief of his wife and because she would then be known by others as the wife of dead Hektor.[25] More than he is pained at the suffering of his people, the fate of his parents, or the deaths of his numerous brothers, Hektor is troubled by the thought of Andromache's fate.

> [T]he thought of you, when some bronze armoured
> Achaian leads you off, taking away your day of liberty,
> in tears; and in Argos you must work at the loom of
>   another,
> and carry water from the spring of Messeis or Hypereia,
> all unwilling, but strong will be the necessity upon you. . . .
> But may I be dead and the piled earth hide me under
>   before I
> hear you crying and know by this that they drag you
>   captive. (VI.454–65)

Their conversation shifts focus to their baby, and Hektor reaches for his son. The boy, who is terrified by his father's war helmet, cries. Both parents laugh, and Hektor removes his helmet to play with his son. He prays that the boy may grow up to be even greater than his father and to "delight the heart of his mother" (VI.466–81). As he hands their son to his wife, Hektor feels pity for her and attempts to comfort her. However fate plays out, he reasons aloud, they each should attend to their own work. He will return to battle, and she must return home: "[G]o therefore back to our house, and take up your own work, the loom and the distaff, and see to it that your handmaidens apply their work also" (VI.482–93). "Beloved" Andromache follows her husband's command, returning to the household where she works while grieving for the death of her still-living husband (VI.494–52).

Seen through a cynical lens, this scene presents the marriage of a glory-seeking warrior who commands his wife to attend to women's work. But it is more than this.[26] Hektor engages with Andromache's concerns and concedes, if only implicitly, that he too has considered the battle strategy that she suggests. Having accepted the legitimacy of Andromache's martial suggestions, he proceeds to demonstrate that he shares her fears for their future, joins her in planning for their son's future, and even acknowledges the importance of her work within their home. Hektor, according to his own estimation, is "proud" to be Andromache's "young husband" (VIII.184–90). Homer at least suggests that this pair shares a form of friendship centered on their common concerns and respect for one another's skills and intelligence.

In addition to the respect that Hektor accords his wife, he also demonstrates love for his immediate family. He takes time away from his martial duties to embrace his son and converse with his wife out of fear that he might never see them again. The thought of the suffering of his wife causes him pain, and Hektor attempts to comfort her. Homer also underscores Hektor's love for his wife and son through subtle descriptions of his physical movements. As Hektor proceeds into the city, to his mother, and on to Alexandros's house, Homer provides no indication of Hektor's speed. But when the husband and father proceeds from Alexandros's home toward his wife and son, Hektor "in speed made his way" (VI.370), and when he looks for them on the city walls he "hastened" (VI.390). Finally, as the brothers leave for battle, Alexandros laughs and moves quickly away from Helen, but Hektor "yet lingered before turning away from the place where he had talked with his lady" (VI.512–16). If Hektor has a particular friend—distinguished from the generalized friendship that he bears for his kin and his fellow soldiers—it is clearly Andromache.

And yet, as Hektor himself concedes to Andromache, he has "learned to be valiant and to fight always among the foremost ranks of the Trojans, winning . . . great glory" for himself and for his father (VI.444–46). Indeed, Hektor indicates that glory drives him on in many instances. For example, when his brother Helenos, the augur, promises that the gods will not permit Hektor to die, Hektor challenges the champion of the Achaians' choice to single combat (VII.41–92). As he makes his challenge to the Achaians, Hektor explains that—if he wins—the burial mound of the defeated warrior will perpetuate his own "glory" (VII.91). Facing Ajax at the outset of the ensuing combat, fear of shame keeps him from running away (VII.214–18). Similarly, as he encourages his army in the next battle, he tells his soldiers that Zeus has assented to his glory and success (VIII.176). When he strips Achilles's armor from Patroklos's corpse, Hektor sends the armor back to Troy "to be his great glory" (XVII.131).

Often Homer juxtaposes Hektor's clearest statements about desiring glory with his competing desire for survival. Hektor challenges an Achaian to single combat when he thinks the gods have promised that he cannot die, and he urges on his army by promising both glory and success. At the end of the same day of battle, he expresses the desire for immortality combined with honor: "Oh, if I only could be as this in all my days immortal and ageless and be held in honour" as a god (VIII.538–41).

Later, as he battles Ajax in an attempt to set fire to the Achaian fleet, Hektor again expresses the desire to be deathless (XIII.824–32). As surely as Hektor desperately wishes to avoid shame and even loves glory, he is painfully aware that the price of this desire may be his life, and he cannot shake the haunting wish that it might be otherwise.

Hektor may ultimately trade his life for a share of glory (or for glory combined with defense of his family and city), but he never makes his peace with this trade. With Andromache and his baby son still alive—and hence the potential for a full life, alive and shared with them—Hektor's options are fundamentally different from those of Achilles. Much less does he ever enjoy the option that Achilles could contemplate before the death of Patroklos—simply leaving to enjoy a long, private life with those he loves. Hektor's discomfort with the price of glory, especially when combined with the importance of his survival to the defense of Troy, helps to explain why the Trojan who does the most to keep the Achaians in check (even while wounded) is simultaneously the Trojan who flees in sheer terror repeatedly (XVI.364–76; XVI.655–58).[27]

In his final moments of life, as he makes his fated choice to remain outside Troy and fight Achilles, Hektor continues to struggle with his competing desires. In anticipation of their confrontation, Hektor both yearns for glory (XVIII.308) and fears for his own life (XX.373–80). In the first of the two encounters in which Hektor advances to oppose Achilles, he does so because his fear has evaporated as he watches his youngest brother die at Achilles's hands: "But now when Hektor saw Polydoros, his own brother, going limp to the ground and catching his bowels in his hands, the mist closed about his eyes also, he could stand no longer to turn there at a distance, but went out to face Achilleus hefting his sharp spear like a flame" (XX.419–23).[28] This moment, although more dramatic because the boy who has been killed is too young for battle, is like many earlier moments when Hektor had taken the lead motivated by the "bitter sorrow" felt over the death of a companion or relative (VIII.115–26; VIII.316; XVII.82; XVII.223–24; XVII.591).

Two books later, when Hektor is caught between the fear of Achilles and the desire for glory for the final time, he stands alone before the gates of Troy. He wishes to find a way out of the situation and feels ashamed of the deaths that his prior recklessness in battle had brought on the Trojan warriors (XXII.104–6). Refusing to hide in the city but unable to face Achilles, he flees until he is persuaded to fight by a trick of the gods. Thinking that his brother Deiphobos offers to stand with him, he turns to fight, as he puts it, against Troy's "greatest affliction" (XXII.287–88). When Hektor discovers that he faces Achilles alone, he knows his death is at hand and determines not to "die without a struggle, inglorious, but do some big thing first, that men to come shall know of it" (XXII.304–5). One hundred lines later, Hektor lies dead in the dust, Achilles has begun to abuse his body, and the wailing of the Trojans has commenced.

Over the course of the *Iliad*, Achilles's loves change. Hektor, by comparison, is a character of mixed loves: his love for his city, his family, his own life, and glory are intermingled—often competing with one another and sometimes reinforcing one another. The most apparent conclusion that can be drawn from his mixed loves is that Hektor's loves do not coincide with Arendt's model of the honor-devoted Homeric hero. Some of Hektor's excellence, in particular his courage, seems attributable to his love of glory. This may be most evident when he rejects Andromache's defensive battle plans and when, perceiving that he cannot escape Achilles, he despairs and makes a final attempt at glory. But thrice-wounded Hektor flees in terror more than once. Not only is Hektor's courage intermittent (although one might argue that this is explained by the intermittency of his desire for glory), but his courage is also motivated by his desire to protect his city and the family that resides therein. His moments of battlefield courage are often motivated by the death of a relative or close companion, and he is more troubled by the thought of Andromache's pain after the eventual fall of Troy than any other aspect of the ultimate defeat that he predicts.

After Hektor's death, the war stops for twelve days while the people of Troy honor him and mourn his death. Every honor they can afford him he receives: he is remembered, as surely he must have known he would be, as Troy's greatest defender. As Hektor made clear in more than one speech, this honor—perhaps even if he could have known his place in Homer's nigh-immortal epics—is not what Hektor had wanted most. Admittedly, his pain would have been alleviated because ultimately the gods forced Achilles to permit him this honor. But what Hektor wanted most—what Hektor would have seen his brother stoned to death to achieve—was the end of the war that brought him this honor.

In other words, what Hektor desired most (and what he knew in his heart he could not have) was enjoyment of the peaceful conditions that would permit Astyanax to grow up to be greater than himself and delight Andromache's heart.[29] In this regard, Hektor is like Achilles—

powerless to bring about what he wanted most. Both men desire a long life shared with their closest companions, with those people with whom they share their private lives.

In the final analysis, Hektor's mixed virtues and mixed loves make him a poor source of insight on the relationship between desire and excellence because it is impossible to clearly attribute his specific virtues and failings to his competing and frustrated desires. Nonetheless, Hektor's presence in the Trojan War does more than demonstrate that a hero need not be motivated solely by the love of honor. Homer uses Hektor as a window on a related aspect of the tension between love of public honor and the preference for one's own private life. Through Hektor, Homer teaches his audience, an audience that he has also taught to marvel at the brilliance of Achilles's battlefield excellence, to mourn the destruction of private life.

The Human Price of the Love of Glory

Hektor's love for his wife and son, like Achilles's desire to live a long, pleasant, and friendship-filled life, demonstrates that private life was esteemed as human and valuable for its own sake and not merely as necessary for public action. The prominence that Homer gives to the grief of Hektor's family, particularly to Andromache's mourning, shows that what has been lost is valuable in human terms. Indeed, Homer narrates the consequences of Hektor's death far more in terms of the loss of husband, father, and son than in terms of the ultimate fall of Troy. For this reason, it is perhaps in his death that Hektor provides the most light on the human experience.

Homer's description of Andromache's response to Hektor's death starts and ends with emphasis on the private aspect of her shared life with Hektor. As Hektor dies and the mourning wails commence, Andromache sits in her home "weaving a web in the inner room of the high house, a red folding robe, and inworking elaborate figures" (XXII.440–41). She calls to her maidens to heat the water for Hektor's bath but then stops. Hearing the cries from the city walls, "her limbs spun, and the shuttle dropped from her hand to the ground" (XXII.447–50). Suspecting that Hektor has been slain, she runs to the city wall like a "raving woman with pulsing heart" (XXII.460–61). Once there, seeing his corpse being dragged toward the ships of her enemies, "she fell backward, and gasped the life breath from her, and far off threw from her head the shining gear that ordered her headdress" (XXII.467–68). Held up by Hektor's brothers and sisters, she catches her breath and then uses it to express her despair.

> Now you go down to the house of Death in the secret places
> of the earth, and left me here behind in the sorrow of mourning,
> a widow in your house, and the boy is only a baby
> who is born to you and me, the unfortunate. You cannot help him,
> Hektor, any more, since you are dead. Nor can he help you. (XXII.482–86)

In her grief Andromache imagines the unhappy future of their son[30] and weeps for the futility of her own labor and that of her household women: they have labored over fine-textured linens, but Hektor's corpse will lie naked.[31] In her final speech, in the final book of the *Iliad*, Andromache makes her formal, public lament for Hektor. Despite the public context of this speech, she emphasizes the tenderness of her relationship with Hektor within the privacy of their own bed. Andromache makes public the private aspect of what she has lost. She loved Hektor, not only as defender of her son, her home, and her city, but also as a loving and beloved husband whose speech she treasured.

> Therefore your people are grieving for you all through their city,
> Hektor, and you left for your parents mourning and sorrow
> beyond words, but for me passing all others is left the bitterness
> and the pain, for you did not die in bed, and stretch out your arms to me,
> nor tell me some last intimate word that I could remember
> always, all the nights and days of my weeping for you.
> (XXIV.741–45)

Andromache's suffering and her predictions for Astyanax's future suffering may be the most obvious, but they are not the only important portrayal of private suffering made public in the *Iliad*. Achilles's story closes in a scene in which he weeps with Priam: Achilles weeps for the father that he will never see again, and Priam weeps not only for Hektor but for so many sons who have died.

> So [Priam] spoke, and stirred in [Achilles] a passion of grieving
> for his own father. He took the old man's hand and pushed him
> gently away, and the two remembered, as Priam sat huddled
> at the feet of Achilleus and wept close for manslaughtering Hektor
> and Achilleus wept now for his own father, now again
> for Patroklos. The sound of their mourning moved in the house. (XXIV.507–12)

These are the last tears that Achilles sheds in the *Iliad*: they flow as the result of the destruction of two private relationships, his relationship with his father and his friendship with Patroklos. Beside him, Priam weeps for his city's greatest champion but also for the loss of boys yet too young to have public significance. Three hundred lines later the *Iliad* concludes with the details of the ceremonies honoring Hektor's burial and the final statement, "Such was the burial of Hektor, breaker of horses" (XXIV.804).

Homer's descriptions of Achilles's and Priam's tears, his focus on Andromache's grief, and his choice of conclusion for the *Iliad* point to the secondary theme that flows through the epic. Homer quietly but consistently underscores the private pain and suffering—the price of this war—to create tension in his portrait of the brilliance of the heroes and the sometimes-breathtaking destruction that they create.[32] Many details in the epic, most too subtle to distract the audience from the brilliance of the battles, support this conclusion. Homer recounts battle deaths in graphic detail, but he also pauses to juxtapose the grim moment of death with references to the resulting loss to the parents and wives of the newly deceased.[33] In yet other instances, Homer reminds his audience of the value of the lost lives through descriptions in which a dying warrior becomes, even as he falls grotesquely into the dust, a beautiful tree or flower.[34]

From nearly the outset of the poem, the object of the quarrel between Agamemnon and Achilles is a woman who pays the price of the war through her captivity and suffering. Andromache, who lost the lives of both her parents and all her brothers to Achilles before the epic began, had her life shattered by this war long before Hektor died. Even before the suffering of Andromache and Briseis becomes apparent, Homer explains that the curse of a priest who has prayed to Apollo for help in recovering his captured daughter, Chryseis, keeps the pestilence in the Achaian camps so that the "corpse fires burned everywhere and did not stop burning" (I.52). Indeed, reconsidering the opening pages and the death descriptions of the *Iliad* in light of the epic's closing pages—in which the suffering of Hektor's family and Achilles's grief are detailed in terms of the loss of intimate human relationships—it becomes evident that Homer has always kept the private suffering caused by the war in sight. Homer thereby demonstrates that he does not limit his understanding of the human significance of the war—and therefore the meaning of human life—to actions that occur in public.

Conclusion

The tapestry of the *Iliad* is dominated by its brilliant and sometimes complex heroes and their immortal public accomplishments. But when we tear our eyes from the glory of the central figures and focus on the scenes into which they are woven, private suffering emerges as a minor theme that runs throughout the *Iliad*—quietly questioning the excellence of the shining hero.

The *Iliad* thus portrays a tension that it does not resolve, a tension that ultimately directs Homer's audience to homecoming—to personal survival, domestic life, and intimate relationships that escape the threat of war—as possible solutions to the unsatisfactory consequences of the pursuit of glory. In other words, the end of the *Iliad* and the elimination of the possibility of homecoming for Achilles and Hektor direct our attention to the *Odyssey*. As a result, Odysseus, who will eventually arrive home to provide Homer's audience with a more detailed portrait of private life, love of one's own, and their consequences for human excellence and politics, emerges as a surprisingly important character in the *Iliad*.

3

Homer's Pausing Hero

Odysseus at Troy

Odysseus escapes easy categorization: he is not the commander of a great host, nor is he a bulwark for his companions. Much less is he, like some of the other heroes of the *Iliad*, the immediate descendant of a god or goddess or a warrior who challenges the gods themselves. He is not consumed by fury, nor is he hopelessly long-winded in counsel. He has no family present, so the audience has no obvious opportunity to observe his relationships in his domestic life. Although he intermittently displays intelligence, self-restraint, and even courage, no simple description can capture his overarching role or dominant trait. More than any other apparent quality, Odysseus is adaptable to the situation—versatile in response to the needs of the moment—and this often manifests in actions that at least appear dishonest or cowardly.[1]

Hence, the first challenge to understanding Odysseus is simply the complexity of his character. Discerning the desire or desires that motivate Odysseus in a particular action or speech—let alone in the campaign at Troy as a whole—is no easy matter. Time and again, for example, the line between prudent strategist and coward is difficult to judge. Odysseus's choice for the placement of his ships among the beached Achaian fleet, mentioned twice in the *Iliad*, illustrates this interpretive challenge. While Ajax and Achilles each "had drawn their balanced ships up at the utter ends, sure of the strength of their hands and their courage," Odysseus chose to position his ships "in the midmost" (VIII.222–26; XI.5–9). Lest this should appear unabashedly cowardly, the text makes evident in both mentions of Odysseus's ships that this location is advantageous for more than security: Odysseus's ships are perfectly located for someone whose skills relate to the use of speech and who therefore needs to "call out to both sides, either toward the shelters of Telamonian Aias, or toward Achilleus" (VIII.223–25; XI.6–8). Such interpretive dilemmas occur often, and each time the reader faces important questions about the dominant loves that drive Odysseus. With regard to his ships, one must ask whether, suffering from a less inflamed love of honor and benefiting from greater intelligence than Ajax, Odysseus merely makes a prudent choice that permits him to put his political skills to their most efficient use. Or is he a coward hiding behind the courage of heroic companions?

A second and particularly pivotal interpretive challenge arises with regard to the trustworthiness of Odysseus's speeches. Redfield and Friedrich argue that, where Achilles speaks the truth (as he perceives it in any given moment), Odysseus speaks to persuade in support of his long-term objective.[2] Accordingly, one must always ask of Odysseus, the man of many designs, whether he speaks what he perceives to be the truth or what he believes will be conducive to his purpose. Odysseus often persuades others with appeals to their love of honor, but he himself rarely pursues honor wholeheartedly in open battle where his gifts of guile provide the least protection. Given this complexity (or duplicity[3]), two principles guide the interpretation of his character. First, although Odysseus's public speeches do not necessarily reveal his true desires, they do reveal what Odysseus knows, what he perceives to be the motivations of others, and what he considers most desirable for the Achaian army. Second, Odysseus's soliloquies, his inner thoughts, and Homer's descriptions of Odysseus are reliable sources of this hero's desires because, unlike his public speeches, no motivation for deception exists in these contexts.

Juxtaposing Odysseus's public speeches with his private thoughts and soliloquies leads to a curious discovery. Within the privacy of his own mind and self-directed speech, Odysseus is never unhesitatingly motivated by a desire for honor; yet in public speech he makes frequent and unequivocal appeals to honor. There is at least a partial disjunction between Odysseus's own love and the love that he appeals to when attempting to persuade others. Examination of his role in the Trojan War shows that Odysseus himself is not motivated to win honor at any price (at least not most of the time), but he believes that appeals to honor will be the most persuasive with his fellow Achaian lords.

Because of these complexities, the approach to Odysseus in this chapter is layered rather than chronological. Public Odysseus—the Odysseus who speaks and persuades in public counsel—appeals to honor and shrewdly manages the honor of the strife-prone lords who determine the course of the war. Inner Odysseus—the warrior and man who must decide whether to risk his own life in battle and how to spend an hour of leisure—is far more complex. Inner Odysseus risks his life for honor in battle, but he also loves a quiet hour more than the acclaim of his peers. Homer does not resolve this tension in the *Iliad*, but he does provide initial clues about Odysseus's desires and excellence. The most restrained and the most intelligent, if not the most courageous, of the heroes is the only Achaian warrior who yearns for at least some aspects of private life *and* whose private life is neither at stake in the war nor destroyed by the war.

Public Odysseus, Like Zeus in Counsel

Among his peers, Odysseus is greatly valued—honored even—but for his mind and his gift with speech rather than for outstanding ability as a warrior or as a leader of a great contingent of ships. Odysseus's epithet in the catalog of ships, in which he and many other characters are initially introduced, provides a good starting point for his character: commanding a mere twelve ships, he is described as "like Zeus in counsel" (II.636).[4] As this epithet indicates, Odysseus is generally trusted and respected for more than his relatively modest prowess in battle. This trust and respect that Odysseus inspires in his peers results from his ability to handle volatile political situations tactfully and to counsel prudently in dire situations.

Although Homer's epics often leave the details to our imagination, Agamemnon's repeated reliance on Odysseus in missions that rely on his ability to persuade, pacify, and coordinate supports this conclusion. Elmer has observed Odysseus's skill at restoring social order and integrity to the Greek army.[5] In the opening book Odysseus "of the many designs" is tasked to lead Chryseis back to her father and assure the proper sacrifices and the soothing of the outraged father and his god (I.430–87).[6] When Menelaus and Alexandros are to engage in single combat in book III, "resourceful" Odysseus flanks Agamemnon and then cooperates with Hektor in arranging the necessary details for the combat (III.267–68, III.314–17). With the Achaian army driven to the ships, "long-suffering great Odysseus" is selected to persuade Achilles to rejoin the war (IX.163–72, 179–81, 676). Indeed, even before the war began, Odysseus was employed both in diplomatic attempts to gain the return of Helen (III.203–24; XI.138–42) and to recruit warriors for the coming war (IX.252–59; XI.765–74). His own value to his allies is supported by the fact that both Agamemnon and Menelaus sail a month out of their way to enlist his help (24.115–19).[7] During the war he appears and speaks at the various Achaian councils far more than his status as warrior or commander of troops justifies. That he was well regarded, at least insofar as his skills and particular abilities were valued, is also implicit in the honor that he is repeatedly accorded by Agamemnon.[8]

Wielding no little power in the Trojan War as a result of his persuasive ability, Odysseus's many public speeches indicate that he knows well the power of the love of honor felt by his companions. Odysseus appeals to his companions' love of honor in many speeches, and he ensures the proper allocation of honor among the Achaians. Three scenes in particular are illustrative: (1) Odysseus's attempt to persuade Achilles to rejoin the war (book IX), (2) the war council of the wounded Achaian war leaders (book XIV), and (3) Odysseus's management of the reconciliation between Agamemnon and Achilles (book XIX). Yet, as much as Odysseus's speeches and actions in these scenes indicate that he is a master manipulator of those who love honor, none of them establishes the extent to which he desires public honor for himself.

Appealing to Achilles

When Agamemnon sends Phoinix, Ajax, and "brilliant" Odysseus to plead "with words of supplication and with the gifts of friendship" for the return of Achilles and his Myrmidons to the Achaian fighting force, Odysseus takes the lead (IX.111–92).[9] Odysseus is the first to address Achilles, and he appeals directly and repeatedly to the estranged warrior's honor, referring in succession to (1) the enormity of the challenge of winning the war, (2) the material honors offered by Agamemnon, (3) the worship that would be accorded to Achilles from the army he could save, and (4) the opportunity to defeat Hektor.

First Odysseus explains that "there is doubt if we save our strong-benched vessels or if they will be destroyed, unless you put on your war strength" (IX.230–31). Continuing in a similar vein for twenty-seven lines, Odysseus reminds Achilles that if he does not come to their aid now it may be too late. Despite the pride of the Trojans and the desperation of the Achaians, superlative Achilles still has the ability "late though it be, to rescue the afflicted sons of the Achaians from the Trojan onslaught"

(IX.244–48). There is honor to be won, Odysseus implies, from the very difficulty of the task of rescuing the Achaian army.

After briefly reminding Achilles of his father's parting instruction, to win honor by controlling his anger and avoiding quarrel (IX.252–58), Odysseus proceeds to a lengthy explanation of the material honors that Agamemnon offers (IX.262–99). Finally, Odysseus concludes his speech with a switch in tactics. If Achilles cannot overcome his anger enough to accept Agamemnon's offer, the estranged warrior should consider the honor that the Achaian troops will afford their rescuer and the honor associated with defeating Hektor.

> But if the son of Atreus is too much hated in your heart,
> himself and his gifts, at least take pity on all the other
> Achaians, who are afflicted along the host, and will honour you
> as a god. You may win very great glory among them.
> For now you might kill Hektor, since he would come very close to you
> with the wicked fury upon him, since he thinks there is not his equal
> among the rest of the Danaans the ships carried hither.
> (IX.300–6)

Odysseus's appeal to Achilles's honor fails, but this is precisely because he has misjudged Achilles's ruling passion. Indeed, Achilles explains to Odysseus that he now values honor at nothing (IX.319–20). Before this new disregard, Achilles had publicly displayed concern for his honor when he quarreled with Agamemnon. Thus, while Odysseus's first public appeal to honor is ill-fated, it is not ill-conceived. The timing of his appeal is bad, but it illustrates Odysseus's often correct perception that the love of honor has the power to motivate many of the soldiers with whom he serves.

Advising Agamemnon

Not surprisingly, given the differences in Achilles's and Agamemnon's loves, Agamemnon more readily changes his course of action in response to Odysseus's appeals to honor. This happens for the first time when

Agamemnon, gripped with panic, suggests dragging their beached ships into the ocean and sailing home. Odysseus, first to respond, asks Agamemnon in disgust, "What sort of word escaped your teeth's barrier?" (XIV.83). He proceeds to insult Agamemnon, calling him unworthy to lead his own army, accusing him of offering a "ruinous" strategy, and warning Agamemnon not to let anyone hear this scheme of dragging the ships into the water (XIV.82–102). The intent behind Odysseus's disdainful speech seems to be twofold. He wishes to make evident to Agamemnon (and to everyone listening) the shamefulness of Agamemnon's plan and the honor that it would afford the Trojans. The greater concern conveyed by Odysseus's speech, however, is the assessment that Agamemnon's plan has no chance of success.

> [A]nd headlong destruction [would] swing our way, since the Achaians
> will not hold their battle as the ships are being hauled seaward,
> but will look about, and let go the exultation of fighting.
> There, O leader of the people, your plan will be ruin.
> (XIV.99–102)

Agamemnon, ever sensitive to his own honor, acknowledges Odysseus's words, retracts his suggestion, and solicits a better plan (XIV.103–8). When Diomedes suggests that the wounded leaders should return to battle in a command rather than a combat role (XIV.109–32), Agamemnon concurs.

Considering that the Achaian resources are already pushed to the breaking point, it seems unlikely that they could successfully drag even some of the ships to sea without being forced to give up yet more ground.[10] Odysseus's observation that the warriors would no longer even try to hold their position if they saw their leaders heading seaward—and that this would lead to immediate "headlong destruction"—is reasonable, perhaps even obvious. This, in itself, does not disprove the possibility that Odysseus desires to stay and fight for glory. Nonetheless, the dangers inherent in Agamemnon's plan for flight provide an adequate alternative explanation for Odysseus's appeal to Agamemnon's love of honor.

If Agamemnon had a good escape plan, would Odysseus have embraced it and happily sailed for home? Neither this scene nor the *Iliad* as a whole provides sufficient evidence for a definitive answer. Appealing to Agamemnon's love of honor is a good way of convincing him and thus provides a sufficient explanation for Odysseus's appeal. Odysseus, tactician that he is, observes the importance of honor to his commander and his culture. Yet his observation and use of his leader's love for honor proves neither that Odysseus shares his leader's love of honor nor that he is motivated by a distinct desire or set of desires.

Brokering the Peace of Agamemnon and Achilles

Odysseus's next speech takes place in the assembly called by Achilles after the death of Patroklos. At the opening of this assembly, Achilles and Agamemnon express the desire to be reconciled, and Achilles demands immediate battle. Before Agamemnon has a chance to respond, Odysseus intervenes, insisting that certain formalities must be publicly observed before the reconciliation is complete and the battle recommenced.[11]

Consistent with his earlier appeal to Agamemnon in book XIV, Odysseus's speech is evenly divided between appeals based on practical constraints and appeals related to love of honor. He starts by detailing the importance of a meal before battle and importuning Achilles to command a meal (XIX.155–70). He then devotes an equal number of lines to explaining to Achilles that pausing for a meal would permit Agamemnon to exhibit his gifts very publicly and take his oath to Achilles (thus effectively restoring the balance of honor between these leaders).

> [A]nd as for the gifts, let the lord of men Agamemnon
> bring them to the middle of our assembly so all the Achaians
> can see them before their eyes, so your own heart may be
>   pleasured.
> And let him stand up before the Argives and swear an
>   oath to you
> that he never entered into her bed and never lay with her.
>   (XIX.172–76)

Odysseus devotes the last few lines of this speech to salving Agamemnon's honor, explaining that "there is no fault when even one who is a king appeases a man, when the king was the first one to be angry" (XIX.182–83).

Agamemnon concurs with Odysseus's plan, assenting to the oath and deputizing Odysseus to manage the transfer of the gifts (XIX.184–97). But Achilles objects: they should not, he argues, pause to eat and deal with gifts when there is fighting to be done (XIX.198–208). At the least, Achilles explains, he will not eat before battle (XIX.209–10). "Resourceful" Odysseus then speaks a second time, revisiting the importance of nourishment to effective fighting and assuring Achilles that he agrees with the importance of both proper mourning and renewed battle (XIX.215–37). Odysseus prefaces his speech with an assertion of superior wisdom, but he softens this assertion by honoring Achilles for supremacy in battle.

> Son of Peleus, Achilleus, far greatest of the Achaians,
> you are stronger than I am and greater by not a little
> with the spear, yet I in turn might overpass you in wisdom
> by far, since I was born before you and have learned more
>   things.
> Therefore let your heart endure to listen to my words.
>   (XIX.216–20)[12]

Thus, even as Odysseus attempts to persuade Achilles to accept his judgment, he is mindful of Achilles's honor in this public setting.

Immediately after finishing this speech, before Achilles can either assent or disagree, Odysseus leaves the assembly, heading to Agamemnon's tent to manage the transfer of property and women on which he has insisted (XIX.238–48). Odysseus has the goods and women brought "into the midst of assembly" and then prompts Agamemnon to take the oath that he has never touched Briseis (XIX.249–65). In turn, Achilles tersely responds by publicly acknowledging divinely inspired madness as the cause of Agamemnon's insult and directs, "Go now and take your dinner, so we may draw on the battle" (XIX.270–75).

Odysseus's participation in this assembly accomplishes two things: the army gets a chance to eat before battle, and the reconciliation between Agamemnon and Achilles is strengthened. The first of these conclusions is obvious, and the second is evident from the text and has been noted by both Donlan and Hammer.[13] Before Odysseus speaks, Achilles is ready to fight for Agamemnon, and Agamemnon is willing to deliver the promised gifts. But no oath has been taken (Agamemnon conveniently forgets to mention it), no sacrifice has been made, and no gifts have been publicly exchanged. Thanks to Odysseus's insistence, Agamemnon is forced publicly, fully, and over sacrifice to admit his wrong to Achilles and make amends. Thus, Agamemnon returns to Achilles (with interest) the honor that he had wrongfully withheld in his quarrel with Achilles over Chryseis and Briseis. Thanks also to Odysseus's intervention, Achilles is forced publicly, fully, and over sacrifice to acknowledge these amends. Achilles, by accepting Agamemnon's amends, thus returns to Agamemnon the honor that he had ceased to afford him (as commander of the army) after their quarrel. Odysseus effectively manages the necessary reapportionment of honor between the two men.

Odysseus's language demonstrates not only his goal but also his understanding that the management of these lords relates to the public honoring of each. As he shepherds the reapportionment of honor, Odysseus calms the insecurities of both men insofar as he can. In the first speech he defends the correctness of Agamemnon's admitting his fault (XIX.182–83). In his second speech he opens by acknowledging the military prowess of Achilles (XIX.216–20). Renewed rift between Agamemnon and Achilles is admittedly conceivable after this assembly, but certainly it is less likely thanks to Odysseus's management.

Is Odysseus more motivated by the desire to ensure the delay necessary for the army to eat before battle or by a belief that the alliance between Achilles and Agamemnon needs reinforcement? As becomes evident in the *Odyssey*, Odysseus's love of a good meal is one of his more prominent characteristics. Yet his brokering of the relationship between Achilles and Agamemnon, illustrating as it does his effective management of the honor of both men, is also consistent with his tendency to use speech effectively to achieve pragmatic ends. Ultimately, he may view the apportionment of honor and food as equally important.[14] Whether he brokers the relationship between Achilles and Agamemnon for the sake of its long-term impact on the Trojan War or takes these steps merely to buy time for the troops to prepare for a long battle, he employs his acumen and his understanding to the advantage of the Achaian army.

Odysseus appears in the *Iliad* as a rhetorician whose intellect and skill in speech permit him to wield a disproportionate amount of power in counsel and negotiation. Through his use of speech, he reveals an understanding that love of honor motivates many of the warriors around him.[15] Both his mixed success with Achilles and his successful manipulation of Agamemnon demonstrate this. Moreover, the attention that he devotes to ensuring that the honor of both Achilles and Agamemnon are correctly reapportioned reveals his judgment that the satisfaction of this desire is important for the efficacy of the Achaian army.

Ultimately, however, Odysseus's strategic use of honor in support of the Achaian cause—intertwined as it is with valid strategic considerations—neither proves nor disproves the existence or power of his own desire for honor.

Inner Odysseus, Great Glory of the Achaians

Odysseus appears most similar to Ajax and Agamemnon in the context of battle. It appears at first blush that Odysseus may merely be a lesser or defective version of the more glorious warriors of the Trojan War. But examination of his thoughts and feelings changes this impression, indicating that his lesser accomplishments are due neither to uncontrollable cowardice nor to inferior battle skills. Rather, his thoughts indicate that he is less devoted to honor and therefore less convinced of the desirability of risking his life in battle. To be clear, Odysseus does not emerge as either less capable of or even disinterested in winning honor; rather, he is less committed to winning honor at any price. This results in a warrior who makes the best use of his skills to win the most honor he can (and the maximum advantage for the Achaian forces) at the lowest risk to himself. Odysseus is strategic, rather than passionate, in his pursuit of honor.

Odysseus of the Hearty Spirit (or Skulking Aside?)

Odysseus's first appearance on the field is described by Helen and Priam. Watching from behind Trojan lines in the calm before the duel between Menelaus and Alexandros, they remark on Odysseus's smaller stature in comparison to Agamemnon and Menelaus, Odysseus's appearance of physical strength, and the way that he ranges through the fighters like a ram through a mass of sheep (III.192–98). He does not have the natural advantages of Ajax or even of warriors of the second rank in height. Instead, he has a physical advantage won by labor—the physical strength that Priam notes by describing Odysseus as "broader, it would seem, in the chest and across the shoulders" (III.194). The final detail in this first portrait of Odysseus further supports the suggestion that the man of many labors is indeed energetic and hardworking: given a potential moment of rest (or sloth) as they await the arrangements for the duel, Odysseus opts instead to continue on some business with the army.

In the following book Homer provides a second look at Odysseus the soldier. As the Achaians prepare for battle, Odysseus and his army "waited, until some other mass of Achaians advancing might crash against the Trojans, and the battle be opened" (IV.334–35). As Odysseus hangs back, awaiting an opportune moment to bring his small army to bear, Agamemnon approaches. Displeased with Odysseus's strategy, Agamemnon first accuses Odysseus of greed and treachery and then proceeds to scold him for failing to be as eager for a prominent place in battle as for a prominent place in feasting (IV.339–48). "Resourceful" Odysseus responds to Agamemnon with a dark look and angry words, neither defending nor apologizing for his tactics (IV.349–55).

> What is this word that broke through the fence of your
>   teeth, Atreides?
> How can you say that, when we Achaians waken the bitter
> war god on Trojans, breakers of horses, I hang back from
> fighting? Only watch, if you care to and if it concerns you,
> the very father of Telemachos locked with the champion
> Trojans, breakers of horses. Your talk is wind, and no
>   meaning. (IV.350–55)

Agamemnon backs down, explaining that he trusts in Odysseus's good intentions (IV.356–63).

When battle commences Odysseus fulfills his promise to Agamemnon. His moment of particular prominence in the battle is prompted by his anger at the death of a "brave companion" who is killed by a spear meant for Ajax (IV.489–93).

> For his killing Odysseus was stirred to terrible anger
> and he strode out among the champions, helmed in bright
>   bronze,
> and stood close to the enemy hefting the shining javelin,
> glaring round about him; and the Trojans gave way in the face
> of the man throwing with the spear. And he made no vain
>   cast,
> but struck down Demokoon, a son of Priam, a bastard,
> who came over from Abydos, and left his fast-running horses.
> Odysseus struck him with the spear, in anger for his
>   companion. (IV.494–501)

Seeing his companion fall, Odysseus is filled with anger and proceeds to force the "champions of Troy [to give] back" (IV.505). In contrast to Odysseus, the other warriors in this battle are relatively passionless. To be sure, Ajax takes down his opponents, brave warriors come forward, and more than one is described in dramatic detail as he falls into the dust. But no other warrior (in this first battle scene) is described as coming forward in anger—let alone anger over a fallen comrade.

As the battle continues in the next three books, Odysseus is less prominent. He continues to appear, coming to the forefront just enough to maintain his status as an important warrior but not nearly enough to raise him to the level of Ajax or Diomedes.[16] Perhaps his bravest action in these books is volunteering to fight Hektor in single combat. Yet "brilliant" Odysseus is described as the last of the nine volunteers to step forward, and the cynical observer notes that he volunteers only after his odds of being selected (by lot) to fight Hektor have become relatively low (VII.161–68).

Less ambiguous is Odysseus's fight, two books earlier (in book V), with the Lykians (troops led by Zeus's son Sarpedon). Seeing Sarpedon and one of the Achaian leaders fall, Odysseus pushes forward. Ready to engage, Odysseus hesitates only over whether to finish off wounded Sarpedon or engage the Lykians.

> [B]ut brilliant Odysseus, who held a hardy
> spirit, saw what had happened, and his heart within was
>   stirred up,
> but now he pondered two ways within, in mind and in spirit,
> whether first to go after the son of Zeus the loud-thundering
> or whether he should strip the life from more of the
>   Lykians. . . .
> Athene steered his anger against the host of Lykians.
>   (V.669–76)

Odysseus proceeds against the Lykians, killing seven warriors in rapid succession (V.677–78). His onslaught is put to an end by the approach of Hektor, at which point the Achaians (Odysseus is not singled out for individual description) begin a controlled retreat (V.699–702).

This scene highlights both Odysseus's similarity to and his difference from his companions. He steps forward to take advantage of his enemy's weakness with a relish that would pass unnoticed in Ajax, but his thoughts distinguish him. Underneath the exterior similarity to Ajax, his "heart within was stirred up" (V.670), and his thoughts do not pertain to the glory to be won. Rather, he is preoccupied with the tactical determination to be made as he "ponders two ways within, in mind and in spirit" (V.671).

Notwithstanding Odysseus's efficacy in some battles, Agamemnon is not the only observer to note that Odysseus is not always at the fore of the most dangerous places in battle. Indeed, Odysseus's behavior during one particular Achaian retreat raises the issue of cowardice quite clearly. Early in book VIII, Zeus sends a storm against the Achaians so that "seeing it they were stunned, and pale terror took hold of all of them" (VIII.76–77). The greatest Achaian leaders begin to flee, including Ajax, Agamemnon, and Odysseus (VIII.78–79). Only Nestor remains, trapped under a dead horse with Hektor closing in on him (VIII.80–91). Diomedes comes to help Nestor, spots Odysseus fleeing, and calls for his help: "Where are you running, turning your back in battle like a coward? Do not let them strike the spear in your back as you run for it, but stay, so that we can beat back this fierce man from the ancient [Nestor]" (VIII.94–96). Odysseus gives no indication of having heard Diomedes: "long-suffering great Odysseus gave no attention as he swept by on his way to the hollow ships" (VIII.97–98). Diomedes remains behind and rescues Nestor by staving off Hektor (VIII.99–129).

The verb used for Odysseus's failure to pay heed to Diomedes can mean either "to hear" or "to pay heed to."[17] This ambiguity leaves unanswered the question of whether Odysseus chooses to ignore Diomedes's plea for help or whether he simply does not hear it. Common sense seems to dictate that if Diomedes saw Nestor's predicament, Odysseus would have too. Consideration of the noise and confusion of battle, particularly during a chaotic retreat, indicates to the contrary. In the final analysis, no definite conclusion can be drawn from Odysseus's flight, except that he was less brave than Diomedes and no more cowardly than the remainder of the army. That one flees with Ajax rather than standing with Diomedes against a sign from Zeus is not a strong indictment of cowardice.[18]

By the end of these early, battle-filled books, Odysseus's behavior and thoughts on the battlefield provide subtle indications of how he differs from Ajax and Agamemnon. In failing to take a consistent place in the front lines, he fails to take advantage of opportunities to win honor from Agamemnon. His approach to battle is strategic and spirited yet lacking in thoughts and references to the various forms of honor mentioned by his fellow warriors.[19] By contrast, he is portrayed as provoked to battle fury by the death of a companion or as preoccupied with the best tactical turn. His courage in battle, while more often than not effective for the Achaians, is moderated by rational consideration and tainted at times by at least the suggestion of cowardice. None of these distinctions, taken alone, indicates that Odysseus does not love honor, but in the aggregate they suggest that this character is less devoted than many of his peers to winning glory at any price.

Great-Hearted Odysseus

Book XI presents Odysseus in open battle in the scene in which he seems the most interchangeable with his fellow warriors. This passage, in which Odysseus makes his most impressive contribution as a warrior (as distinguished from counselor), is also the only action scene in the *Iliad* in which the narration indicates that Odysseus is thinking and speaking of battle in terms of his own desire to win honor and avoid shame. For the first time, his willingness to risk his life in battle is explicitly linked—as it is for Ajax and Agamemnon—to love of honor. Even here, however, Odysseus questions whether this desire should rule.

It is perhaps helpful to think of this passage as presenting two Odysseuses. Odysseus-the-pondering-strategist questions the value of the glory for which he risks his life and hangs back from the engagement. Odysseus-the-action-hero, on the other hand, appears as a lesser Ajax or Agamemnon—a man with the same drives and, to a lesser degree, the same skills as his peers in rank. Like Ajax and Agamemnon he is motivated in this battle to put himself at risk for the glory to be won. Unlike Ajax and Agamemnon he pauses in the midst of open battle to query his own motivation. As he weighs the options before him, his thoughts bear resemblance to those of Hektor and Achilles in the moments when those warriors contemplate the alternative paths of public honor and death or relative obscurity and long life.

Book XI opens with the Achaians pushed back to their ships. Agamemnon initially drives the Trojans back, but then he is wounded. After Agamemnon's wounded retreat from battle, "there might have been havoc and hopeless things done, now the running Achaians might have tumbled back into their own ships had not Odysseus" acted (XI.310–12). Odysseus, apparently grasping the gravity of the situation, calls out to

Diomedes, "Come here and stand with me, brother. There must be shame on us, if Hektor of the glancing helm captures our vessels" (XI.314–15). Together they stave off the Trojans until Diomedes is wounded in the foot (XI.320–400). Odysseus then protects the wounded and retreating Diomedes until he is "left alone, nor did any of the Argives stay beside him, since fear had taken all of them" (XI.401–2). With the Trojans fast bearing down upon him, Odysseus considers how to respond.

> And troubled, he spoke then to his own great-hearted spirit:
> "Ah me, what will become of me? It will be a great evil
> if I run, fearing their multitude, yet deadlier if I am caught
> alone; and Kronos' son drove to flight the rest of the Danaans.
> Yet still, why does the heart within me debate on these
>   things?
> Since I know that it is the cowards who walk out of the
>   fighting,
> but if one is to win honour in battle, he must by all means
> stand his ground strongly, whether he be struck or strike
>   down another." (XI.403–10)

Odysseus stands "pondering these things in his heart and his spirit," but the Trojans surround him before he reaches a decision (XI.411–20). The battle thus initiated by his foes, Odysseus, now "insatiable of guile and endeavour" (as he is described by one of his attackers), performs with admirable effectiveness, killing or wounding five Trojans (XI.419–33).

As the battle proceeds, Sokos—the brother of one of the men Odysseus has just felled—wounds Odysseus (XI.426–38).[20] Odysseus's hesitancy, if it still lingers, vanishes completely. It becomes evident that he is now fueled by his desire to win glory. For the first time he speaks like Ajax and Agamemnon, relishing the allotment of glory anticipated in exchange for courage and possible death. First, he promises death to Sokos, explaining, "[B]eaten down under my spear you will give glory to me and your life to Hades of the horses" (XI.444–45). Fulfilling his promise of death to Sokos, Odysseus then boasts over the fallen warrior, comparing his enemy's lack of burial rites with the treatment that he expects in the case of his own death: "If I die, then brilliant Achaians will bury me in honour" (XI.450–55).

But the moment of battle fury passes, and Odysseus's "heart was sickened" at the sight of his own blood (XI.456–58). He is alone, wounded, and surrounded by enemies who, when they see his vulnerability, "cried aloud through the close battle and all made a charge against him" (XI.460). Retreating slightly, Odysseus calls for help and is overheard by Menelaus (XI.461–63). Menelaus, bringing Ajax with him, defends Odysseus, around whom the Trojans "crowded, as bloody scavengers in the mountains crowd on a horned stag who is stricken" (XI.465–83). Odysseus had been beating off the "pitiless death-day" with his spear, but when Ajax arrives "carrying like a wall his shield, and [stands] forth beside him" the Trojans flee (XI.483–86). Ajax pushes forward after the fleeing Trojans, and Menelaus leads Odysseus from the battle (XI.487–97).

Book XI marks the highpoint of the power of Odysseus's love of honor, and his wounded exit from this scene marks his final battle in the *Iliad*.[21] Odysseus's performance, thoughts, and actions in this scene are *almost* interchangeable with those of Ajax in battle and Agamemnon in relationship to the war. The qualification is important: before he proceeds to contend for glory with his enemies, Odysseus pauses to question the decision. Hence, even in the one sequence in which Odysseus's actions and speeches most clearly denote his love of honor, Homer indicates that honor does not hold complete sway over Odysseus. Rather, as when Hektor finally faces Achilles, it is a close matter whether Odysseus's love of honor is strong enough to overcome his fear of death and compel him to pursue glory.

Patient Odysseus

The night before the battle in which Odysseus is wounded, he participates in a mission, often called the Night Raid, that showcases his more distinctive qualities. The subject of an entire book, the raid is sandwiched between battles in which tactics generally amount to nothing more than determining whether to pause to strip a fallen warrior's armor or which opposing champion to challenge. By contrast, in book X Odysseus and Diomedes sneak like stalking lions into the enemy camp, kill a spy and sleeping enemies, steal fresh horses, and then rush back behind friendly lines to be cheered by their companions.

The Night Raid is a singular incident in the *Iliad*. But the *Odyssey* includes the story of the wooden horse (4.271–89) and Odysseus's spy mission in Troy (4.240–58) and thus reveals that such covert tactics were not singular in the Trojan War. Moreover, Odysseus's central role in every such endeavor in both epics indicates that such tactics are more representative of Odysseus's contribution to the war than is apparent from the *Iliad* alone.

The Night Raid takes place after the Achaians are first pushed back to their ships and while Achilles still refuses to return to battle. Nestor proposes the raid as a spy mission intended to gather information: he promises glory and gifts to the man who can return with the Trojan plans (X.204–17). Diomedes, fresh from a brilliant day of superlative battlefield exploits (including wounding a goddess), volunteers at once and requests a companion to accompany him. Many volunteer to go with him, including "patient" Odysseus, "since forever the heart in his breast was daring" (X.227–32). Diomedes selects Odysseus without hesitation.

> If indeed you tell me myself to pick my companion,
> how then could I forget Odysseus the godlike, he whose
> heart and whose proud spirit are beyond all others forward
> in all hard endeavours, and Pallas Athene loves him.
> Were he to go with me, both of us could come back from
>   the blazing
> of fire itself, since his mind is best at devices. (X.242–47)

Diomedes's praise of Odysseus, after Odysseus's headlong retreat on the preceding day, raises questions about Diomedes's sincerity. Yet, discounting the possibility that he would intentionally select an inferior companion for a dangerous mission, Diomedes must at a minimum believe that Odysseus is the best man for this specific exploit.

For his part Odysseus shows no interest in Diomedes's public praise (mock or otherwise). Perhaps there is even a hint of chagrin or fear of a detailed explanation of his failure to help rescue Nestor in Odysseus's response to Diomedes: "Son of Tydeus, do not praise me so, nor yet blame me. These are the Argives, who know well all these matters you speak of. But let us go: for night draws far along, and the dawn nears" (X.249–51). However the preceding day may color their remarks, it is clear that Odysseus speaks with focus on the practical necessities of their mission. Unwilling to delay to listen to more praise, he gives no indication that the public flattery offered by Diomedes gives him any pleasure.

From the outset their mission is grim. Odysseus and Diomedes move "like two lions into the black night through the carnage and through the corpses, war gear and dark blood" (X.297–98). As they proceed Odysseus supplies strategy and focus, and Diomedes follows his lead. Odysseus spots Dolon, a Trojan spy, who "in the thoughtlessness of his heart ran swiftly by them" (X.350). Formulating a plan, "illustrious" Odysseus[22] tells his companion how to capture Dolon (X.341–48), and Diomedes carries out his instructions (X.360–81). Once they capture him, "resourceful" Odysseus questions their captive, ignoring Dolon's requests for ransom and exercising his gift for deception in truth: "Do not fear, and let no thought of death be upon you" (X.382–84). Protesting and pleading, Dolon tells all that he can about the Trojan encampment and plan (X.390–445). Although Odysseus's questions seem aimed only at tactical information, Dolon unbidden suggests a raid on the newly arrived allies of the Trojans, the Thracians (X.426–41). Dolon explains that the Thracians, who are camped in a vulnerable spot, have excellent, fresh horses and carry armor fit for gods (X.433–41).

Diomedes then steps forward, taking the lead for the only time during the raid. He explains to their prisoner, "[I]f you lose your life now, then you will nevermore be an affliction upon the Argives" (X.452–53). Diomedes decapitates the unhappy prisoner as Dolon moves to cling in supplication (X.454–57). In the moments between Diomedes's statement and the actual decapitation, Odysseus does not act or speak. The text does not indicate either Odysseus's approval or disapproval—unless we should take the decision to strip Dolon to denote approval (X.457–59). Odysseus pledges Dolon's gear to Athena and asks her guidance in the next stage of their raid (X.460–64).

Odysseus and Diomedes next thread through enemy lines to the Thracian camp. Odysseus again sets forth the plan: one of them must kill the men, and the other will untie the horses (X.477–81). Diomedes stands over the sleeping men, killing them with his sword, while "resourceful Odysseus . . . would catch each dead man by the foot from behind, and drag him away" (X.488–90). As he drags away the dead, eminently practical Odysseus had "this thought in mind, that the bright-maned horses might pass easily through and not be shaken within them at stepping on dead men" (X.491–93).[23] While "patient" Odysseus prepares the horses for their flight to the Achaian camp and remains focused on the next step in his plan (X.498–502), Diomedes becomes distracted and considers the potential for further exploit. But Athena intercedes where needed, directing Diomedes to head back (X.503–11). Their "ghastly work done," Odysseus manages the horses as they head back to their army (X.513–14, 23–25).

The returning marauders are greeted warmly by the Achaians, who "rejoicing congratulated them with clasped hands and with words of welcome" (X.541–42). Nestor overflows with praise of the raiders, calling Odysseus "honoured Odysseus, great glory of the Achaians" (X.544). But when Nestor conjectures that the Thracian horses must be of divine origin (X.545–53), Odysseus will have nothing of the comparison. He politely explains, "[L]ightly a god, if he wished, could give us horses even better than these, seeing that the gods are far stronger than we are" (X.556–57). Having brought the praise of the animals into its proper sphere, he explains their actual value: they are fresh (X.558–59). Odysseus then tells Nestor about the raid, omitting the fact that they killed sleeping enemies and giving "brave" Diomedes credit for the deeds that Odysseus had planned and helped execute (X.559–63).[24]

The night's grisly work done, the book concludes with an oddly domestic scene. Odysseus, "laughing aloud" as he goes, takes the newly acquired horses to Diomedes's ship (X.565). Rather than the communal feasting typical of postcombat scenes, this interlude concludes with Diomedes and Odysseus stashing their spoils and then enjoying a good scrub.[25] The only bath in the *Iliad* (Hektor never comes home to take the bath that Andromache prepares for him),[26] this one is described in relative detail. First they scrub off crusted sweat in the sea, cleaning not only their bodies but also finding relief in an "inward heart . . . cooled to refreshment" (X.572–75). Then they indulge in tub baths and an olive oil rub (X.576–78). Fully refreshed (though doubtless exhausted), they sit down to a comparatively private meal and pour forth an offering to Athena (X.568–70).

The Night Raid is one of the few times in the *Iliad* when Odysseus becomes the poet's primary focus for more than a few consecutive lines. The episode recounts what could be considered Odysseus's most important achievement as a warrior in the *Iliad*. As the text makes clear, Odysseus's superior good sense, restraint, and a healthy dose of courage are necessary for the success of the mission. It seems highly unlikely, for example, that Diomedes and Menelaus would—absent Odysseus's tactics and self-control—have returned alive (let alone with fresh horses and detailed information). Diomedes knows that, in this particular context, Odysseus is his superior, and he willingly accepts Odysseus's leadership for the duration of the exploit. Book X thus highlights Odysseus's particular excellence, a mixture of intelligence, self-restraint, ruthlessness, and courage. This combination of virtues and his resulting contribution to the Trojan War might otherwise remain dormant in the *Iliad* and appear only in the *Odyssey*'s mention of the wooden horse and Odysseus's spy mission in Troy.[27] In other words, this incident reveals an important continuity with his character in the *Odyssey*.

Despite the fact that the Night Raid demonstrates Odysseus's usefulness from a military perspective, this exploit fails to clothe him in public honor akin to that to be won on the battlefield. The context of war may justify the spy mission, the killing of Dolon and sleeping soldiers, and the theft of horses. Thus, a degree of honor is accorded in exchange for the aid that the information and horses bring to the Achaians. But, Nestor's hollow claims to the contrary aside, this is not a glory-enhancing event on a par with the daytime exploits of the Trojan War. Nor does Odysseus seem interested in being honored for his willingness to volunteer or even for his success. He abruptly cuts off Diomedes's praise before the mission and then rejects Nestor's hyperbolic praise of the horses after his return. His retelling of the raid to Nestor skirts the issue of the murdered sleepers, but it also shifts much of whatever honor might be gained by the mission to Diomedes. Most tellingly, Odysseus literally cuts short the honor offered by Nestor and the soldiers, preferring a quiet bath and a private meal to public honor.

Loving Father of Telemachos

Notwithstanding the Night Raid and his moment of glory in book XI, Odysseus's aggregate battle record does not come close to that of Ajax, Agamemnon, Hektor, or Achilles. Nor does he seem to have any outstanding physical ability or skill—like the speed of Lesser Ajax or the archery of Teukros—that could attract honor for supremacy in a specific warrior skill. Odysseus's famed mental abilities, although important during the Night Raid, play a comparatively minor role in the battles, leaving him relatively undistinguished as a warrior. Odysseus does not emerge as one of the best of the Achaians during battle, and yet he does emerge as one of the best during the public competitions held in honor of Patroklos, where he pursues and wins as much glory as any of his peers.[28] He first ties Ajax in wrestling and then, albeit with Athena's help, takes first place in the footrace.[29] For these feats Odysseus is publicly honored in front of the assembled Achaian army,[30] and his performance reveals Odysseus's love of glory (why else compete?[31]) as much as any scene in the *Iliad*. Perhaps more surprising in light of his middling battlefield performance, Odysseus demonstrates for the first time that he has the ability to win the highest honors among the most elite warriors. This uncharacteristically excellent accomplishment, in particular matching Ajax in a contest involving physical strength, thus emphasizes something about Odysseus's performance on the battlefield. Odysseus's lesser love of honor—not his lesser ability—explains his less than superlative performance in battle.

If Odysseus thinks and speaks of honor in relation to his own battlefield prowess *less* often than Ajax and Agamemnon (rather than not at all), the natural implication is that he is *less* motivated by love of honor. Indeed, his lesser performance in battle—as compared to his exemplary performance in the funeral games—is best explained by a lesser rather than a nonexistent desire for honor. Less motivated by love of honor than Ajax and Agamemnon (rather than less able), he performs less brilliantly when the risk is greatest. Still suffering from some love of honor, he excels when the risks to his life are less extreme[32] (as they are in the competitions at the funeral games) or when his own intelligence and self-control provide him with a distinct advantage (as they do in the Night Raid). Similarly, Odysseus, gifted as he is in intelligence and speech, usually excels in the relatively low-risk, low-honor tasks of counsel, strategy, negotiation, and diplomacy.

Is there anything in his character, besides superior intellect or cunning, that explains why honor is less appealing to him than to his peers? Cowardice cannot fairly be said to explain his motivations consistently. Calculation—or superior intellect combined with self-restraint—may come closer to capturing how he differs from honor-loving Ajax and Agamemnon. But, if calculation does accurately describe the difference, this conclusion still leaves unanswered the question of what Odysseus seeks via his calculation. The Night Raid provides some indication of Odysseus's preferences. Before and after the raid, Odysseus's thoughts are directed to practical, tactical, and even mundane matters rather than any honor that might be associated with the mission. Instead of basking in the honor offered first by Diomedes and later by Nestor and the army that welcomes him back, Odysseus directs his attention initially to ensuring time for their mission, and afterward he prefers to spend the remaining precious hours of the night refreshing his spirit with a good bath and a quiet meal.

Odysseus shows a strong interest, relative to his peers, in that which is distinctively his own. This can be observed first in his focus on two physical and therefore private aspects of life—physical comfort (food and bathing) and survival. The *Iliad* also hints, although it does not definitely prove, that Odysseus thinks more of his own home and family than his honor-dominated peers think of theirs. The epic demonstrates this in two ways. First and most simply, Odysseus is the only character in the *Iliad* to refer to himself as the father of his own child. Odysseus refers to himself as Telemachos's father twice in the *Iliad*.[33] In the first instance Odysseus calls himself "Telemachos's father" (II.260, Τηλεμάχοιο πατὴρ), and in the second he indicates love, referring to himself as "Telemachos's loving father" (IV.354, Τηλεμάχοιο φίλον πατέρα).[34] Moreover, although his fellow Achaians call Odysseus the "son of Laertes," Odysseus never refers to himself in this more common way.[35] Odysseus's unique form of self-identification through reference to his relationship with Telemachos suggests that he loves his son. At the very least, Odysseus's references to Telemachos demonstrate that his son is not completely absent from his mind.

An additional indication that Odysseus's competing desire is that which is his own—personal survival, home, and family—appears near the beginning of the *Iliad*. Hoping that the army will refuse to sail home, Agamemnon announces to the army that he thinks they should sail for home (II.53–75, 110–54). Contrary to his wishes, the soldiers take Agamemnon at his word and begin hurried preparations to leave. If not for the intercession of Athena and the actions of Odysseus, "[t]hen for the Argives a homecoming beyond fate might have been accomplished" (II.155–56). In this pivotal moment, with the army on the verge of sailing for home, Athena finds Odysseus standing still, neither assisting the men in their flight nor attempting to stop them: "There she came upon Odysseus, the equal of Zeus in counsel, standing still; he had laid no hand upon his black, strong-benched vessel, since disappointment touched his heart and his spirit" (II.169–71). Athena commands Odysseus to stop the flight of the Achaians (II.156–69). When Odysseus recognizes the goddess's voice, he puts an end to both his indecisiveness and his inaction; he takes Agamemnon's scepter and forces the men to a second assembly (II.182–210).

Having stopped the flight of the army, Odysseus steps forward in the assembly and speaks to Agamemnon in defense of the army's near departure. He describes—as no one else does in the *Iliad*—the desire to return to one's wife.

> For as if [the soldiers] were young children or widowed women
> they cry out and complain to each other about going
>   homeward.
> In truth, it is a hard thing, to be grieved with desire for going.
> Any man who stays away one month from his own wife
> with his intricate ship is impatient, one whom the storm
>   winds
> of winter and the sea rising keep back. And for us now
> this is the ninth of the circling years that we wait here.
>   Therefore
> I cannot find fault with the Achaians for their impatience
> beside the curved ships; yet always it is disgraceful
> to wait long and at the end go home empty-handed.
>   (II.289–98)

As in all of Odysseus's public speeches, this speech serves an overt political purpose: Odysseus, acting as Athena has directed, lays the groundwork for the reassertion of Agamemnon's authority over the army and hence the continuation of the war. But, as in Odysseus's other speeches, the immediate purpose accomplished via his words do not disprove their value as an indication of Odysseus's understanding.

Odysseus's short speech in defense of wishing to return to one's wife is the most—arguably the only—tender reference in all of the *Iliad* made by an Achaian about the wives left at home.[36] In claiming not to blame the men for their impatience to see their wives, Odysseus endorses their impatience and seems to indicate that he shares the desire that he describes. It is hard to imagine that he speaks these words without thinking of his own Penelope.[37] It is possible that the speech is all expediency—the right argument made in front of the right people at the right moment. Indeed, this speech poses the same interpretive challenges as the appeals to honor discussed in the first section of this chapter: just because Odysseus makes an appeal to the desire to return to one's wife (or the desire for honor) does not prove that he shares that desire.

But even if Odysseus does not share the desire that he describes so poignantly, it is still noteworthy that he is able to articulate a longing for and a love of one's wife that is otherwise absent from the Achaian leaders in the *Iliad*. In Odysseus's description, a man parted from his family yearns to return home in the same manner that the women and children mentioned by Agamemnon yearn for their departed husbands and fathers. According to Odysseus (surrounded though he is by the enslaved women preferred by Agamemnon), "any man" would prefer to be at home with his wife. In this moment his speech bears a striking resemblance to Hektor taking leave of Helen for the sake of spending time with Andromache. Similarly, he seems to share (or at least understand) the longing for pleasant domestic life that Achilles articulates before the death of Patroklos.

It is possible that the desires thus described by Odysseus may not be his own, but at the very least he reveals an understanding of and sympathy for love of one's family and wife that is alien to Ajax and Agamemnon. Moreover, if Odysseus does feel some desire to see his young son and a longing for Penelope, this would explain the hesitancy—the intermittent hanging back—that he exhibits in battle in the *Iliad* and when the army is on the verge of heading for home in book II.[38] Odysseus's desire to turn homeward does not overcome his desire for honor or even become explicitly adopted as *his desire*, but it may pull him into moments of stillness in which his competing loves are at war with one another.

Conclusion

Odysseus emerges from the *Iliad* a very different hero from Ajax, Agamemnon, Achilles, and Hektor. Most obviously, Odysseus like Zeus in counsel surpasses his companions in persuasive speech and strategy because of his superior intellect, and he puts these skills to use for the Achaian cause. Indeed, inasmuch as Ajax and Achilles each prove necessary to the survival of the Achaian army, Odysseus's vital role in the eventual Achaian victory should not be overlooked. Homer does not explicitly credit Odysseus (or anyone else) with the idea for the wooden horse, but he does explain that Odysseus was necessary to restrain the soldiers hidden in the horse and then valiant (and focused) in his assistance to Menelaus in ensuring the actual recovery of Helen (4.271–89; 8.514–20; 11.523–37). At least equally important, when Odysseus minimizes the strife between Agamemnon and Achilles, his superior intellect serves to preserve the political alliance necessary to ultimate victory.

Odysseus distinguishes himself, not only as strategic advisor and negotiator, but through his performance as a warrior: he reveals himself to be susceptible, but to a lesser degree than Ajax and Agamemnon, to the love of honor. In contrast to the warriors with whom he is juxtaposed in the Myth of Er, Odysseus literally hesitates in the midst of battle. His most remarkable feats occur either when the risk is lowest (as in the funeral games for Patroklos) or when glory does not seem to be a strong motivating force (as in the Night Raid). When public honor is offered him before and after the Night Raid, he minimizes it—preferring first extra time to pursue the mission and later the pleasures of a good bath, a meal, and rest. More surprisingly, Odysseus evinces an awareness foreign to his Achaian peers of the longing for wife and home, as well as a cognizance of his role as a father. Odysseus's sensibility to a wife and son at home, while arguably minimal, is remarkable in contrast to the utter lack of thought and tenderness for family evinced by Agamemnon and Ajax.

In the aggregate Odysseus proves to be more self-possessed—inclined to weigh his decisions rather than to act out of sudden passion—in comparison to his anger-prone peers. Through his superior self-control and intellect, Odysseus checks and lessens the consequences of the strife caused by Agamemnon's unmoderated love of honor. Odysseus also moderates the effects of Achilles's loss of moderation after Patroklos's death by insisting on a more complete rebalancing of honor in the Agamemnon-Achilles relationship and by ensuring that the army eats before battle. Tellingly, Odysseus's public appeals indicate that he has a good understanding of how the desire for honor and the desire to return to one's family can both motivate men.

Although the *Iliad*'s treatment of Odysseus is not full enough to permit a complete identification of his loves during the Trojan War, it does suffice to support a conclusion with regard to Odysseus's love of honor and family: his love of honor is less than that of Ajax and Agamemnon, and his love of family life is more than theirs. This state of his loves provides an excellent explanation for Homer's portrayal of Odysseus as a pondering, pausing hero. Unlike many of his peers, Odysseus neither rushes forward at the prospect of glory nor falls victim to great passions that cause him to lose the ability to ponder the consequences of his decisions. At the end of the *Iliad*, Odysseus may not yet be the man that he is portrayed as by Socrates in the Myth of Er, but he is certainly the likeliest candidate for the method of choosing—taking his time, considering his options, and deliberating fully.

Distinguishing Odysseus from two characters omitted from the Myth of Er, Achilles and Hektor, relates more to their differences in situation than in their loves. Unlike Achilles, Odysseus has no particular friend with him. The war thus does not destroy—although it clearly hinders and threatens—his chance of private happiness. The *Iliad* does not reveal whether Odysseus's desire for private life, to the extent that it may exist, could lead him to act with either Achilles's courage or his immoderation. Similarly, Odysseus and Hektor present obvious points of similarity and of difference. Each has a wife and young son, but only Hektor fights to save his family in the Trojan War. Odysseus, to the extent that he loves his family, has clearer incentives to focus on survival, to direct his strategic efforts toward a successful conclusion of the war, and to permit his peers to bear a disproportionate share of danger.

In the *Odyssey* Homer completes the portrait begun in the *Iliad*, deepening and developing the character of Odysseus and his relationship with his own private life—as well as providing insight into his competing desires and their consequences. In a sense, the reader follows Odysseus home to learn about more than just Odysseus. The *Odyssey* provides at least some answers to the "what if" questions that Achilles and Hektor will never answer: What if Achilles and Patroklos had both survived the war? What if Hektor had successfully defended Troy and returned home to whisper in Andromache's ear and watch his son grow and flourish? Would they be heroes worthy of admiration?

Part II

The Odyssey

4

A Hero's Story

Odysseus emerges from the Trojan War a hero—particularly after providing the restraint necessary for the wooden horse ruse and helping Menelaus reclaim Helen during the sack of Troy. Yet the courage, cunning, and moderation that he provides to the Achaian cause remain less admired than the exploits of men like Ajax, Agamemnon, Achilles, and Hektor because of the very qualities that make Odysseus so effective. In other words, Odysseus's preeminence in strategy and counsel over straightforward action—not to mention his tendency to question before charging forth for glory—grant him a particular advantage, but they simultaneously undermine his claim to prominence among those with whom he leads. While courage and spiritedness are evident in much of his action, the suggestion of intermittent cowardice (even if often arguably justified by superior strategy) weakens his claim to honor among the most glorious warriors. The practical self-possession and intelligence of Odysseus distinguish him from his peers even as they threaten to undermine his status: his fellow Achaians and Homer's readers alike accord less glory to the warrior who insists on pausing to make plans for dinner.

This reading of Odysseus as generally courageous yet more moderate than his fellow Achaians is only a partial portrait. The *Iliad* does hint that Odysseus may indeed feel the desire to see his son and wife working against his desire for honor, but the text is not definitive on this point. Put in different terms, the *Iliad* suffices to distinguish Odysseus from the honor-loving, public-acting, immortal-name-seeking culture that Arendt so vividly describes and that Agamemnon and Ajax exemplify, but the *Iliad* alone cannot explain what Odysseus loves instead. To deepen this inquiry (and to learn more about the implications of the intermittent yearnings of Hektor and Achilles for a peaceful, domestic life), one must turn to the *Odyssey*, in which devotion to private life is a slowly escalating major theme and in which the love of honor quietly recedes into the backdrop.

Of course, the *Odyssey* poses its own interpretive challenges, and some of these challenges require preliminary attention. If the *Iliad* and the *Odyssey* bear a resemblance to tapestries, then one may fairly say that the *Odyssey* is the more complexly woven of the two. The first twelve books chronicle Odysseus's voyage home and the plight of the family waiting for his return. The second twelve books are devoted to Odysseus's return, his reclaiming of his home and position, and his reunion with wife, son, father, and servants. The complexity of the epic stems from Homer's sophisticated narrative techniques: the story shifts among points in time and speakers so often and so effortlessly that, unless conscious attention is paid to the implications of these shifts, they are lost in the many turns, many tales, and many wonders of the adventure. Because the middle of the story of Odysseus's voyage is told first, followed by various and disordered pieces of the beginning (frequently interrupted by tales of the hero's wife and son and the homecomings of other Achaian warriors), neither the sequence nor the timing of the story is evident from a start-to-finish reading. Indeed, because important portions of the story are told by Odysseus rather than the narrator, before proceeding to issues of timing and sequence, it is necessary to determine the truthfulness of Odysseus's account of his first two years after leaving Troy.

Accordingly, Homer's web of narrative must be questioned and straightened to create a firm foundation from which to interpret Odysseus's loves and virtues.[1] Without such a detailed examination of Homer's tale, Odysseus's desires during his ten-year voyage are easy to misunderstand. Many readers conclude that Odysseus spent ten years wandering—in the sense of aimlessly seeking adventure and avoiding home—before suddenly deciding, if somewhat passionately, that he wanted his homecoming at last. This conclusion arises in part from the complexity of the timeline, which tends to disguise both how quickly Odysseus sought his homecoming and how powerless he was to expedite it after the early years of his voyage. The suspicion that Odysseus willfully wandered for ten years can also arise from an understandable skepticism about the honesty of Odysseus's accounts of his own voyage.

Lest it be thought that Odysseus's desire to reach Ithaka poses too obvious a question, it should be noted that scholarship diverges widely on the question of Odysseus's desire for his homecoming. Seth Benardete argues that, far from coming to value home and private life, Odysseus's "strongest and deepest desire is not for home but for knowledge."[2] In his account, Odysseus's rejection of Kalypso's offer of immortality does not indicate a preference for Ithaka, longing for family, or desire for Penelope.[3] In partial agreement with Benardete, Patrick Deneen concludes that Odysseus is fundamentally and perpetually torn between his own private life and longing for transcendence.[4] Although Deneen argues that Homer's poem ultimately portrays Odysseus as choosing the "particular" and "local" goods of home and wife, his Odysseus simultaneously reaches a kind of "limited transcendence" in which the "cosmopolitan" and "universal" goods of knowledge and immortality remain the objects of Odysseus's desire.[5] The ongoing tension between *oikos* and *cosmos*, in Deneen's view, remains alive in the poem and in its hero despite Odysseus's homecoming.

Jacob Howland and Jenny Strauss Clay both conclude that Odysseus eventually comes to love his private life, but they depict this as a more distinct character shift. Howland's Odysseus longs for home but develops this desire only relatively late in his journey home. For Howland, Odysseus must explore and overcome other desires before his love of his own becomes a powerful motivating force.[6] The knowledge gained from life and death teaches Odysseus that human life is inseparable from pain, hearth, and home.[7] Thus, an acutely human Odysseus emerges from his many labors suffering from "painful homesickness" and comes to place a dearer value on home and family.[8] Clay interprets Odysseus as suffering a less radical shift in desires. In her reading Odysseus develops by becoming more aware of the consequences of his own actions and thereby gaining greater self-restraint. Clay's Odysseus becomes more cautious as his hardships increase his desire for homecoming.[9] She argues that Odysseus's rejection of the honor prized by the heroes of the *Iliad* represents "a new kind of *kleos*" directed toward "[r]eturn and long life."[10]

None of these interpretations of the *Odyssey*, save perhaps Clay's, gives sufficient weight to the desire that Odysseus has for his homecoming even as he sets out for Ithaka after the Trojan War. This chapter examines the desire for return to Ithaka that Odysseus evinces even in the early years of his voyage, revealing the continuity between the restrained war hero of the Trojan War and the suffering voyager of the first half of the *Odyssey*. Homer's telling of the voyage chronicles his hero's development in constancy of desire and strength of self-control, two qualities essential to Odysseus's eventual homecoming.

The first four books of the *Odyssey* underscore the importance of the question of whether Odysseus should be blamed for the length of his voyage by focusing the audience's attention on the consequences of his twenty-year absence from his family and kingdom. Suitors who abuse the rules of hospitality and hound Penelope to select a new husband threaten to permanently destroy Odysseus's home. The same men begin to plot Telemachos's death, and Telemachos (making his initial steps into manhood) begins to wander in search of news about his father. Ithaka's first assembly since Odysseus's departure raises the question of who will be king next, and the possibility of bloodshed looms. At the outset of the *Odyssey*, Homer thus reminds his audience of the private suffering and political unrest that is prolonged by Odysseus's continued absence.[11]

The length of Odysseus's voyage, his capacity to tell convincing lies, and the stakes in Ithaka constitute the primary case against Odysseus's desire to expedite his homecoming. The case in favor of his desire to reach Ithaka expeditiously is found in the sequence and timing of his adventures, the distinction between his lies and his true accounts, and the poetic focus on his reasons for suffering during the voyage. In fact, Odysseus did not wander aimlessly for ten years. His initial near misses with homecoming and the resulting despair over his inability to return to Ithaka demonstrate that Odysseus longed for his homecoming—whatever that might entail—even during the months immediately after leaving Troy. After the first two years, Odysseus never prolongs his voyage. To be clear, Homer shows that Odysseus's desire for homecoming was powerful—but intermittent—even during the initial months of his voyage.

Consistent with his desires in the *Iliad*, Odysseus's intermittent competing desires prove to be his love of honor and his love of physical comfort. This is most powerfully illustrated through two incidents that occur in the first two years of his voyage: his altercation with the Cyclops and his decision to stay at Circe's table for a year and a half. These two interludes account for nearly all the avoidable prolongations of Odysseus's voyage.

Telling a True Homecoming Story

When Odysseus finally arrives home near the beginning of book 13, half of the *Odyssey* has been devoted to the story of his voyage and the dramatization of his family's precarious position in Ithaka. During the course of these first twelve books, the *Odyssey*'s storytellers include Athena, Zeus, Helen, Menelaus, Penelope, the "Old Man" encountered by Menelaus, Agamemnon, Nestor, Demodokos, Antikleia, Kalypso, Circe, and Teiresias.[12] Among the resulting stories one is particularly important relative to the adventure as a whole. After his ten years of voyage and on the eve of his return to Ithaka, Odysseus is shipwrecked on the island of the Phaiakians, who take him in as their guest. Having bestowed gracious hospitality on the still-unidentified stranger, the king and then the queen request that Odysseus tell them who he is and why he is filled with sorrow. Odysseus's response to his hosts' requests is a four-book account of his voyage. This account is not only the longest speech within the poem but also the most vital to the construction of a sequence of events and a rough timeline of Odysseus's ten-year voyage home.[13]

In light of Odysseus's famed wiliness and—to be blunt—dishonesty, the importance of his story causes a significant interpretive problem.[14] In the second half of the *Odyssey*, Odysseus tells complex lies to Athena, his swineherd, Penelope, and his father. Athena herself tells Odysseus that he is full of "ways of deceiving and . . . thievish tales" that are "near to you in your very nature" (13.291–95).[15] Odysseus lies frequently and with great skill. And yet, if one is to have a complete account of his ten-year voyage, the story that Odysseus tells the Phaiakians in books 9–12 must be consulted.

Fortunately, while Odysseus's propensity and ability to lie raise this issue, Homer's consistent textual indications distinguish Odysseus's true speeches from his false ones. In every instance in which Odysseus lies or misleads, Homer alerts his audience.[16] Examination of Homer's narration of Odysseus's lies throughout the *Odyssey* repeatedly confirms this observation. When Odysseus first meets Athena after his arrival home in Ithaka, for example, the narrator explicitly states that Odysseus lies to her by explaining that he "did not tell her the truth, but checked that word from the outset, forever using to every advantage the mind that was in him" (13.254–55). After Athena and Odysseus recognize one another, Homer then forecasts the many lies that will follow by explaining that Athena disguised Odysseus and commanded him to "tell no one out of all the men and the women that you have come back from your wanderings" (13.307–9).

This practice of overtly identifying Odysseus's lies continues in the following books even though the audience—privy to Odysseus's true identity, the preceding adventures, and Athena's command not to reveal himself—knows that Odysseus is fabricating his stories. When Odysseus lies to his loyal swineherd, Eumaios, the disguised master and his servant engage in a conversation in which they discuss the possibility that the "stranger's" tale is a lie (14.360–409). When Odysseus, disguised as a beggar and still undetected, tells his false history to Penelope in book 19, the line following his speech explains that he "knew how to say many false things that were like true sayings" (19.203). A few lines later, Penelope's suffering moves him to pity, and Homer explains that Odysseus hides his tears and "deceived her" (19.212).

In short, while Odysseus lacks credibility, Homer retains it. Even when the point might seem too obvious to bother emphasizing, Homer's narration marks his hero's deception.[17] In contrast to these scenes in Ithaka, Odysseus's speech in books 9–12 is accompanied by very little comment (and no indication of guile or dishonesty) from the narrator. When Odysseus starts to tell his story, the narrator merely notes, "Then resourceful Odysseus spoke in turn and answered" (9.1; 11.377). When he pauses and when he finishes the story, the narrator comments only on the audience's reaction: "So he spoke, and all of them stayed stricken to silence, held in thrall by the story all through the shadowy chambers" (11.333–34;13.1–2). In light of the *Odyssey*'s general practice of signaling Odysseus's lies, this narration indicates that Odysseus tells the truth in his longest and most complete version of the story of his voyage.

This conclusion is supported by two additional factors. To the extent that any of the events in Odysseus's story are mentioned elsewhere in the poem (if with less detail), the additional references corroborate Odysseus's version of events. These sources include the narrator, Athena, and a second telling by Odysseus. To commence with the most unimpeachable testimony, the opening plea to the Muses outlines how Odysseus lost his companions through their own folly on Thrinakia (1.6–10).[18] As the narrator's voice picks up from the initial plea to the Muses, the opening lines verify Odysseus's unwillingness to stay with Kalypso on Ogygia, Odysseus's "longing for his wife and his homecoming," and Kalypso's desire "that he should be her husband" (1.13–15). The opening lines also vouch for the difficulty of the final stage of Odysseus's voyage (1.16–19).[19] Athena and Zeus each attest to several episodes from Odysseus's story. When Athena mentions Odysseus's captivity on Ogygia to her father, Zeus explains that Odysseus is not yet home because he has angered Poseidon, "who, ever relentless, nurses a grudge because of the Cyclops, whose eye he blinded" (1.55–69). The entirety of book 6, told directly by the narrator, details Odysseus's voyage from the moment when Hermes arrives to bid Kalypso set him free until he arrives in Phaiakia. Many of the references to the events in Odysseus's story confirm portions of his account, and there are no references within the *Odyssey* that contradict his account. Odysseus's story thus adds to the reader's knowledge of his voyage in important respects, but—unlike the lies he tells the Cyclops or while disguised in Ithaka—it in no way contradicts those aspects of the voyage mentioned by more obviously credible sources.

Another internal consistency lies in the fact that Odysseus later tells the same story to Penelope in book 23 after his disguise is removed and she has acknowledged his return.[20] As with Odysseus's story in Phaiakia, when Odysseus tells Penelope about his voyage from Troy, Homer provides no evidence that Odysseus is lying or telling less than the complete story of his adventures. Indeed, as is discussed in more detail in chapter 6, the original Greek is emphatic to the point of redundancy about the completeness of Odysseus's tale to Penelope (although Lattimore's English translation greatly understates or makes ambiguous this aspect of their conversation). Given how the epic has clearly indicated Odysseus's many lies, this alone provides evidence that Odysseus has told his story accurately to his wife and thus, insofar as this story coincides with the story he tells the Phaiakians, corroborates that story as well.

It is also worth noting that Odysseus never tells the same lie twice. Despite strikingly similar contexts, each of his lies—told earlier in book 19 to Penelope and also to Athena, Eumaios, Polyphemos, and Laertes—is a wholly unique fabrication. In light of his propensity to create a unique story where none is needed (because the context and the audiences have much in common with one another), it seems yet more unlikely that Odysseus would opt to tell the same lie—were it such—to the Phaiakians and to Penelope. In a word, it seems out of character for him to tell the Phaiakians and Penelope the same story unless that story is the truth.

Taken as a whole, although Odysseus clearly could lie to the Phaiakians if he wished to do so, the *Odyssey* provides no reason to believe that he does. On the contrary, attention to narrative details provides many reasons to conclude that Odysseus's account of his voyage in books 9–12 should be relied on when constructing a chronological outline of the events of his voyage home. The straightforward narration of Odysseus's story juxtaposed against Homer's general practice of indicating Odysseus's deceptions provide strong initial support for the conclusion that he is telling the truth to the Phaiakians. Considerations of internal consistency and the character of Odysseus's known lies point to the same conclusion. Many of the adventures that Odysseus relates to the Phaiakians are also confirmed by seemingly unimpeachable sources, including the prayer to the Muses, the narrator, and the gods. Finally, Odysseus's book 23 tale to Penelope provides significant corroboration, due both to Homer's indication of the completeness of this second and corresponding story and to Odysseus's general practice of creating unique stories when lying.

The True Homecoming Story

The *Odyssey*'s opening pages attest to Odysseus's "longing for his wife and his homecoming,"[21] but this assertion is subtly undermined by the complex structure of the epic. Over the course of the first twelve books, the length of his ten-year voyage is emphasized while the sequence in which the voyage is recounted—with its beginning withheld until nearly the end—obscures the answer to an important and natural question: if Odysseus wants to get home so desperately, why does he not get himself home? A timeline of his voyage is an essential tool for understanding his desires and thus for answering the question why it takes a man who genuinely wants to get home ten years to do so.

THE LAST EIGHT YEARS: WORKING BACKWARD

Creating a sequence and timeline demands painstaking backtracking and cross-referencing.[22] Moreover, because the *Odyssey* omits the duration of many of the incidents that take place early in the voyage, creating a precise chronology by working forward from Odysseus's departure from Troy is impossible. Working backward, however, from his arrival in Ithaka is feasible because the story specifies the duration of later events—such as the length of his stay on Ogygia with Kalypso and with the Phaiakians.

At the very end of his voyage, Odysseus spent the night before landing in Ithaka at sea and the three previous nights with the Phaiakians negotiating his passage home. Before his stay with the Phaiakians, Odysseus had passed twenty days at sea and, immediately before this, eight years stranded with Kalypso (5, 7.259–61). Although Odysseus's "entrapment" by Kalypso is the subject of many a smirk, the *Odyssey* leaves no room to question either the hero's desire to depart or his inability to do so without divine assistance.[23]

Before Odysseus's arrival alone on Ogygia, he and his companions had sailed at the mercy of storms and monsters for one month and eighteen days, stopping at land only when necessary. During the last ten days of this period, Odysseus loses his last ship and the remainder of his companions and then struggles to remain alive alone in the sea (12.403–49). Immediately before this, Odysseus (against his own urgings) lets his crew convince him to take shelter on Thrinakia, the island of the cattle belonging to the god Helios (12.260–402). This stay, intended to be a one-night stop, stretches into a month and a week due to storm winds that make departure impossible (12.325–403).[24] Odysseus has been warned by prophecy and Circe not to eat the god's cattle found on the island, but ultimately he is able to restrain only himself: his men doom themselves to their subsequent deaths at sea by eating the cattle (12.374–419).[25] Prior to this unhappy stay on Thrinakia, Odysseus and his companions had spent one eventful day (in which they encountered the monsters Scylla and Charybdis and sailed past the Sirens) en route from Circe's island (12.144–259).

To summarize these events and order them chronologically, Odysseus's final eight years and three months of travel are spent as follows: (1) one month and eighteen days—after leaving Circe—before landing alone on Ogygia (one day at sea, five weeks trapped on the island of Helios's cattle, a storm of unspecified duration in which his final companions die, and ten days alone at sea); (2) eight years stranded with Kalypso on Ogygia; (3) twenty-four days until his arrival in Ithaka (twenty days at sea, three nights in Phaiakia, and a final night at sea). Thus it is ultimately possible to create a clear sequence of events and a rough chronology, even if the textual support is as tedious as it is important. The value of this tedium lies most evidently in demonstrating that during the last eight years and three months before arriving in Ithaka the poem gives no reason to believe that Odysseus could have done anything to expedite his return. Odysseus did not simply "wander" or delay his homecoming for ten years. But this timeline and sequence of events also direct attention to the initial year and nine months, the period when Odysseus alternately struggled for homecoming and made voluntary decisions that would threaten and delay his eventual return.

Desiring Home

Because the poem does not specify the exact duration of the individual events or the time spent at sea in the portion of his voyage before his arrival on Circe's island, Aiaia, a precise breakdown of the timing of this first year and nine months is not possible. Hence, when recounting the first part of the voyage it is more helpful to work forward from Odysseus's departure from Troy.

During the first year and nine months of his journey, Odysseus displays more control over the length of his voyage than at any other point in the story. He shows himself to be a man of varied impulses—many of which are strong but none of which is consistently dominant. More specifically, Odysseus has three desires during this period: (1) homecoming, (2) honor, and (3) physical comfort.

Some of the delays in the early months of the voyage can be attributed to Odysseus, but many cannot. After one false start and a return to Troy, Odysseus leaves Troy permanently (3.155–64; 9.39). He and his companions are forced ashore at Ismaros by bad winds, but they stay to sack the town, taking treasure and capturing women (9.40–43).[26] After staying an extra day at the behest of his men, Odysseus departs with his companions the day after their arrival (9.43–44).[27] Brief episodes follow—taking shelter on the mainland and sailing through a storm—but when Odysseus and his companions almost reach Ithaka, bad winds drive them past home (9.79–81).[28]

After this initial brush with early homecoming, they are blown off course for nine days. Another short sequence of adventures follows: they encounter the Lotus-Eaters, spend five days in the land of the Cyclops, and then feast for a month on the Aiolian island (9.82–10.26). After leaving the Aiolian island at Odysseus's prompting, they sail toward Ithaka again (10.13–18).[29] This time Odysseus has a secret advantage: King Aiolos has given him a bag with all the winds unfavorable to their homecoming trapped in it (10.17–27). As Odysseus describes it, the voyage home was hard but nearly over.

> Nevertheless we sailed on, night and day, for nine days,
> and on the tenth at last appeared the land of our fathers,
> and we could see people tending fires, we were very close
>   to them.

> But then the sweet sleep came upon me, for I was worn out
> with always handling the sheet myself, and I would not
>   give it
> to any other companion, so we could come home quicker
> to our own country. (10.28–34)

With relieved and exhausted Odysseus asleep, his men are filled with jealousy and curiosity, and they open the bag holding the winds. Once the winds are released, the ships are blown off course once again. Waking and discovering what his men have done, Odysseus despairs of his homecoming and considers suicide as an alternative to continued wandering.

> Then I waking
> pondered deeply in my own blameless spirit, whether
> to throw myself over the side and die in the open water,
> or wait it out in silence and still be one of the living;
> and I endured it and waited, and hiding my face I lay down
> in the ship, while all were carried on the evil blast of the
>   stormwind. (10.49–54)

Were it not for the exhaustion caused by this devotion to homecoming, Odysseus would have arrived home about three months after departing from Troy.[30] Odysseus admittedly displays poor leadership and bad decision-making during this incident. But far from being ambivalent about homecoming—let alone consumed by wanderlust—Odysseus's desire for homecoming dominates both his actions and his emotions after his second brush with homecoming. Like Achilles in the wake of Patroklos's death, Odysseus contemplates suicide. But for Odysseus, unlike for Achilles, this blow is a setback and does not permanently preclude achieving his desires.

Desiring Honor

In the interim between Odysseus's two near arrivals home, his altercation with Polyphemos reveals that his love of honor exists in tension with his desire to arrive home. Odysseus arrives in the land of the Cyclops very early in his voyage, perhaps as quickly as a few weeks after leaving Troy. After spending a day hunting and feasting on plentiful wild game, he leads some of his men on a search for inhabitants (9.156–76).[31] They find the monster Polyphemos's cave and, despite Odysseus's premonition of trouble and the insistence of his men that they depart, they permit themselves to be trapped inside once the monster returns (9.213–15, 224–30, 239–44).

In the competition between force and wit that follows, Odysseus's love of honor emerges as his spiritedness is roused. As self-possession and cunning give way to spiritedness, his love of honor emerges and, more than at any other moment in the *Odyssey*, takes command. When Polyphemos initially asks Odysseus who he is, before any violence has ensued between monster and men, Odysseus cautiously answers, "We are Achaians coming from Troy, beaten off our true course" (9.259–60). After Polyphemos kills and eats two men and then falls asleep, Odysseus's spirit arises, prompting him to act rashly.

> Then I
> took counsel with myself in my great-hearted spirit
> to go up close, drawing from beside my thigh the sharp
>   sword . . .
> but the second thought stayed me;
> for there we too would have perished away in sheer destruction,
> seeing that our hands could never have pushed from the lofty
> gate of the cave the ponderous boulder he had propped
>   there. (9.298–305)

Still in command of his actions at this point, Odysseus contents himself with "mumbling . . . black thoughts" of how he will punish Polyphemos and with hoping that Athena might grant the "glory" of defeating the monster (9.316–17). In this state between spirited action and self-possession, Odysseus plans and executes the blinding of the Cyclops (9.318–94). When Polyphemos asks for Odysseus's name again, Odysseus gives more information than he did originally, but he still disguises his identity in a pun on his own "famous name" and the word for "nobody": "Nobody is my name. My father and mother call me Nobody, as do all the others who are my companions" (9.364–67).

Odysseus's plan to blind the Cyclops and his pun having worked equally well, Polyphemos calls out for help from his fellow Cyclopes and tells them in his rage that "Nobody" is attacking him (9.395–413). Odysseus observes his wounded adversary, and his spirit is filled with glee:

"the heart within me laughed over how my name and my perfect planning had fooled him" (9.413–14). Escaping to his ship with his surviving companions, Odysseus's high-spiritedness finally conquers the remnants of his self-control. His companions beg him to be silent, and the near miss of a rock flung by Polyphemos warns him of the continued danger (9.471–99). Despite these sobering reminders of the need for moderation, Odysseus cannot control himself. He tells Polyphemos his name in the hope that he will become known for this victory.

> Cyclops, if any mortal man ever asks you who it was
> that inflicted upon your eye this shameful blinding,
> tell him that you were blinded by Odysseus, sacker of cities.
> Laertes is his father, and he makes his home in Ithaka.
>   (9.502–5)

Polyphemos throws another rock at Odysseus's ship, but he misses. Yet Odysseus and especially his men still pay dearly for Odysseus's inability to keep his name to himself (9.526–42). Polyphemos prays to his father Poseidon: if the god permits Odysseus to come home at all, it should be "late, and in bad case, with the loss of all his companions, in someone else's ship, and find troubles in his household" (9.534–35).

Odysseus does not initially seek glory, but as his spirit rises his willingness to incur risk in pursuit of honor increases.[32] His inner dialogue during this adventure is similar to his inner dialogue in his most glory-seeking moment during the Trojan War. But, unlike the battles of the *Iliad*, here Odysseus's temporary loss of self-control and his desire for honor have a grave cost. His momentary loss of self-possession and his pursuit of renown dooms him to continued suffering, the loss of his comrades, troubles at home, and the great length of his voyage.

Desiring Comfort

Succumbing to the temptation of gluttony and oblivion at Circe's table is the cause of Odysseus's second-longest avoidable delay on the way home. Moreover, because he could not have predicted the voyage-lengthening consequences of proclaiming his name to Polyphemos, remaining with Circe easily ranks as Odysseus's longest intentional extension of his voyage. As he admits, it is his own enjoyment at Circe's table that keeps him enthralled, forgetful of home until his companions remind him that they should continue their journey homeward (10.467–75).[33] It is important to note that although this episode represents his longest voluntary delay in the voyage home, Odysseus goes to great lengths to avoid Circe's snares before her table conquers him. The year and a half that he squanders feasting is much less than he and his men might have lost on her island had he not followed the advice given to him by Hermes and later ultimately listened to the pleas of his men for departure.

Upon arriving on Circe's island, Aiaia, Odysseus and his men rest, hunt, and eat (10.140–86).[34] Lost and fearing the possible savagery of the island's inhabitants, Odysseus splits his companions into two groups to seek out the source of the smoke he has seen (and a potential source of directions) (10.187–209). When half the men find Circe in her house, she lures them to a meal mixed with herbs that "makes them forgetful of their own country" and then changes them into pigs (10.236). One crewmember escapes and returns to Odysseus with this report (10.244–48).

As Odysseus approaches Circe's house to rescue his men, the god Hermes meets him (10.274–79). Hermes gives Odysseus a root to eat to defeat Circe's magic and explains in exacting detail what Odysseus must do to protect himself and save his men.

> As soon as Circe with her long wand strikes you,
> then drawing from beside your thigh your sharp sword, rush
> forward against Circe, as if you were raging to kill her,
> and she will be afraid, and invite you to go to bed with her.
> Do not then resist and refuse the bed of the goddess,
> for so she will set free your companions, and care for you also;
> but bid her swear the great oath of the blessed gods, that she
> has no other evil hurt that she is devising against you,
> so she will not make you weak and unmanned, once you are
>   naked. (10.293–301)

Odysseus, his heart "a storm" in his chest, follows these instructions, procures an oath from Circe that she will devise no evil against him, and joins her in her bed (10.307–47). Circe's maids then offer Odysseus every creature comfort his heart could desire: luxurious table, plentiful food, and a bath with "hot and cold just" to his taste (10.348–75). With all this before him, Odysseus remains unmoved until Circe, in response to his complaint, changes his comrades back into men (10.371–96).[35] At Circe's suggestion Odysseus then returns to his ship to invite the entire crew to feast at her table (10.428–48).[36] When they return to her house, Circe invites Odysseus to set aside lamentation and refresh his spirit before continuing his voyage.[37] Odysseus accepts Circe's offer of renewal, which leads—whether he anticipates it or not—to his forgetting his longing for home.

It is unclear how long Odysseus would have continued at Circe's table, or indeed whether he would ever have torn himself away, had his men not prompted the continuation of their homeward journey: "Then my eager companions called me aside and said to me: 'What ails you now? It is time to think about our own country, if truly it is ordained that you shall survive and come back to your strong-founded house and to the land of your fathers.' So they spoke, and the proud heart in me was persuaded" (10.466–75). But from this moment forward, Odysseus's desire to continue homeward controls his actions. Never again does preference for comfort or honor lead him to delay or risk his homecoming. At times, both before and after he reaches home, he is tempted by physical comfort or by the desire to assert himself in ways that might threaten his ability to reclaim his place, but he is—from this moment forward—always able to remind himself of the danger and to resist. His preference for home has prevailed and taught him to restrain and stifle—to rule—any competing desire that emerges.

Accordingly, he insists to Circe that he must depart, explaining, "[T]he spirit within me is urgent now, as also in the rest of my friends, who are wasting my heart away, lamenting around me" (10.484–86). The strength of Odysseus's newly remembered desire to continue homeward is underscored by his willingness to travel to the underworld when Circe explains that he must visit Hades to "consult with the soul of Teiresias the Theban" before continuing toward Ithaka (10.488–95). Odysseus is terrified at the thought: "and the inward heart in me was broken, and I sat down on the bed and cried, nor did the heart in me wish to go on living any longer, nor to look on the sunlight" (10.492–502). Despite his extreme dread, however, Odysseus assents and travels to Hades to ensure his homecoming.

Odysseus is initially ensnared by Circe because of his desire to save his companions, but he remains on her island because he is captivated by the pleasures of her luxurious home and table. Although he eventually leaves, this interlude suggests that the hero who longs for his homecoming likewise has a desire for physical comfort. Yet, Odysseus's choice to leave indicates that whatever he seeks in his own home is not merely pleasure, the absence of physical deprivation, or the end of danger. There is something distinct that Odysseus seeks in Ithaka.

Conclusion

The sequence and timing of Odysseus's adventures demonstrate that the length of his voyage is not due to an initial absence of desire for homecoming or to ten years of wanderlust. During most of his voyage, there is nothing that Odysseus can do to expedite his homecoming. Odysseus has less than two years—about a year and nine months—at the outset during which he could have shortened his journey; after this, he is continually trapped, driven by storm, or unfailingly sailing and negotiating his way homeward for the final eight years and three months. Admittedly, Odysseus exhibits some curiosity and resulting desire to explore the unknown. But, contrary to Deneen's and Benardete's interpretations, neither the search for transcendence nor the search for knowledge comes close to dominating among his desires. Much less is there any evidence that either of these tendencies prolongs his voyage or grows in strength over the course of the story.

Close observation of his character in the early months and initial years of his voyage reveals instead that Odysseus lacks consistency of desire and self-restraint. His voyage is significantly lengthened and his companions are lost in part because of his lack of self-possession when seized by a momentary desire for honor and when his love of physical comfort lulls him to forget his home. These tendencies in his character were first revealed in the Trojan War when his spirited love of honor became strongest in combat and when he insisted on the importance of food before battle (and took the only bath of the epic). During the voyage home, both the love of honor and the love of comfort emerge as impediments to his homecoming. In order to reach Ithaka and reclaim his home, Odysseus's mindfulness and self-possession must become constant in the face of such enticements.

As Clay and Howland both note, there is a definite growth in the power of Odysseus's desire to reach Ithaka. Leaving Circe (and perhaps encountering the souls of the dead in Hades at her direction) may indeed be the most pronounced moment of this growth in Odysseus. After his ensnarement by Circe, Odysseus appears to have learned to beware of the danger of forgetting his homecoming when physical comfort presents itself as an alternative. Never again does he forget his homecoming by acting in a way that threatens or delays his arrival in Ithaka. Yet Odysseus's character growth, as Clay observes, is not the birth of a new love or virtue. Self-restraint and desire for homecoming are preexisting characteristics; the strength of Odysseus's self-restraint and the constancy of his desire for homecoming are new. This continuity in his character underscores the fact that it is not simple chance or poetic whim that makes Odysseus the Trojan War hero who develops into a more restrained and consistently homeward-looking individual.

Odysseus's growth is not the simple result of time and trials, as much as time and trials may be necessary ingredients. Agamemnon and Ajax, had they experienced voyages like that of Odysseus, could not have become like Odysseus because they never had his preexisting loves and his related mixture of intelligence, moderation, courage. As his desire for homecoming becomes more constant and his ability to restrain his initial impulses grows stronger, Odysseus develops into a man who steadily prioritizes his private life and who, consequently, has the ironclad self-control necessary to reclaim his home.

5

Remembering Home

At the end of the first half of the epic, as Odysseus finally sets foot in Ithaka, the audience has learned that he did not merely wander aimlessly for ten years. In order to reach home, Odysseus faced many dangers and has rejected feasting with Circe, immortal life with Kalypso, and marriage to Nausikaa in luxurious Phaiakia—each of which offered obvious bodily pleasures and safety compared to the risks involved in reclaiming his home in rugged Ithaka. The epic thus confirms and reconfirms not only that Odysseus passionately desires his homecoming, but also that survival and pleasure are not what he loves most—at least not any longer. Yet ambiguity remains at the beginning of book 13 because the audience still remains uncertain about why Odysseus has forgone so many pleasures for the sake of his homecoming. Penelope, after all, is a queen as well as a wife, and Ithaka is a kingdom as well as the location of Odysseus's house.

Perhaps it is this ambiguity at the moment of his homecoming that has led some readers to conclude that Odysseus does not desire his homecoming wholeheartedly—let alone passionately. Horkheimer and Adorno, arguing that Odysseus is a proto-bourgeois, conclude that Odysseus "survives only at the cost of his own dreams."[1] In this account, he conquers the beauty and mystery of nature—that which inspires dreams—at the cost of a life cut off from passion in "bourgeois disillusionment."[2] Similarly, Ahrensdorf argues that Odysseus operates from calculation, superior pleasure taken in his dalliances, and fear of acknowledging the truth of divine injustice.[3] To the contrary, the last two episodes during the voyage homeward demonstrate that Odysseus prefers neither sexual dalliance nor physical comfort over his own rough home and kingdom. Odysseus's desire to leave Kalypso to return to his homeland and his family is perhaps the most repeated and the most passionate aspect of the first half of the *Odyssey*. Despite the many pleasures proffered by life in Phaiakia and Odysseus's frank appreciation of these pleasures, he remains steadfast in his preference for return to a relatively rustic home. And in his farewells to the Phaiakians, he focuses on the joys of marriage and family, confirming what the *Iliad* had suggested: Odysseus fully understands that love for one's own spouse and family are an important and positive human phenomenon. During these interludes Homer begins to reveal—or at least suggest—why Odysseus wishes so passionately to return to Ithaka: Penelope and the rugged land of his fathers emerge as at least part of what Odysseus associates with his homecoming.

Distinguishing Home from Pleasure

Among the many wonders of Odysseus's voyage from Troy to Ithaka, Homer emphasizes one adventure more than any other. His descriptions of the eight years that Odysseus spends with Kalypso are recurrent, prominent, and poignant. The emphasis placed on this aspect of Odysseus's voyage begins in the opening lines of the poem, which describe Odysseus as "longing for his wife and his homecoming . . . detained by the queenly nymph Kalypso, bright among goddesses" (1.13–14). In the following pages Athena provides a similar description of how Kalypso "detains the grieving, unhappy man, and ever with soft and flattering words she works to charm him to forget Ithaka; and yet Odysseus, straining to get sight of the very smoke uprising from his own country, longs to die" (1.55–59). Books later, when the narration returns to stranded Odysseus, Athena explains to Zeus that Odysseus "lies away on an island suffering strong pains in the palace of the nymph Kalypso, and she detains him by constraint, and he cannot make his way to his country, for he has not any ships by him, nor any companions who can convey him back across the sea's wide ridges" (5.13–17).[4]

Although many incidents from the voyage are described in detail only by Odysseus, the poem is structured so that this particular portion of his story is corroborated by numerous sources and told in the greatest detail. Following the narrator's detailed account of Odysseus's departure from Ogygia in book 5, Odysseus describes his shipwreck with Kalypso, her infatuation with him, and his departure from her island three times in the course of describing his voyage to the Phaiakians (7.243–66; 9.29–33; 12.447–53). Odysseus draws attention to this repetition: when he concludes his story to the Phaiakians, he refuses to tell this part of his journey again because it "is hateful . . . to tell a story over again, when it has been well told" (12.452–53). Odysseus may dislike repeating this part of his story, but Homer certainly does not.

The importance of this particular episode stems from the enticing offer made by Kalypso, Odysseus's rejection of her offer, and the hero's newly steadfast desire to depart for home.[5] The narrator—not Odysseus— explains that although resisting a goddess's seduction is not possible at night, Odysseus weeps all day on the beach, pining for home.

> [H]is eyes were never
> wiped dry of tears, and the sweet lifetime was draining out
>   of him,
> as he wept for a way home, since the nymph was no longer
>   pleasing
> to him. By nights he would lie beside her, of necessity,
> in the hollow caverns, against his will, by one who was
>   willing,
> but all the days he would sit upon the rocks, at the seaside,
> breaking his heart in tears and lamentation and sorrow
> as weeping tears he looked out over the barren water.
>   (5.151–58)[6]

Smitten with Odysseus, Kalypso had hoped to make him "immortal and all his days to be endless" (5.135–36). She showers every physical comfort and pleasure on him, wishing to make him her immortal husband, and cares for him "as if he were truly a god" (8.453–54). Despite her personal charms and the many amenities of life with a goddess, Odysseus's heart remains steadfast in his preference of home over immortality.

> [Kalypso] received me
> and loved me excessively and cared for me, and she promised
> to make me an immortal and all my days to be ageless,
> but never so could she win over the heart within me.
> There seven years I remained fast, but forever was drenching
> with tears that clothing, immortal stuff, Kalypso had given.
>   (7.255–60)

Confused and frustrated by Odysseus's refusal of her offer, Kalypso compares her own beauty to Penelope's and asks Odysseus why he insists on returning home to his mortal wife. Why does he insist on enduring "many hardships . . . before getting back to [his] country" for the sake of a wife who could not possibly be superior in "build or stature" (5.203–13). Odysseus responds with an easy admission of Kalypso's superiority and a stubborn insistence upon his genuine desire for home.

> Goddess and queen, do not be angry with me. I myself know
> that all you say is true and that circumspect Penelope
> can never match the impression you make for beauty and stature.
> She is mortal after all, and you are immortal and ageless.
> But even so, what I want and all my days I pine for
> is to go back to my house and see my day of homecoming.
> And if some god batters me far out on the wine-blue water,
> I will endure it, keeping a stubborn spirit inside me,
> for already I have suffered much and done much hard work
> on the waves and in the fighting. So let this adventure follow. (5.215–24)

Although Odysseus does not specify longing for Penelope, Kalypso is right to raise the issue. On the opening page of the poem, the narrator verifies what Odysseus is too politic to state to the goddess's face: Odysseus is "longing for his *wife* and his homecoming" (1.13, emphasis mine).[7]

On Ogygia Odysseus does not lament the odium of a secluded life with a goddess; he suffers pain from his prolonged absence from home and his admittedly shorter and less beautiful wife. The character growth between Odysseus's ensnarement with Circe and the entrapment by Kalypso is important. On Aiaia Odysseus forgot his homecoming, having too successfully submerged his soul's sorrow in the solace of physical pleasures. On Ogygia—which offers no less pleasure—Odysseus does not need his companions to remind him of home. He has learned that safety, pleasure, and physical comfort pose a particular danger: it has the potential to dull his memory of the cause of his pain and suffering. Armed with this knowledge, Odysseus remembers his home, his family, and his pain every day on the beach, straining for sight of home. Once the gods facilitate his departure, Odysseus diligently prepares his raft (with tools provided by Kalypso) and sails away from immortality, safety, and creature comfort—"happy" because the good winds carry him toward Ithaka (5.262–75).

Remembering to Remember Home

Eighteen days of sleepless sailing and three days of storm-tossed survival after leaving Ogygia, Odysseus is again shipwrecked and enticed to abandon his homeward journey. In Phaiakia Odysseus is offered many enticements to stay, but he continues steadfast in pursuit of passage home. Neither the beauty of Nausikaa, the wealth of her father's kingdom, the many physical comforts lavished on him, nor even spirited competition distracts Odysseus from his goal: passage home. In contrast to his earlier adventures, in which luxury induced forgetfulness of homecoming and love of honor could arouse Odysseus to reveal his identity imprudently, in Phaiakia Odysseus always remembers his homecoming. In the only instance when emotion overpowers his reason, the desire for homecoming overcomes his otherwise iron self-restraint.

The first and most obvious pleasure offered is the princess Nausikaa. Nausikaa, "like the immortal goddess for stature and beauty," is the first and only human woman who wishes to prevent Odysseus's homecoming (6.16).[8] Not only does Odysseus note her beauty, but he is clearly sensitive to her marriageable age and intelligence—denoting at least appreciation for the fact that he could choose worse for a new marriage. He tells her, albeit as he tries to win her assistance, that "blessed at the heart . . . is that one who, after loading you down with gifts, leads you as his bride home" (6.158–60). As Odysseus's interactions with Nausikaa and her parents develop, it appears that a beautiful bride and honorable position (if not the most honorable position) in a land far wealthier than rocky Ithaka could be his for the asking.[9]

Phaiakia offers Odysseus much that Homer has shown could lead this particular hero astray. Nausikaa's homeland is a kingdom of plentiful tables, soft beds, fine clothing, sophisticated baths, and excellence in song (6.209–50). Odysseus's pleasure in the luxury afforded him is evident. Perhaps the most striking example is his reaction to the bath that the queen offers him: "and he with joy in his heart looked on the hot water" (8.449–54). Odysseus accepts food and a comfortable bed with similar, if less exuberant, satisfaction.[10] But his enjoyment of these bodily pleasures does not eclipse Odysseus's ability to appreciate the cultivated beauty of the kingdom and its arts. At several points during his stay,

Odysseus pauses to wonder at the magnificence of town, gardens, palace, and dancing.[11] More than fifty lines describe the beauty and opulence of the royal household and Odysseus's admiration: "But when his mind was done with all admiration, lightly he stepped over the threshold and went on into the palace" (7.133–35). The beauty and richness of Phaiakia earn Odysseus's attention and admiration, but they lack the power to diminish his urgency for the voyage homeward.

Indeed, perhaps it is because of the pleasure that he takes in Phaiakia's luxuries and culture that Odysseus's response reveals a wariness of the threat that these pleasures pose to his homecoming. Odysseus has not lost his love of physical comfort and the cultivated arts, but he has learned to restrain his enjoyment so that he may obtain his first priority. Thus, for example, bemoaning the demands of the belly, Odysseus explains to his hosts that his physical needs force him to cater to his body. Caring for his body, as any mortal must, poses a danger of which experience has made him wary: the danger of forgetfulness of even his great sorrow.[12] Despite this great sorrow, his stomach still demands to be fed, and satisfaction of this demand threatens to induce forgetfulness.

> But leave me now to eat my dinner, for all my sorrow,
> for there is no other thing so shameless to be set over
> the belly, but she rather uses constraint and makes me
>   think of her,
> even when sadly worn, when in my heart I have sorrow
> as now I have sorrow in my heart, yet still forever
> she tells me to eat and drink and forces me to forgetfulness
> of all I have suffered, and still she is urgent that I must fill
>   her. (7.215–21)

Now aware of his hunger's power to diminish his ability to strive for home, Odysseus rules his mortal weakness. As he had been unable to do when offered food by Circe, Odysseus insists that he must continue his struggle the very next day.

> But you, when dawn tomorrow shows, see that you make
>   speed
> to set unhappy me once more on my own land, even
> when I have much suffered; and let life leave me when I
>   have once more

seen my property, my serving people, and my great high-
  roofed house. (7.222–25)

Odysseus's labors have not only taught him awareness of the threat posed by physical pleasures, they have also strengthened his ability to moderate or control his own desire for them.

Similarly, if somewhat less demonstrably, Odysseus continues to exhibit his intensified focus on homecoming when the Phaiakian youths provoke his spirited love of honor in their games. On Odysseus's second day in Phaiakia, after feasting and singing, athletic games follow. The king's son, Laodamas, calls Odysseus "father stranger" and asks him why he does not compete and comments, "There is no greater glory that can befall a man living than what he achieves by speed of his feet or strength of his hands" (8.145–48). In response, Odysseus explains to the young prince that suffering and longing have taken the place of glory and games for him.

> Cares are more in my mind than games are,
> who before this have suffered much and had many hardships,
> and sit here now in the middle of your assembly, longing
> to go home, entreating your king for this, and all of his
>   people. (8.154–57)

Another young Phaiakian begins to taunt Odysseus, accusing the visitor of "grasping for profits" and of lacking athletic ability (8.163–64). At this, Odysseus's spiritedness starts to emerge as he looks darkly at the youth and explains that his own gift in speech is more valuable than good looks that are unaccompanied by good sense (8.165–77).

At first it appears as if Odysseus's love of honor—once more—will triumph over the self-restraint that he maintains when his spiritedness lies dormant. In response to the young man's goading, Odysseus determines to compete in the discus throw.

> Now you have stirred up anger deep in the breast within me
> by this disorderly speaking, and I am not such a new hand
> at games as you say, but always, as I think, I have been
> among the best when I still had trust in youth and hands'
>   strength.
> Now I am held in evil condition and pain; for I had much
> to suffer: the wars of men; hard crossing of the big waters.

> But even so for all my troubles I will try your contests,
> for your word bit in the heart, and you have stirred me by
> speaking. (8.178–85)

Odysseus steps forward and makes the best discus throw of the day. As he had done on the battlefield and after escaping Polyphemos, Odysseus rejoices and begins to vaunt: "Let any of the rest, whose heart and spirit are urgent for it, come up and try me, since you have irritated me so, either at boxing or wrestling or in a foot race, I begrudge nothing" (8.204–6).[13] Yet this time Odysseus stops short of announcing his name, heritage, and homeland in connection with his victory. This time, he is spirited but retains his self-possession. He maintains his decision not to reveal his identity.

This new self-restraint might be due to the fact that, this time, Odysseus is not struggling for his life. Yet even in light of this distinction, the incident is noteworthy because for the first time Odysseus's spirit is roused, but he retains control of his impulses. This test of his self-restraint may be comparatively mild, but it signals a turning point for his character and foreshadows the self-control that will be required to reclaim his home once he returns to Ithaka.

Shortly after Odysseus maintains his restraint when tempted by love of honor, Homer reveals the desire that does have the power to overcome Odysseus's restraint. When the games give way to dancing and thence to feasting and storytelling, Odysseus requests that the bard Demodokos tell the story of one of his own glorious exploits from the Trojan War—the story of the wooden horse (8.517–20). Demodokos complies, describing Odysseus's valor in battle after the infiltration of Troy as he aided Menelaus to find Helen in some of the grimmest fighting of the war. At this, Odysseus begins to weep in one of the most painful outbursts of emotion described by Homer.[14]

> So the famous singer sang his tale, but Odysseus
> melted, and from under his eyes the tears ran down, drenching
> his cheeks. As a woman weeps, lying over the body
> of her dear husband, who fell fighting for her city and people
> as he tried to beat off the pitiless day from city and children;
> she sees him dying and gasping for breath, and winding her
>   body

about him she cries high and shrill, while the men behind
    her,
hitting her with their spear butts on the back and shoulders,
force her up and lead her away into slavery, to have
hard work and sorrow, and her cheeks are wracked with
    pitiful weeping.
Such were the pitiful tears Odysseus shed. (8.521–31)

As Odysseus sits in the court of Alkinoos, listening to his own story, his glory turns to ashes. Despairing of an eventual homecoming, he feels that he is one of the unhappy widows that he created. It seems to Odysseus that spouse, child, and homeland are as far beyond his power to reclaim as they were for the women whom he has witnessed being dragged from the ruins of their war-ravaged families.

In response to Odysseus's breakdown, King Alkinoos puts an end to Demodokos's singing and asks his guest to provide his name, family, and homeland so that he may send him home. The king closes his request for information about Odysseus by inquiring if he lost a relative in the Trojan War and asking Odysseus to tell him why the war story causes him to "weep in your heart and make lamentation" (8.577–86). Odysseus ignores the king's request for details about his connection to the war and reveals that he was lamenting over his own sufferings and sorrows.

> But now your wish was inclined to ask me about my mournful
> sufferings, so that I must mourn and grieve even more.
>   What then
> shall I recite to you first of all, what leave till later?
> Many are the sorrows the gods of the sky have given me.
>   (9.12–15)

After giving his name and claiming to be "known before all men for the study of crafty designs," Odysseus declares himself "at home in sunny Ithaka" and proceeds to describe the rugged, humble beauties of his home (9.19–27). He turns eventually from description of his island to his desire to return.

> [A] rugged place, but a good nurse of men; for my part
> I cannot think of any place sweeter on earth to look at.

...   So it is
that nothing is more sweet in the end than country and
   parents
ever, even when far away one lives in a fertile
place, when it is in alien country, far from his parents.
   (9.27–38)

Just as Penelope is shorter and less beautiful than Kalypso, rugged Ithaka is less fertile than Phaiakia. Yet Ithaka is dear to him because it is his and the land of his parents. Now, at the end of his voyage, desire for this land of his fathers causes Odysseus to speak his name to his hosts. Having remained mindful of homecoming when surrounded by beauty and comfort and restrained when provoked to reveal his identity by the love of honor, Odysseus's longing for home finally overwhelms him and causes him to reveal his identity.

The Meaning of Home on the Eve of Homecoming

After Odysseus reveals his identity to his hosts, he tells them the story of his voyage since his departure from Troy. His choice of how to tell his story, starting and ending with his entrapment by Kalypso and his great desire to go home, emphasizes love for his home. When Odysseus tells the Phaiakians the story of his trip to Hades, his emphasis within the story reveals that he considers the prophecy relating to his homecoming and the news of his family's troubles to be more noteworthy than his encounters with the famous deceased heroes who were once his comrades in arms. Indeed, Odysseus does not even consider his encounters with Achilles, Agamemnon, and Ajax worthy of recounting. He ceases his story before describing these encounters, begging to be permitted to sleep (11.330–32). Only when King Alkinoos specifically asks to hear about his famous companions from the war does Odysseus describe these encounters (11.362–84).

Left to his own devices, Odysseus chooses to recount his conversation with the prophet Teiresias (who prophesizes his homecoming), his newly dead crewman Elpenor, and his mother.[15] As he tells the story of his encounters in Hades, it becomes apparent that Odysseus prioritizes his mother, Antikleia. During his trip to the underworld he defers conversation with her until after he hears the prophecy for which he has descended (11.84–89), but his first question after the prophecy denotes more interest in his mother than the prophet's prediction and advice. He asks Teiresias no follow-up questions and probes for no extra advice, merely noting, "All this, Teiresias, surely must be as the gods spun it" (11.138–39). Then he presses for instructions about how to speak with his mother.

> But come now, tell me this and give me an accurate answer:
> I see before me now the soul of my perished mother,
> but she sits beside the blood in silence, and has not yet deigned
> to look directly at her own son and to speak a word to me.
> Tell me, lord, what will make her know me, and know my presence? (11.140–44)

Odysseus's urgency in wishing to speak to Antikleia (as compared with his interest in Teiresias's prophecy) may be explained by a distinction between how prepared he is for what he learns in the two conversations.[16] By this point in his journey, Odysseus does not yet know how long it will take him to get home, but surely he understands that the task is not easy and that he is beset by sufferings. But until he speaks with Teiresias and his mother, he does not know that his household suffers from his absence.

Antikleia can and does tell Odysseus more about his family than the prophet. Her initial explanation of her presence in Hades is unexpected. She died of grief, longing for her son: "[T]hat was the reason I perished . . . shining Odysseus, it was my longing for you, your cleverness and your gentle ways, that took the sweet spirit of life from me" (11.197–203). Odysseus responds to the description of his mother's death by "pondering in [his] heart" for the only time during his visit to Hades (11.204–5).

Antikleia helps Odysseus understand the suffering that will accompany his homecoming. Odysseus asks his mother about his father, son, property, and wife. Of Penelope in particular, he specifies his desire to know "about the wife I married, what she wants, what she is thinking, and whether she stays fast by my son, and guards everything, or if she has married the best man among the Achaians" (11.176–79). Antikleia responds with reassurance as to Telemachos and his property but has troubling news about his wife and father. Penelope, although faithful, suffers from the same grief as Antikleia: "All too much with enduring heart she does wait for you there in your own palace, and always with her the wretched nights and the days also waste her away with weeping" (11.180–87). The news about Odysseus's father, Laertes, is yet more disturbing: he avoids the city, lives like a "thrall" without the comforts of his wealth, and "lies, grieving, and the sorrow grows big within him as he longs for [Odysseus's] homecoming, and harsh old age is on him" (11.187–96). She bids her son to "remember these things for your wife, so that you may tell her hereafter" (11.223–24). This conversation deepens the reader's awareness of the possibility of genuine tenderness and personal affection among the members of Odysseus's household. Antikleia expresses concern for the suffering of her husband and Penelope, as well as affection for the son whose clever and "gentle" ways she treasures. Odysseus, his heart filled with pity and "thronging sorrow" at the sight of his mother, wishes to hold her and is distressed when he cannot (11.87–88, 204–14).

The focus on family that Odysseus exhibits in his account of his conversations in Hades pervades his interactions with Phaiakia's royal family. His speech consistently indicates that marriage is on his mind.[17] In his initial meeting with Nausikaa, he describes the joy of the man who will be her husband. Later, he waxes yet more poetic, wishing the young woman a happy marriage.

> [A]nd then may the gods give you everything that your
>   heart longs for;
> may they grant you a husband and a house and sweet
>   agreement
> in all things, for nothing is better than this, more steadfast
> than when two people, a man and his wife, keep a harmonious
> household; a thing that brings much distress to the people
>   who hate them
> and pleasure to their well-wishers, and for them the best
>   reputation. (6.180–85)

Nor is it just with the marriage-minded young Nausikaa that Odysseus speaks of happiness in marriage.[18] As he bids her goodbye, he wishes Queen Arete joy in both her family and public relationships: "joy here in your household, in your children and your people, and in your king,

Alkinoös" (13.61–62). In his parting words to the king, Odysseus blends his own heart's yearning for Penelope with wishes for the king to find happiness in marriage.

> [A]nd yourselves fare well, for all my heart desired is now made
> good, conveyance and loving gifts. May the sky gods make these
> prosper for me. May I return to my house and find there
> a blameless wife, and all who are dear to me unharmed.
> May you
> in turn, remaining here, bring comfort and cheer to your wedded
> wives and your children, and may the gods grant success in every
> endeavor, and no unhappiness be found in your people.
> (13.40–46)

Far from forgetting Penelope, it appears that the subject of marriage is very much on Odysseus's mind before he departs for the final night of his voyage.

As the first half of the *Odyssey* draws to a close, Homer has yet to fully answer the question of why Odysseus wants his homecoming and why he considers his wife and marriage important. At this midpoint no element of the poem has excluded the possibility that Odysseus may wish to reforge family connections for the sake of reclaiming his political position as king and thereby the honor associated with political rule. Nonetheless, as Odysseus leaves Phaiakia, the frequency and nature of his references to family have begun to set the stage for a homecoming in which private life constitutes more than a necessary support to public life.

Conclusion

In the *Iliad* Odysseus can be observed to pause and ponder, but ultimately he pursues honor; in the first twelve books of the *Odyssey*, Odysseus seeks his own home and family, sometimes pausing for pleasure or to follow an imprudent impulse prompted by his desire for honor. By the end of his voyage, however, Odysseus's desire for homecoming has a newly acquired dominance in his soul, and the corresponding growth of his self-restraint permits him to continue homeward when offered enticements that might have delayed his earlier self.

Homer has shown that Odysseus passionately desires his homecoming, but the reader does not yet know whether Odysseus seeks private life, public kingdom, or some combination thereof. Still, Homer has ruled out several possibilities. Odysseus's many eloquent references to marriage suggest that he places great value on this aspect of homecoming.[19] More obviously, Homer has demonstrated, through the inducements that Odysseus forgoes, that desire for survival and physical pleasure cannot be Odysseus's foremost desires. Odysseus does not seek his home because it is the most splendid or powerful or his wife because she is the most beautiful. His frank admiration of Phaiakia's magnificent wealth and architecture (particularly in juxtaposition to the meager twelve ships he led to Troy and his reference to "rugged" Ithaka) demonstrate the former, and his easy concession to Kalypso in favor of the nymph's superior personal charms demonstrate the latter. Whatever excellence Odysseus seeks in Ithaka, it is not primarily the power and wealth of his kingdom or the physical beauty of his wife.

On the eve of Odysseus's departure from Phaiakia, Homer provides one final indication of the strength of his hero's desire for homecoming through imagery that emphasizes Odysseus's yearning for home. As the Phaiakians make final preparations for departure, "Odysseus turned his head again and again to look at the shining sun, to hasten its going down, since he was now eager to go" (13.28–31). He yearns for sundown, the time set for departure, like an exhausted laborer yearning to return to his home at the end of a long day.

> [A]nd as a man makes for his dinner, when all day
> long his wine-colored oxen have dragged the compact plow for him
> across the field, and the sun's setting is welcome for bringing
> the time to go to his dinner, and as he goes his knees fail him;
> thus welcome to Odysseus now was the sun going under.
> (13.31–35)

Although we do not yet know whether Odysseus will finally overcome his love of honor in favor of a private life of minding his own business in Ithaka, in one sense Homer has already demonstrated that Odysseus is a model of excellence in private life. Over the course of the first half of the *Odyssey*, Odysseus struggles alone—and thus in private—for his homecoming. During the final portion of his voyage, Odysseus—alone at sea and fighting for survival during the two storms that nearly kill him—is a private hero in the most obvious sense because he is completely alone (5.269–493;12.403–58). In these moments Odysseus is shown to the reader as a man with no audience, with no current presence in the public world, where fame and postmortem immortality are possible. By Arendt's calculation, Odysseus alone and struggling for survival at sea is neither human nor excellent. But through Homer's portrayal of him, it is clear that the audience is meant to admire the intelligence, self-restraint in the face of fear, and courage—the excellence—of Odysseus as he struggles to the utmost of his physical and mental abilities to navigate these dangers and achieve his homecoming, risking an unsung and anonymous (and therefore private) death. Moreover, although our ability to admire him depends on the story being told, Homer's telling of the story indicates that Odysseus, even had he died and the story died with him, would remain excellent. In other words, Odysseus is not dependent on Homer for his excellence. Contrary to MacIntyre's definition of Homeric excellence, Homer reveals in Odysseus a hero whose excellence depends on the virtue with which he faces the challenge—not on the successful completion thereof.

In juxtaposition to Odysseus's private excellence, however, a theme of public consequences runs through the backdrop of the first half of the *Odyssey*. Odysseus, through his own excellence (and with the help of his companions and the gods), is returning home. But Odysseus's companions, through a combination of Odysseus's poor leadership, their own lack of self-restraint, and the will of the gods, will not return home. As the prowess of the glory-earning heroes took center stage in the *Iliad* and the private suffering they caused, while present, remained largely in the backdrop, so in the *Odyssey* the private excellence of Odysseus—which is perhaps most powerfully illustrated initially as Odysseus battles the elements alone at sea—takes center stage. The public suffering that results from his poor leadership—the death of an entire army—remains primarily in the backdrop.

6

At the Heart of Homecoming

Having taken ten years and twelve books to travel home from Troy, Odysseus proceeds to reclaim his position in Ithaka in the course of several days and an additional twelve books. The plot in these twelve books is relatively simple, but Homer's art lies in his masterful orchestration of the resolution of intertwined questions about his characters' desires and relationships. Among the issues facing Odysseus, his family, and their household at the moment of his return are (1) their personal safety and public positions, (2) the security of their physical home and wealth, and (3) the harmony—or lack thereof—among the members of the family and household.

This chapter focuses on Penelope, making the case for Odysseus's marriage as a central component of his homecoming. Understanding Penelope—her critical role in Odysseus's homecoming, her individual virtues, and the love that her husband bears her—is essential to understanding the *Odyssey*'s ultimate portrait of the potential for excellence in private life. Penelope's political importance is not difficult to perceive: without a wife and queen with her specific qualities, Odysseus is not likely to survive, much less to regain either his household or his kingdom. But Penelope is not just politically convenient. Homer portrays Penelope as an excellent individual, and both the existence and nature of her excellence have critical implications for the Homeric presentation of private life, the preference for one's own, and the value of Odysseus's homecoming. Perhaps most importantly, the poet shows that Odysseus loves his wife. Homer presents marriage as a variant of friendship in which the virtues of both partners are essential to private and political success.

The threshold issue of Penelope's political importance and efficacy can most clearly be demonstrated by examining her virtues in comparison to the virtues and failings of the two characters with whom she has the most in common, Klytaimestra and Helen. Although some scholars claim that her virtue—at least insofar as her virtue denotes more than fidelity—is of relatively little political significance, Penelope's intelligent, brave, and self-restrained actions prove necessary for both the private success of her marriage and her joint public success with Odysseus. In other words, Odysseus's success requires Penelope's active employment of her own individual excellence.

According to MacIntyre and Adkins, Penelope's virtue is defined by her social role, limited to fidelity. As a result, Penelope and Odysseus are friends, but their friendship is based on difference and the successful completion of their respective social roles. For Arendt, on the other hand, Penelope can only be found virtuous insofar as her public, queenly role permits her to exhibit herself in the world of public action. But Penelope's actions, words, and thoughts do not coincide with either of these interpretations. Examination of her character reveals a politically powerful woman whose virtues, whether categorized as public or private, are essentially the same as the virtues of her husband. Indeed, when read through the gendered lens demanded by her cultural context, the virtues that most define Penelope are the same as those that define Odysseus. Insofar as Penelope exhibits the "masculine" strengths of intelligence and courage, Odysseus exhibits the cunning intelligence and self-restraint that one might easily categorize as "feminine." Homer thus escapes the gendering of virtue, even in a world with gendered social roles, through his portrait of the spouses' parallel virtues. In sum, Penelope is not only relevant politically, she is also excellent and worthy of admiration—a hero in her own right. The story of the heroes and virtues in Homer's epics is not complete without the inclusion of Penelope.

Homer's elevation of Penelope results in a corresponding elevation of private life. Odysseus and Penelope are united by more than erotic longing and their partnership in protecting household and kingdom. They are friends. This friendship elevates private life, transforming it into a venue for speech and the love of that which is good, the excellence of the friend. Odysseus and Penelope's private sphere is thus the antithesis of Arendt's vision: far from a subhuman sphere of animal necessity in which excellence and therefore friendship are equally impossible, Homer presents Penelope and Odysseus's marriage as one in which the similarity of the spouses' virtues permits eros and friendship to coexist in private.

This view of marriage, love of one's own, and private life is powerfully presented at the end of the *Odyssey* through Odysseus's desire to be not only reunited with but also recognized by his wife. Homer affirms the strength and quality of his hero's desire for his wife by showing his audience the overwhelming joy Odysseus finds in their reunion. Homer's description of the night of the couple's reunion completes the portrait of a very specific type of love. Penelope is the only friend in Ithaka with whom Odysseus shares the true story of his adventures and his plans for the future. Attention to additional details in Odysseus's relationship with Penelope reveals that he considers her to be—in addition to a valuable public ally—a precious friend with whom to love, talk, plan, and rest in private. When necessary, he reemerges into the public world. But Odysseus loves the space that he shares with Penelope, and he leaves her company for the sake of preserving that which he most highly values. Marriage and friendship with a like-minded individual are at the center of the *Odyssey*'s portrait of human happiness.

Lion at Bay

Although the variety of queens, wives, and noblewomen in Homer does not begin to approach that of the kings, husbands, and warriors, the epics include female characters who play meaningful roles in the political dramas that surround them.[1] In this story about the consequences of a war instigated by the theft of one queen and wife, the political significance of women is indeed an obvious and contentious premise.[2] Yet, just because possession of one beautiful queen may cause political havoc, it does not necessarily follow that individual women (with their individual virtues and characteristics) are politically important as either examples of political efficacy or human excellence. While Homer often leaves at least this reader frustrated over the lack of detail with regard to the thoughts of his female characters, he presents women as agents whose individual qualities—their virtues, passions, temperaments, and skills—are pivotal in both the domestic and political dramas that surround them.[3] Their social (and sometimes political) roles as queens, wives, mothers, and objects of desire are undeniably important, as they are in a parallel (if lesser) fashion for their male counterparts: who could deny that a portion at least of Agamemnon's political power arises from his status as a son of Atreus and a king? But, as with male characters (again, if to a lesser degree), the individual qualities of Homer's Penelope (not just her social functions) are critical to her success and to the success that she makes possible for Odysseus.

The evidence for reading Penelope as a model of passive, loyal, and traditional feminine excellence is substantial: as the *Odyssey* commences, weeping Penelope yearns for her presumably deceased husband, negotiates a strained relationship with a beloved son who has begun to assert his role as head of the household, and—her one effective ploy having lost its effectiveness—seems nearly defenseless. The epic's early depictions of Penelope stress her continued faithfulness to Odysseus and her vulnerability. Her first words in the *Odyssey* describe her longing for the husband who has yet to return: "[T]he unforgettable sorrow comes to me, beyond others, so dear a head do I long for whenever I am reminded of my husband" (1.342–44). As Telemachos explains in public assembly, Penelope remained steadfast for twenty years: "[M]y mother, *against her will*, is beset by suitors, own sons to the men who are greatest hereabout" (2.50–51, emphasis mine). When she finally agrees to remarry, she does so in light of her well-founded belief that this act is necessary to save Telemachos's life and in response to the threats of the suitors who have already impoverished her household and diminished his inheritance (18.288–89; 21.52–79). She tells Odysseus (while he is disguised) that when her husband left, all of her "excellence . . . beauty and figure, were ruined" (19.124–25).

This impression is not controverted by the epic's ambiguous picture of Penelope's political role in Ithaka, an issue on which the scholarship remains divided.[4] Although Penelope claims that Odysseus left her in charge in his absence, their servant Mentor is introduced by the narrator as the man to whom Odysseus had turned his household over "so that all should obey him" (2.224–27; 18.266). It is conceivable that both references might be accurate: Odysseus may have left his wife in command and yet commissioned a man to enforce her commands. Still, a broader question—the question of the continuance of politics in Odysseus's absence—complicates the matter. The assembly held in book 2 is the first in Ithaka since the king's departure, and Homer provides no additional indications of political activity since the army departed with Odysseus. If it is difficult to ascertain the character of politics in Ithaka, it is doubly difficult to pinpoint Penelope's role therein.[5]

Her ambiguous political role and pronounced vulnerability (both emotional and political) in the early books of the *Odyssey* provide the grounds for those who argue that Penelope's virtue, insofar as one may call it that, is synonymous with her fidelity. But Homer's aggregate portrait of the queen is far more nuanced, and the simile with which he closes his initial portrait of her situation in Ithaka underscores the aspect of Penelope that an exclusive focus on her vulnerability ignores. When Penelope learns, in book 4, of the suitors' plot to kill Telemachos, Homer describes her as a lion encircled by hunters (4.787–94). This imagery takes into account both Penelope's power, which her scholarly detractors discount, and her overwhelmingly powerful enemies. Of course, one simile is not sufficient to demonstrate Penelope's prowess, but it is certainly suggestive that neither passivity nor loyalty sums up her character.

The nature and consequences of Penelope's lionlike virtues begin to come into focus when her actions are juxtaposed with those of Klytaimestra and Helen, whose particular shortcomings as individuals (and thus also as queens) are partially responsible for both marital and political instability. These two queens, the wives of Agamemnon and Menelaus, serve as obvious counterpoints to Penelope (and she to them). Agamemnon loses first his throne and then his life because his wife, Klytaimestra, either could not or would not fend off suitors during the Trojan War. Helen, who left Achaian Menelaus for Trojan Alexandros, doomed her husband and all of Achaia to the Trojan War through a failure in fidelity that was caused by the inability to recognize the identity of her own husband.

Klytaimestra, who never appears in person in either epic, remains in the backdrop of the *Odyssey*.[6] The subject of secondhand accounts that leave unresolved the question of her willingness to remarry, she is never permitted by Homer to take center stage in her own drama. Whatever her state of mind may have been at the time of her second marriage, Klytaimestra was courted by and eventually married her husband's usurper, Aigisthos, while Agamemnon was still absent (3.234–310). Klytaimestra's remarriage permits Aigisthos to take her husband's place as king, and when Agamemnon returns from the war Klytaimestra participates in his murder (11.410–26).[7] After his death, Agamemnon—admittedly not an objective observer—describes Klytaimestra's faults to Odysseus in Hades. He focuses on his queen's mind, claiming that "there is nothing more deadly or more vile than a woman who stores her mind with acts that are of such sort" (11.427–34). Agamemnon condemns all women because of the mind of his wife, which is filled "with thoughts surpassingly grisly" (11.427–34).

As scholars have noted, Klytaimestra's story—undeniably one of a failure in loyalty and possibly (depending upon her complicity in becoming Aigisthos's wife) also one of weakness—highlights the faithfulness *and* the strength of Penelope.[8] When Agamemnon attempts to reassure Odysseus that Penelope will remain faithful, he again focuses on the mind, telling Odysseus that Penelope's "mind is stored with good thoughts" (11.446). Athena too emphasizes the importance of Penelope's mind, telling Odysseus upon his arrival in Ithaka that his wife plays the suitors against one another.

> [C]onsider how you can lay your hands on these shameless suitors,
> who for three years now have been lords in your palace,
> and courting your god-like wife, and offering gifts to win her.
> And she, though her heart forever grieves over your homecoming,
> holds out some hope for all, and makes promises to each man,
> sending them messages, but her mind has other intentions.
>   (13.376–81)

The chief tactic by which the queen avoids the suitors is through an ongoing refusal to either reject or accept any particular suitor.[9] As Penelope explains to Odysseus (disguised as a beggar), her suitors try to hasten the marriage, but she "weave[s]" her "own wiles" (19.137). She first persuaded the suitors that respectability required that she finish a funeral shroud for Odysseus's father before remarriage. Then, for three years, she managed to hold the suitors at bay by undoing each day's weaving each night (19.149–56). This use to which Penelope applies her intellect in defense of her marriage and home demonstrates that it is not merely her willingness to remain faithful to Odysseus that differentiates her from Klytaimestra.[10]

When Agamemnon tells Odysseus of Klytaimestra's betrayal, Odysseus's response relates to the political aspect of a queen's decision to take a new husband. He calls her action "treason" (11.439), thus highlighting the political ramifications of Klytaimestra's betrayal. In Ithaka Penelope's betrayal would have likely brought about the same political consequences.

Had Penelope remarried before Odysseus returned, Odysseus might have been slain by her new husband and king.[11] That some of the suitors seek the crown and intend to kill Odysseus, should he return, becomes clear when they challenge Telemachos's likelihood of claiming the throne (1.383–401). One of the suitors, Leokritos, explains openly to Telemachos that "even if Odysseus of Ithaka himself were to come back . . . his wife would have no joy of his coming, though she longs for it greatly, but rather he would meet an unworthy destiny" (2.246–51).

Penelope's success in her efforts to maintain her home and kingdom during Odysseus's absence hinge, it is true, on her ability to maintain her fidelity to Odysseus, but her ability to maintain this fidelity requires the strength of her intellect as surely as her warrior husband's ability to defeat his enemies in battle requires courage. Penelope employs her mind to defeat the suitors. A lion at bay though she may be when Odysseus returns, the strength of mind that earns her this image proves a necessary (if not sufficient) condition of their joint success and the primary reason why Odysseus does not meet the same end as Agamemnon.

Like the juxtaposition of Penelope with Klytaimestra, the juxtaposition of Penelope with Helen highlights the qualities necessary for Penelope's success and underscores their political implications. Penelope herself draws the comparison to Helen, but she does so in a light more favorable to Helen than one might expect.[12] Penelope believes that Helen was tricked into following Alexandros to Troy and thus blames not Helen but the gods for the war that followed. It was, she explains to Odysseus, "a god who stirred [Helen] to do the shameful thing she did, and never before had she had in her heart this terrible wildness" (23.218–23). Although Homer never details how, Helen too implies that her failure was one of perception and not, as one might otherwise think, succumbing to seduction.[13] In the *Iliad*, when a disguised Aphrodite entices Helen to Alexandros's bed, Helen accuses the goddess of a past deceit. Recognizing Aphrodite, Helen accuses the goddess of playing a *second* trick on her: "Will you carry me *further yet* somewhere among cities fairly settled? . . . Is there some mortal man there *also* who is dear to you?" (3.399–402, emphasis mine). Later, in Sparta with Menelaus, Helen repeats this implicit accusation against Aphrodite (4.261–64).

Penelope, afraid of making the same mistake as Helen, is deliberate in her attempts to avoid being deceived by appearances.[14] When Eurykleia, Odysseus's old nurse, first comes to tell Penelope that Odysseus has returned and killed the suitors, Penelope expresses delight but then immediately moderates her initial impulse. She cautions the old nurse that the man claiming to be Odysseus must be an avenging god: "[R]ather, some one of the immortals has killed the haughty suitors in anger over their wicked deeds and the heart-hurting violence" (23.62–68). When the nurse persists, Penelope reminds her that cleverness is no guarantee of immunity from a god's plan (23.81–82).

Penelope's concern that she might be tricked by a god (or by a man disguised by a god) and thus become a second Helen explains why she hesitates to acknowledge Odysseus even after she believes that she has recognized him. The poet explains that Penelope "came down from the chamber, her heart pondering much, whether to keep away and question her dear husband, or go up to him and kiss his head, taking his hand" (23.85–87). Her hesitation is so pronounced that Telemachos rebukes her for her failure to greet Odysseus (23.100–3). She defends her unwillingness to forgo caution, explaining, "I am not being proud, nor indifferent, nor puzzled beyond need, but I know very well what you looked like when you went in the ship with the sweeping oars, from Ithaka" (23.174–80). When Penelope is finally convinced that the man before her is her husband, she explains to him her fear "that some one of mortal men would come my way and deceive me with words" (23.213–17). Homer describes her hesitation, deliberation, and questioning of Odysseus in great detail, but it is only if one reads the scene from Penelope's perspective of genuinely fearing divine ensnarement that her behavior makes sense.

Where Helen was deceived, Penelope directs all her attention and self-restraint to discerning what is truly her own. She thus applies her intelligence with equal vigilance to fending off the overt threat of the suitors and to the more subtle potential assault of deception. Juxtaposing Penelope with Klytaimestra and Helen highlights the political ramifications of Penelope's choices and thus underscores the importance of her distinct qualities. While in a sense it is true that Penelope's political efficacy is tied to her constancy, this constancy is only possible because of characteristics specific to her, her individual virtues or excellence.

King Penelope

Thus far, I have made the case for Penelope's relevance as an individual whose particular qualities—not just the successful maintenance of her fidelity or status as a queen—create the necessary conditions for her joint success with Odysseus. Her loyalty, intelligence, and attention to discerning what is her own are necessary to Odysseus's regaining his crown (and home) and to the likelihood of his surviving his return. To clarify the nature of her virtues, it is helpful to consider Odysseus as a point of reference.[15] Like Odysseus, Penelope's most renowned virtue is her intelligence. And like Odysseus, the intelligence for which she is renowned is tinged with a degree of trickery, dishonesty, and wiliness. Also like Odysseus, if in a less obvious fashion than her husband, Penelope displays her intelligence in tandem with courage. Perhaps most importantly, she displays a degree of self-restraint—an ability to moderate her impulses—that echoes that of her husband. The basis of Penelope's political efficacy is thus a set of virtues that extend beyond those traditionally viewed as feminine.

If Penelope initially appears masculine through the strengths of courage and intelligence, Odysseus initially mirrors her by appearing feminine through his particularly calculating form of courage, his wily intelligence, and a moderation that are out of place among the paragons of masculinity with whom he is surrounded in the *Iliad*. This suggests that their virtues, although expressed somewhat differently for husband and for wife due to cultural constraints and resulting differences in circumstances, can best be understood as gender neutral. In sum, Homer avoids the gendering of virtue through his portrait of the parity in virtue that undergirds their marriage. Admittedly, the actions of wife and husband (Penelope's sexual fidelity and Odysseus's skill with his bow, for example) differ and are indeed highly gendered. But their virtues—what we admire in them and what Homer wants us to admire in them—are not their successes or their actions but rather the underlying characteristics that, barring overwhelming force or the contrary will of a god, make their successes possible. In other words, their virtues are not their actions; their virtues are the individual qualities that power their actions: one might call this personality, character, inner strength, or even strength of soul. Because Penelope and Odysseus exhibit matching virtues, they create—in the midst of a gendered world of human action—a gender-neutral portrait of the human excellence that directs their actions.

Intelligence

The argument that Penelope's intelligence makes her similar to Odysseus might seem to belabor an obvious point. If Odysseus is the hero of many wiles, all but Penelope's most aggressive detractors concede that she is the heroine of at least one wily trick.[16] Yet the text shows in many ways that her midnight unraveling is not her only claim to clever intelligence. Her suitors, although clearly attracted to Penelope's position, wealth, and beauty, describe her mind as one of her outstanding qualities. Even Agamemnon (not the most sympathetic observer of women) encourages Odysseus when they meet in Hades, telling him that "her mind is stored with good thoughts" (11.446). The point of this analysis, then, is not to establish the existence of Penelope's intelligence but to show how her intelligence resembles the intelligence of Odysseus.

That their intelligence manifests similarly can be surmised from many aspects of the story: (1) it is evident in the way that both spouses manipulate the love of honor of those around them; (2) it is implicit in their many tacit (or at least longstanding) agreements about the individuals around them; and (3) it provides the best explanation for Odysseus and Penelope's ability to coordinate with one another without speaking openly (whether or not Penelope is already aware of Odysseus's identity).[17] Further evidence of their similarity can be found in Odysseus's understanding of and pleasure in the clever wiles of his wife, as well as in Penelope's assessment that the stranger in her home (Odysseus in disguise as a beggar) is a man of good sense.

Like her husband, Penelope manipulates the desire for honor of those who surround her.[18] Even as Odysseus uses his grasp of the same motivating factor to navigate the political alliances among the Achaians, Penelope appeals to the suitors' love of honor to partially thwart their "harsh courtship" (2.199). In order to delay her remarriage, she initially persuades the suitors that she must weave Laertes's shroud "lest any Achaian woman in this neighborhood hold it against me that a man with many conquests lies with no sheet to wind him" (2.101–2). Her explicit appeal is to her own honor, but she simultaneously makes an indirect appeal to the honor of any suitor who thinks he may eventually marry her (and thereby link his own honor to hers).[19]

Later, Penelope uses both public shame and the suitors' love of honor to renew her delays. She asserts the power of choice, explaining that Odysseus empowered her to choose a new husband once Telemachos had grown to manhood.[20] After asserting this authority, Penelope publicly insults their courtship: "But this thing comes as a bitter distress to my heart and spirit: the behavior of these suitors is not as it was in times past when suitors desired to pay their court to a noble woman and daughter of a rich man, and rival each other" (18.274–77). Noble suitors, Penelope goads them, "bring in their own cattle and fat sheep, to feast the family of the bride, and offer glorious presents. They do not eat up another's livelihood, without payment" (18.278–80). Antinoos takes this speech—as Penelope evidently intends—as a challenge to their honor and leads the other suitors in sending home for an impressive array of gifts.

Still disguised, Odysseus's reaction as he watches Penelope is instructive. He both understands his wife's ruse and takes pleasure in observing her craftiness. At the outset of the scene, Athena has inspired Penelope to speak with the suitors "so that she might seem all the *more* precious in the eyes of her husband and son even than she had been before this" (18.161–62, emphasis mine). Athena conspires to accomplish this by bestowing goddesslike beauty on Penelope so that the suitors' "knees gave way, and the hearts in them were bemused with passion, and each one prayed for the privilege of lying beside her" (18.212–13). Odysseus's reaction to his wife, by contrast, is not described until *after* she incites the suitors to send for gifts: "She spoke, and much-enduring great Odysseus was happy because she beguiled gifts out of them, and enchanted their spirits with blandishing words, while her own mind had other intentions" (18.281–83).[21] Penelope becomes more precious in the eyes of her husband not due to divinely bestowed beauty or the wealth that she procures but in response to her exhibition of the craft in which these two individuals surpass all others.

Odysseus and Penelope also display their similarity of judgment through a series of common conclusions about the individuals who surround them.[22] Although making their discernments independently, they reach the same conclusions when identifying enemies and friends. For example, each demonstrates trust in the pig farmer Eumaios and high regard for Odysseus's old nurse, Eurykleia. Each singles out the serving woman Malantho as an enemy. Moreover, they are in agreement as to the most worthy of the suitors, Amphinomos.[23]

Particularly in the nuances of the negotiation that build toward their adoption of the plan, Odysseus and Penelope's agreement about the test of the bow demonstrates their similarity in reasoning. On the day that Odysseus returns to his house, even as he is considering how to rid his house of his rivals, Penelope despairs of discovering a new means to thwart her suitors and preserve Telemachos's life and inheritance. Although her appeal to the suitors' love of honor had been partially successful (gaining a short delay and helping to replenish the wealth they had used up), the suitors continue to menace her (18.288–94). Later in the same evening, Penelope and Odysseus have their first conversation since his departure for Troy. Before this conversation even begins, the couple's negotiation as to its time and place suggests the similarity in their thought processes. Penelope had sent Eumaios to "tell the stranger to come, so I can befriend him, and so I can ask him if he has somewhere heard any news of steadfast Odysseus or seen him in person. He seems like a man who has wandered widely" (17.508–11). Odysseus agrees but delays until they may have a more private interview: "I am afraid of rough suitors. . . . Tell Penelope, therefore, for all her eagerness, to wait for me in the palace until the sun has set" (17.560–73). When Eumaios delivers this response, the queen concurs with Beggar/Odysseus's reasoning: "So it shall be. The stranger's thought is not without good sense" (17.584–88).

When evening comes their first conversation commences. In a poem that began nineteen books earlier with a man "longing for his wife," the reader begins—much like Odysseus and Penelope—to be rewarded for the preceding patience. Yet, with the possibility of unfriendly ears listening and at least the semblance of Penelope's acceptance of Odysseus's disguise, this first reunion is greatly inhibited (on his side at least, even if she suspects nothing).[24] Penelope and Odysseus commence by trading stories. She praises her absent husband and describes her own past "wiles" (19.136–61). She despairs of her next move: "Now I cannot escape from this marriage; I can no longer think of another plan" (19.136–61).[25] Odysseus compliments his wife: "Lady, no mortal man on the endless earth could have cause to find fault with you; your fame goes up into the wide heaven, as of some king" (19.107–9). Mutual compliments exchanged, Penelope presses for Odysseus's identity. He claims to be a younger brother of one of the great Achaians of the Trojan War, Idomeneus, and describes how he saw Odysseus on the Ithakan's way to Troy (19.162–202). Penelope, listening to Odysseus's account of himself, melts into her most momentous display of emotion (save when she and Odysseus finally embrace two books later). She "melts" like the snows on a mountain melt until the "rivers run full flood" (19.207). Penelope weeps: "her beautiful cheeks were streaming with tears" for Odysseus, "for her man, who was sitting there by her side" (19.208–9). The tears that Penelope weeps for Odysseus nearly prompt him to weep in his turn for her; he can barely hold back his own tears. "But Odysseus in his heart had pity for his wife as she mourned him, but his eyes stayed, as if they were made of horn or iron, steady under his lids. He hid his tears and deceived her" (19.203–12).[26]

Penelope next questions the stranger about how Odysseus had looked, and he responds with a compliment on the finery in which Penelope had arrayed him (19.232–35). Her response to this praise includes a promise of friendship but also an explanation of how she prepared the finery that Odysseus has just complimented (19.253–57). These emotional words and more expressions of Penelope's fears that she will never see her husband again pass between them. Odysseus then shifts the conversation to more immediate concerns, as he begins to explain to Penelope how and why Odysseus will return. The transition in the conversation from an emotional exchange of identity proofs to planning a response to the present danger is marked. Penelope immediately follows his lead. He tells her, "But now, give over your lamentation, and mark what I tell you, for I say to you *without deception, without concealment, that I have heard of the present homecoming of Odysseus*" (19.268–70, emphasis mine). The disguised Odysseus explains to Penelope that Odysseus is near, but alone—having lost his men (19.271–78). The purported stranger reveals that Odysseus has been greatly enriched by the Phaiakians and has hidden possessions that "would feed a succession of heirs to the tenth generation" elsewhere (19.279–95).[27]

Acquiescing to her husband's change in tone, Penelope calls for her maids to provide a good bed and bath. When Odysseus refuses the bath "unless there is some aged and virtuous woman whose heart has had to endure as many troubles" as his has, Penelope proposes that Odysseus's old nurse wash his feet (19.317–56). She calls Eurykleia's attention to the similarity between Odysseus and the stranger, commenting to the nurse, "Odysseus must by this time have just such hands and feet as you do, for in misfortune mortal men grow old more suddenly" (19.357–60). Eurykleia's stifled recognition of Odysseus follows during the footbath, and then Penelope restarts the conversation with the question of their current situation. After dismissing a dream ostensibly portending Odysseus's successful but violent return as unreliable, Penelope—mirroring her husband's earlier change in tone—signals that the heart of her communication is about to commence: "And put away in your heart this other thing that I tell you" (19.570).

Penelope details her plan for an elaborate archery contest for her hand. Although she predicts a day of "evil name," she proposes to risk her remarriage: "I will set up . . . a contest before my suitors, and the one who takes [Odysseus's] bow in his hands, strings it with the greatest ease, and sends an arrow clean through all the twelve axes shall be the one I will go away with" (19.571–80). Odysseus assents, agreeing to the excellence of the plan: "O respected wife of Odysseus, son of Laertes, do not put off this contest in your house any longer" (19.582–84). Indeed, Odysseus prophesizes his own return in time to play a role in the plan: "Before these people can handle the well-wrought bow, and manage to hook the string and bend it, and send a shaft through the iron, Odysseus of the many designs will be back here with you" (19.585–87). The plan agreed to, their conversation ends.

Odysseus and Penelope demonstrate much about their similarity in this conversation. Each expresses admiration for the other. Each feels sorrow for the other: she at the thought of his absence and labors, he for the grief that she suffers because of him. He explains Odysseus's tactical situation to her, and she reveals her strategy to him. One cannot help but wonder whether Penelope has the comfort of knowing that she has agreed upon this plan with Odysseus (or at least a god disguised as Odysseus). Or is she just grateful for the opportunity to speak with a stranger whom she has judged to be of intelligence and good will (and who predicts the imminent return of Odysseus)? In either event, the readiness of their agreement and the ease with which they navigate the conversation establishes the similarity of their crafty minds.[28] It cannot surprise readers that Odysseus, like Zeus in counsel, and circumspect Penelope agree on their plan.

Courage

Penelope's courage is not as obvious as that of her warrior-husband, but it is all the more exceptional in a cultural context in which the courage of a woman is neither as expected nor as evident as that of a man. Penelope's many tactics demonstrate her ability to remain levelheadedly courageous in dangerous circumstances. Although admittedly not the same expression of courage as that of a battlefield hero, it should be remembered that Penelope takes great risks to protect the life of her son and to avoid a marriage that she finds more distasteful than death (20.79–83).[29]

As the epic progresses, Penelope's courage becomes increasingly evident in her open defiance and belittling of the men who seek to force themselves on her as husband. Two of the men whom she most pointedly shames are the two most likely to claim her as wife. She speaks plainly to the suitor who first proposed murdering Telemachos, publicly calling him "evil" and accusing him of the attempted murder of Telemachos and of taking "no heed of suppliants, over whom Zeus stands witness" (16.418–22).[30] Later Penelope becomes more pointed, telling Eurymachos that he has so little honor that he no longer has any need to "be concerned over reproaches" (21.330–34). In addition to these pointed public insults, Penelope makes no secret of her desire not to marry at all. Even as she offers the contest of the bow to the suitors and promises to marry the winner, she continues to assert the superiority of and her own preference for her first marriage (21.75–79).[31]

How is it that these insults—Penelope's hot words—constitute a form of courage? Penelope, unlike Homer's readers, does not know that she will not be taken home as wife and captive to one of the men whom she has repeatedly, publicly, and correctly put to shame. Rather, she has reason to flatter and please these men, one of whom may soon be the tyrant of the remainder of her life. The more resistance, disdain, and superior intellect and virtue she displays while she retains her independence, the more hostility, resentment, and anger she can expect once the doors of her new bedchamber close behind her.

Even if by the time Penelope most pointedly insults Eurymachos she suspects or knows that Odysseus is home and listening to her, she has no guarantee that Odysseus will still be able to string the bow that he used in his youth—or that he will survive the confrontation with the suitors that surely must follow. Indeed, initiating the contest of the bow is itself a particularly daring move: Telemachos or Odysseus (if indeed she suspects his presence or imminent arrival) may win her, but the risk of falling into the hands of Antinoos or Eurymachos becomes greater too.[32] It would be safer to give up her stalling techniques (how long, at any rate, can the bow save her if Odysseus fails or if he is not at least near?) and concede to marry the relatively benign and (according to her own estimation) sensible Amphinomos. Indeed, the best move for a risk-averse Penelope would have been to marry Amphinomos years before.

Penelope displays her courage again when she refuses to recognize Odysseus immediately after his slaughter of the suitors and the disloyal members of the household. When Eurykleia runs to tell Penelope of the terrible vengeance wrought by Odysseus, the nurse's description emphasizes the fearsomeness of the purported husband.

> There I found Odysseus standing among the dead men
> he had killed, and they covered the hardened earth, lying
> piled on each other around him. You would have been
>   cheered to see him,
> spattered over with gore and filth, like a lion. (23.45–48)

Despite the threat implicit in this bloody figure, Penelope risks his wrath in her insistence on avoiding Helen's mistake. Although Odysseus initially defers to her, at first seemingly amused as Penelope attempts to be sure of his identity, there can be no doubt that if he chooses to claim her without her consent he has the power to do so. The floor is still wet from washing away the gore of the scores of men and women that Odysseus and those under his command have killed. Nonetheless, even as his growing impatience gives way to anger, Penelope courageously takes her time to be sure of his identity. Only when sure does she beg her husband, "Do not be angry with me" (23.209).

Self-Restraint

Odysseus's self-restraint or moderation, at least in contrast to his anger-prone peers, is prominent. In particular, this is a quality in which he exceeds his male peers of the Trojan War and is crucial for his survival. Penelope, whose epithet (περίφρων) is most frequently translated "circumspect," "prudent," or "discreet," also boasts a larger-than-ordinary degree of self-restraint.[33] A preliminary suggestion of this characteristic can be observed in Penelope's frequent use of the metaphor of "weaving" for planning.[34] If her husband is the "much devising Odysseus," Penelope might well be thought of as "constantly weaving Penelope."[35]

But the best evidence of Penelope's self-restraint—if one discounts twenty years of overcoming grief and fear while tending to her daily duties and obstacles—is her self-controlled test of Odysseus after his defeat of the suitors. As previously argued, it is conceivable that she may already be certain of the stranger's identity. If this is the case, by the time he proclaims himself she has already exhibited impressive self-control by speaking to Odysseus without outwardly indicating her suspicion. This possibility aside, the moderation of her initial impulse that she demonstrates between the moments of Eurykleia's announcement of the return of Odysseus and her own confirmation of this truth is a remarkable feat.

When Eurykleia, sent to Penelope's chamber by her master to tell Penelope of his return, announces Odysseus's return and his vengeance, Penelope tells the faithful servant that she must have fallen prey to a divine ruse: the gods are able both to "change a very sensible person into a senseless one, and to set the light-wit on the way of discretion" (23.11–14). When Eurykleia continues in earnest to describe Odysseus's return, Penelope betrays her joy for a moment but then continues questioning (23.32–34). Eurykleia provides a description of Odysseus's ferocity and urges Penelope, "Come with me then . . . now at last what long you prayed for has been accomplished" (23.52–54). But Penelope stifles any premature joy: "Dear nurse, do not yet laugh aloud in triumph" (23.59–68). She consents to go down to the hall "to see my son, so that I can look on these men who courted me lying dead, and the man who killed them" (23.83–84). As she descends, the poem gives us a rare glimpse of Penelope's thoughts as she struggles with competing impulses: her heart is "pondering much, whether to keep away and question her dear husband, or to go up to him and kiss his head, taking his hands" (23.85–87).

Penelope remains cool and observant as Telemachos asserts his father's identity.

> But then, when she came in and stepped over the stone threshold,
> she sat across from him in the firelight, facing Odysseus,
> by the opposite wall, while he was seated by the tall pillar,
> looking downward, and waiting to find out if his majestic wife would have anything to say to him, now that she saw him.
> She sat a long time in silence, and her heart was wondering.
> Sometimes she would look at him, with her eyes full upon him,
> and again would fail to know him in the foul clothing he wore. (23.88–95)

She insists that she will know Odysseus by "signs that we know of between the two of us only" (23.109–10). Odysseus smiles and sends Telemachos away. Still patient, he commands a bath. But when, "looking like an immortal, he strode forth from the bath, and came back and sat on the chair from which he had risen, opposite his wife," Odysseus's patience wears thin. He restarts the conversation, accusing (or praising?) his "strange" wife of having a heart made by the gods "more stubborn than for the rest of womankind" (23.166–67). Odysseus demonstrates his own self-control by accepting Penelope's refusal to acknowledge him and asks for a separate bed (23.168–72).[36] "Iron" Penelope holds her ground. She claims to be neither "proud, nor indifferent, nor puzzled beyond need," and she remembers quite well what the man who left her twenty years ago looked like (23.174–76).

Seeming to agree with her husband's decision to go to a separate bed, she commands Eurykleia to move "that very bed that he himself built" outside the bed chamber (23.178–79). Having found a way of "trying him out," Penelope is rewarded for her careful weaving of this conversation by Odysseus's "angry" and pitiable outburst: "What you have said, dear lady, has hurt my heart deeply" (23.183). He proceeds to describe the immovable, secret bed, focusing on his own role in fashioning the bed: "I myself, no other man, made it" (23.188–89). Mixed with his proud description of the bed that he had constructed from a live olive tree and his doubts as to whether any man living could move it, his fears that it might indeed have been destroyed betray themselves in a demonstration of vulnerability: "There is its character, as I tell you; but I do not know now, dear lady, whether my bed is still in place, or if some man has cut underneath the stump of the olive, and moved it elsewhere" (23.202–4).

Penelope is satisfied "with the clear proofs that Odysseus had given." Her restraint (and his) vanish in the moment that the poem has built to since the poet revealed the hero's longing for his wife in the opening lines (23.205–6; 1.13). Penelope begs Odysseus not to be angry and explains her fears of becoming like Helen as she embraces and kisses her husband (23.207–30). As for Odysseus, Penelope "still roused in him the passion for weeping. He wept as he held his lovely wife, whose perception he cherished" (23.231–32).[37] The degree of Penelope's relief and joy in these moments of reunion should be taken as the measure of the strength of her self-restraint in the moments that preceded. As Odysseus experiences one of his most pronounced moments of weeping, Penelope figuratively becomes Odysseus and he the land to which sea-wrecked Penelope clings.

> And as when the land appears welcome to men who are swimming,

> after Poseidon has smashed their strong-built ship on the open
> water, pounding it with the weight of wind and the heavy
> seas, and only a few escape the gray water landward
> by swimming, with a thick scurf of salt coated upon them,
> and gladly they set foot on the shore, escaping the evil;
> so welcome was her husband to her as she looked upon him,
> and she could not let go from the embrace of her white arms.
> (23.233–40)

This scene, which has tested the courage, intelligence, and restraint of circumspect Penelope, thus ends in a mutual lowering of guards between husband and wife. Their reunion elicits an emotional response that is only partly due to the twenty-year wait, extreme dangers, and many labors of the pair: the beauty of the moment stems in part from the knowledge that they are well matched with similar strengths and from their mutual recognition of those strengths in one another. If it was specifically Penelope who made Odysseus's homecoming possible, it is in great part the virtues of Penelope—so well matched to his own—that make Odysseus's homecoming good. Signaling approval of the priority of the moment, divine intervention (for the one and only time in either epic) holds back the dawn to permit Penelope and Odysseus to fulfill the promise of this moment with the words and acts implicit in their joy and understanding.

> Now Dawn of the rosy fingers would have dawned on their weeping,
> had not the gray-eyed goddess Athene planned it otherwise.
> She held the long night back at the outward edge, she detained
> dawn of the golden throne by the Ocean, and would not let her
> harness her fast-footed horses who bring the daylight to people . . . (23.241–44)

Beloved Penelope

Demonstrating that Penelope is worthy of being an object of love does not prove that Odysseus loves her, but it provides background that consistently suggests this conclusion. That Odysseus has reason to be grateful to Penelope is evident from the kingdom, household, and family that she preserved. His sense of partnership with Penelope can be gleaned from the manner in which he coordinates with her as they make the joint decision to invoke the test of the bow (as well as in the negotiations in which they determine when and how to communicate under dangerous circumstances). Odysseus reveals his respect for his wife's judgment and intelligence in many scenes—when he is pleased by her prompting of the gifts from the suitors, in his initial amusement at the deliberation that she employs before acknowledging him in book 23, and in his deference to her timing in determining to assent to his identity. Odysseus's affection—at the very least—is also displayed in many of these scenes. When she weeps during their book 19 conversation, the pity that he feels and the difficulty that he experiences in hiding his emotion speak of the strength of Odysseus's feeling for Penelope.

The structure and imagery of the *Odyssey* imply the mutually love-driven nature of Odysseus and Penelope's relationship. Odysseus's longing for his wife first appears in the opening lines, forming a part of the very premise of the epic. Penelope's echoing yearning appears soon after, and their mutual longing fuels the plot and the emotional tension of the *Odyssey*.[38] Homer also links the couple repeatedly through imagery in which they switch genders: she is a male lion, king, and sailor, and he is a grieving war widow, a mother dog, and finally the land that Penelope the sailor clings to.[39] There is a reason, after all, that the *Odyssey* has a claim to the title of the first novel, and it is not Penelope's passion alone that prompts the comparison between this ancient Greek epic and modern romance.[40]

The suspense reserved for Penelope's recognition of her husband, the couple's embrace, and the reunion that follows provide further evidence that Odysseus's love for Penelope is not only genuine but also of great importance within the poem as a whole. Indeed, the only reason for us as readers not to skip forward to the events of the next day at the beginning of book 23 (when the suitors are vanquished and the king and queen face one another without disguise for the first time) is the desire to be sure of the fulfillment of Odysseus's still unmet desire for Penelope (and hers for him). In the books leading up to the reunion scene, the *Odyssey* leads its readers through a set of emotional experiences that echo those of Odysseus: we long for him to return to Penelope, but once he returns to his home—through the six and a half books in which he is under his own roof but unacknowledged by Penelope—impatience for his triumph and reunion coexist with dread over the possibility of the loss of the almost grasped fulfillment of his longing. As Argos's death reminds Odysseus and Homer's readers, the gods may deny the couple's reunion at the very last moment. In other words, neither the plot, nor the imagery, nor the structure of the epic makes sense unless Odysseus's love for Penelope is one of his strongest desires.

For some readers, therefore, the strength of the couple's mutual regard and love is obvious—explicit in Homer's description of the couple's desires and joys and woven into the very fabric of the poem. Yet, to others, their attachment, at least insofar as it entails more than mutual regard for the fulfillment of a social role, is nothing more than a ploy managed by Odysseus on Penelope and by Homer on overly sentimental readers.[41] Thus, while the thesis that Odysseus loves Penelope may be painfully obvious to some, I set forth additional evidence for the sake of the skeptical.

During the night after Odysseus and Penelope's fireside conversation (book 19), the poem chronicles the couple's separate nights, alternating between description of husband and wife as they spend the evening at least partially concerned with one another. The queen returns to her chamber and weeps for Odysseus until Athena eases her to sleep (19.600–4). Odysseus lies restless and awake, worried about how he will overcome the suitors and escape the backlash that he knows will follow his vengeance, but Athena puts him to sleep too (20.1–55). As Odysseus is released from his cares, "at that time his virtuous wife wakened in turn, and cried, sitting up in her soft bed" (20.57–58). Penelope weeps again, remembering an "evil dream": "For on this very night there was one who lay by me, like [Odysseus] as he was when he went with the army, so that my own heart was happy. I thought it was no dream, but a waking vision" (20.88–90). As Dawn rises, the poem transitions back to Odysseus, who lies listening to Penelope crying (20.92). Before he arises for the day, he drifts once more into sleep and is visited by a dream of her: "It seemed to him in his mind that now [Penelope] was standing by his head, and had recognized him already" (20.93–94).

When Odysseus's words and actions coincide with what the narrator reveals as his thoughts or solitary words, the room for creative interpretation narrows significantly. Odysseus's nighttime preoccupation with Penelope (like her preoccupation with him) implies that his attachment to her is not based primarily on political strategy or manipulation.

As in the opening lines (and in the many references to his joy in her), Odysseus's solitary thoughts of Penelope do not indicate that he is considering how best to trick her or reveal that he is plotting how to regain his household through manipulation of her emotions. Much less is he diverted with thoughts of the need to resume the relationship as an element in solidifying his place as ruler in Ithaka. In contrast to these possibilities, in the midst of the danger that surrounds him, as he lies alone in bed (with no one to persuade and hence no incentive for deception) Odysseus dreams fitfully of his desire to be reunited with his wife. For Odysseus, Penelope is an individual and an end in herself.

This conclusion is consistent with and reinforced by attention to the details of the following night, the prolonged night of Odysseus and Penelope's reunion. Odysseus finds relief in their reunion, and Homer connects Odysseus's happiness to the hero's appreciation of his wife's excellence of mind (23.231–32). It is evident that they both take pleasure not only in making love but also in conversing and even in sleeping side by side (23.295–96).[42] Moreover, he hides nothing from her, explaining immediately, "Dear wife, we have not yet come to the limit of all our trials" (23.248–49). When he calls her to their bed, he pauses at her request to explain his remaining voyage (as foretold to him in Hades by Teiresias), agreeing, "Yet I will tell you, concealing nothing" (23.265). Their entire night's conversation would be superfluous—nay, inconsistent—with the story, if Odysseus was primarily concerned with Penelope as an element in securing his claim on his kingdom or as an element in ensuring dynastic purity.

This point bears underscoring: Odysseus tells Penelope everything—or at least everything that the poet has told the reader. He repeats nearly verbatim the still unfulfilled portion of the prophecy he heard in Hades (simply changing second to first person in his repetition of Teiresias's words) and tells Penelope the version of his adventures that he had earlier told to the Phaiakians. Odysseus's only arguable addition to the prophecy is a one-line preface explaining that he must "go among many cities of men" (23.267–68). This comment is an interpretation of what is necessary to fulfill the prophecy, which requires him to journey until he finds men who know nothing of the sea. It adds nothing to what Teiresias had outlined.

The narrator's outline of the story of his voyage that Odysseus tells Penelope later in the night, reported in the third person, is also completely consistent with Odysseus's earlier report to the Phaiakians.

Homer could not be clearer about the completeness of Odysseus's tale. The narrator explains that when "Penelope and Odysseus had enjoyed their lovemaking, they took their pleasure in talking, each one telling their story" (23.300–1). After Penelope recounts her experiences to him, Odysseus in turn "told of *all* the cares he inflicted on other men, and told too of *all* that in his misery he had toiled through, *telling her all*" (23.306–8, emphasis mine).[43] This is not Odysseus's claim; this is the narrator's description of Odysseus's speech. Finally, the poet vouches a final time for Odysseus by explaining that Penelope "listened to him with delight, nor did any sleep fall upon her eyes *until he had recounted his entire story to her in full*" (23.308–9, emphasis mine).[44]

The *Odyssey* goes to great lengths—indeed it lengthens the night—to show us that Penelope is not merely a strategic component of Odysseus's reclaiming his kingdom or primarily appreciated and respected for her competence in performing the role of faithful wife. A focus on the text's many examples of Odysseus's displays and feelings of respect, pity, and desire for his wife—as well as a consideration of his desire for her as integral to the imagery, plot, and sequencing of the epic—demonstrates the strength of Odysseus's love for Penelope. The couple's use of their prolonged night, passed partially in lovemaking and rest but also partially in conversation, points to the friendship found in their marriage and successful alliance. Only to Penelope does Odysseus recount all his adventures and explain that he must depart again.[45] Neither Telemachos nor Laertes nor the faithful swineherd with whom Odysseus spends so much time hear either this fuller, more accurate version of his adventure or take any part in planning, discussing, or even learning about the journey that Odysseus must undertake once matters are settled in Ithaka. Indeed, in comparison to Penelope, Odysseus spends relatively few lines conversing with his son and father. Penelope is not only a virtuous and therefore worthy object of desire; she is Odysseus's greatest friend.

Conclusion

Examination of Penelope's actions, words, and thoughts reveals a woman of cunning intelligence, courage, and self-restraint who resembles—far more than any other character in Homer—Odysseus of the many devices. Odysseus and Penelope, moreover, share a similarity resulting from their shared excellence that brings into focus an important aspect of Homeric virtue. The virtues of Penelope and Odysseus—the underlying excellence that drives their actions—resist categorization by gender. Penelope shines outside the feminine, domestic sphere by displaying both courage and strength of intellect, and Odysseus reveals a self-restraint and calculating aspect in his use of intellect that is absent from the heedless form of courage embraced by most of his male peers. Penelope's virtues—her qualities as an individual—create the conditions necessary for Odysseus's successful homecoming, but they also bear an importance that is not linked to public utility. It is in great part the virtues of Penelope—so well matched to his own—that make Odysseus's home and his homecoming good. Homer portrays Odysseus's reunion with his wife and Odysseus's own happiness about this event as a central aspect of the hero's homecoming—an aspect that the hero does not desire primarily as a strategic component of his public goals.

The marriage of Penelope and Odysseus, the foundation of their household and the center of their private sphere, contains a component of erotic longing for one another—as illustrated by the centrality of their lovemaking and their common concern for Telemachos's welfare.[46] But alongside this element exists something dependent upon the similarity of their exceptional virtues and perhaps at least partially responsible for Socrates's praise of Odysseus's desire for a private life: they are friends. Revealing that their home houses more than mere necessity, Penelope and Odysseus spend a portion of their precious night of reunion in speech—exchanging stories and planning together for the future. The *Odyssey* thus demonstrates that the ancient Greeks did not entirely confine private life to the provision of necessary goods. On the contrary, Odysseus chooses to return home at least in part to rejoin the true friend who shares his virtues—Penelope.

7

The Meaning of Homecoming

At the close of the *Odyssey*, Odysseus exhibits his prioritization of private life and his love for that which is his own. This is most evident not in any particular act, speech, or thought but rather in the consistent prioritization of his family and his household over the longevity of the memory of his name. To some extent, therefore, the proof lies in his silence and his inaction—in all that he does not say and does not do. On the one hand, he is demonstrative in the happiness that he finds in the resumption of his relationships with his wife, son, father, and servants. On the other, he is all but silent with regard to the public and the potentially glory-earning aspects of his homecoming—such as his victory over the suitors who menace his home and the resumption of his role as king in Ithaka. The success of his homecoming and the security of all that is his own require his participation—even, to some extent, imposing order—beyond the doors of his household. But Homer consistently reveals that Odysseus's happiness and his inner struggles all relate to his desire to reclaim that which is his own and, in the case of Penelope, that which is both like himself and his own.

Discerning Odysseus's loves as he reclaims his place in Ithaka remains complex because Odysseus's homecoming relates to marriage, family, household, and his role as king of Ithaka. Odysseus's private and public life cannot be completely distinguished from one another analytically because of their actual interconnections and dual functions. While it is true, for example, that he speaks to Penelope in private and confronts the suitors' families in public, the consequences of these private and public actions cannot be neatly severed from one another. Odysseus's love for what is his own, in part, motivates him in the public sphere, and the consequences of his actions in public will be felt in all aspects of his life. Tracing the desires that cause Odysseus to act (and to refrain from acting), therefore, provides more insight than merely examining what he does.

Socrates's description of Odysseus's soul's determination to live a private life of minding his own business is subject to an obvious objection: Odysseus remains king at the end of the story. Without arguing that Homer presents Odysseus as having chosen an exclusively private life, it is helpful to commence by contextualizing the meaning of Odysseus's public position—*basileus*. As numerous scholars have concluded, an examination of Homer's use of the term *basileus* indicates that the title "king" (as it is often translated) in Ithaka is less permanent, less exclusive, and generally less glorious than the meaning commonly attributed to the position. *Basileus* might well be better translated as "nobleman" or "lord." Insofar as the position is less one of exclusive, permanent, and autocratic rule and more akin to that of a prominent citizen, Odysseus's position as *basileus* is less inherently antithetical to a preference for private life.[1]

Even with his public role better clarified, however, Odysseus's virtual war with the suitors raises reasonable questions about what he seeks from his homecoming. The same events give reason to question the excellence, particularly the self-restraint, that Socrates ascribes to Odysseus. Is his slaughter of the suitors (and the resulting near war with their families) a step in his plan to win power and glory through political dominance that could spread the renown of his name? Or are Odysseus's bloody measures merely necessary steps in defending that which is his own? This question can be answered by carefully distinguishing the actions that Odysseus chooses for himself from those directed by Athena. With this distinction in mind, it becomes apparent (1) that her dominant desire is punishment of the suitors, and (2) that Odysseus's dominant concerns are the reclaiming of his house (which requires, among other actions, ridding it of the suitors) and the personal relationships housed therein. This insight springs initially from attention to the source of Odysseus's actions, but it is confirmed—subtly and consistently—by reference to Odysseus's thoughts and emotions. Even setting aside his relationship with his wife and queen, Odysseus's strongest moments of joy and anger relate to reunions with members of his family and his household. Contrary to Ahrensdorf's recent characterization, Odysseus's ire at the suitors and his happiness in victory are relatively muted. Nor does he so much as consider his own name, his crown, or his rule in Ithaka.

Throughout, Odysseus has as much need of his courage, his intelligence, and—most particularly—his ability to moderate his initial impulses as at any other point in his many labors. As he exhibits these virtues, now responding to and interacting with his actual home, Odysseus confirms what he seeks—what he loves—in Ithaka. Thus, at the end of the epic of homecoming, Odysseus finally reveals his own potential for excellence in private life and his love of his own. In the process, Homer shows his readers the meaning of the homecoming for which they too have waited.

Nonetheless, Homer's second epic—like his first—ends on a complex note, reminding his audience of the limitations of human happiness. There is no fairytale ending: the permeability of the partition between private and public remains, and Odysseus must leave that which is his own—everything housed in his private sphere—once more. His reason for doing so, as Homer shows through his hero's happiness and his sufferings, is to secure yet another, longer reunion with his family and with Penelope. Because Odysseus ultimately prefers that which is his own, the public is necessary and the private is the source of his humanity, his excellence, and his greatest—although always limited—happiness.

"King" in Ithaka

Although it is not possible to pinpoint what being "king" denotes in Ithaka, it is possible to discern some of what it is not. As Donlan and Raaflaub both conclude, Homer's term *basileus* means something far closer to nobleman than absolute monarch.[2] The king does not necessarily hold a permanent position, as illustrated by the still-living Laertes.[3] Laertes either chose to or was required to hand the crown to his successor, suggesting that the same might be true in Odysseus's case. Nor does the position necessarily descend from father to son. Telemachos is a contender, but the exclusivity of his claim is never clarified.[4] In the first book of the *Odyssey*, Antinoos tells Telemachos that he hopes that the boy will never be "our king" but concedes, "To be sure that is your right by inheritance" (1.384–87). This might seem to resolve the matter in favor of Telemachos's right as son of the reigning *basileus*, but Telemachos's response to Antinoos muddles the issue. Without making clear whether he speaks of a rightful challenge, Telemachos responds to Antinoos that "in fact there are many other Achaian princes, young and old, in seagirt Ithaka, any of whom might hold this position, now that the great Odysseus has perished" (1.394–96).

This touches on an additional issue—the multiplicity of *basileus* in Ithaka. The term that Telemachos uses for "prince" in the English translation of the preceding conversation is the same Greek word (βασιλεύς) used for Odysseus's title, "king," and "prince." With the distinction between king and prince removed from the conversation, a distinction that only appears in translation, the question emerges as to the number of kings in Ithaka. Antinoos seems to be referring to one king who rules, and Telemachos to many kings. How it is that they determine who is, for lack of a better term, "head king" (if such a position truly exists) is never mentioned. Despite the fact that only the Greek word βασιλεύς, and words derived from it, are used, other references lead to a similar distinction in meaning. In the assembly held in book 2, Telemachos refers to Odysseus as "one who was king once over you" (2.46–47). After Antinoos is slain, Eurymachos attempts to shift all the blame to him and tells Odysseus that Antinoos had planned to kill Telemachos in order to become "king" (22.53). On the other hand, Antinoos and Eurymachos are between them referred to as if they were currently "king" three times—which could only make sense if, as Telemachos claims, there are many kings in Ithaka (18.64; 24.179).

It appears from these and other references both that there are many *basileus* and yet that Odysseus's position is in some way superior to that of the others. The difficulty for understanding Odysseus's role is that the relationship between the various *basileus* is never clarified.[5] To what extent are the other *basileus* subordinate to (rather than merely lesser than) Odysseus? The issue is further complicated by the existence of an assembly. Ithaka's assembly and, within it, the role of the people raise important questions related to the powers of the *basileus*.[6] At the beginning of the *Odyssey*, Homer reveals that the assembly has not been invoked since Odysseus left for Troy. This may indicate a rupture in political activity during Odysseus's absence, or it may merely indicate the extraordinary nature of the assembly in Ithakan politics. In either event, the existence of the assembly, like the existence of many *basileus*, indicates that Ithaka is something less than an absolute monarchy.

The nature of Odysseus's political position is far easier to problematize than to clarify. The powers he wields, how long he is to be *basileus*, and the likelihood that his son will be *basileus* after him are issues that resurface periodically in the poem. They are not directly resolved and are only rarely (and usually indirectly) referenced. Whatever the political structure of Ithaka, it is clear—for all the lack of clarity—that "king" means something different in Ithaka than in medieval European politics or modern imagination. On the one hand, Odysseus is foremost among the leaders in Ithaka and therefore an important public figure. This cannot be denied. But because of the many ambiguities in the degree of his power, the suggestion that he might not be *basileus* for the remainder of his life, the ambiguity of Telemachos's claim to inherit the throne, and the existence of other (if admittedly lesser) *basileus*, Odysseus may not—depending on how he relates to his title—be so entirely removed from the life of a private man as a nuanced consideration of his title indicates.

"King" in Ithaka is not inherently the opposite of a private life. Rather, "king" in Ithaka, at most, seems to mean being foremost among an elite group of prominent, wealthy, and powerful citizens. As such, Socrates's description of Odysseus in the Myth of Er as choosing to lead a private life of minding his own business—given a very broad understanding of "his own business"—is potentially correct. Given the inconclusiveness of Odysseus's title, examining the hero's thoughts, emotions, and actions as he navigates his homecoming is the best way to discern whether Odysseus has overcome his love of honor and prefers a private life. Does Odysseus relate to Telemachos as a future king or a son? To his house as a palace or a home? To his fellow Ithakans as men he will rule or as neighbors with whom he must have peace in order to pursue his own ends? Does he foresee a famous name and honored burial resulting from his actions and future in Ithaka? Despite the dual role of most (if not all) of the people and objects in his life, Odysseus reveals a definitive, consistent preference.

Athena's Commands and Odysseus's Desires

When Odysseus first arrives from Phaiakia, he exhibits caution by keeping his identity to himself.[7] Ignorant of where he is, he continues to express the longing for his homecoming and the concern about his wealth that preoccupied him while in Phaiakia (13.197–216). When Athena meets him and reveals that he is finally in Ithaka, Odysseus's joyful response implies that his happiness is closely related to his love of his family. Kissing the ground, he prays to the nymphs that Athena will grant him "to go on living here myself, and sustaining my dear son" (13.359–60).[8]

Before Odysseus can devise his own plans, however, Athena takes command. She assigns Odysseus his mission and explains how to achieve her objectives.[9] She does not give Odysseus the option to be gentle. She commands him to "lay your hands on these shameless suitors" and specifies her wish "for endless ground to be spattered by the blood and brains of the suitors" (13.376, 394–96). Athena disguises Odysseus as an old and helpless beggar to hide him from "all the suitors and your wife and child" (13.398–403).[10] The goddess twice emphasizes that Odysseus may not reveal himself to anyone. Nor should he expect the task to be easy: "But you must, of necessity, endure all, and tell no one out of all men and women that you have come back from your wanderings, but you must endure much grief in silence, standing and facing men in their violence" (13.307–10).

Odysseus assents to Athena's direction, telling her, "Come then, weave the design, the way I shall take my vengeance upon them; stand beside me, inspire me with strength and courage" (13.386–87). He seems grateful for Athena's guidance and expresses a willingness to obey, but he does not actually endorse or express approval of her plan. Some similarity in approach between goddess and hero can be discerned, particularly because of his initial impulse toward concealing his identity and their mutual concern for his wealth.[11] But the focus on total secrecy and the insistence on a complete and bloody vengeance come from Athena.[12]

In this initial conversation with Athena, Odysseus reveals little about his own inclinations in Ithaka. Before she appears, it is evident that he will proceed cautiously, demonstrating that he has no interest in meeting a death similar to that of Agamemnon. He also has a firm eye to the protection of the wealth with which he returns. Generally, Odysseus's concern for Telemachos appears greater than Athena's, and indeed Telemachos is the cause of his objection to Athena's plan. When he learns that Telemachos is in Sparta, Odysseus unhappily asks Athena whether his son had been sent on a voyage "so that he too wandering over the barren sea should suffer pains, while others ate up his substance" (13.417–18).

The accuracy and the relevance of this initial distinction between Athena's commands and Odysseus's impulses are confirmed as the story unfolds. As he prepares to execute Athena's plans for vengeance, Odysseus's greatest moments of joy occur in his reunion with members of his household, and his greatest misgivings, which he expresses both to himself and to the goddess, relate to the prudence of Athena's plan. This pattern first emerges in Odysseus's feelings toward his loyal swineherd and in his reunion with his son, and it continues as he returns to and regains control over his household. Although these relationships (like all aspects of Odysseus's life in Ithaka) have public implications, it is in the goodwill of his servant and in his personal reunion with his son that he finds happiness and begins to taste the joys of the homecoming for which he has suffered.[13] In comparison, the strategic value of their support to the goals dictated by Athena seems an afterthought.

Odysseus initially goes, as Athena had commanded, to his swineherd's dwelling to "ask him all questions" (13.404–15).[14] While there, Odysseus relies on Eumaios for clothing, food, shelter, and the tactical information to which Athena had referred. In addition, however, to the use that he makes of Eumaios, Odysseus repeatedly exhibits a warm satisfaction arising from his swineherd's piety and loyalty.[15] Odysseus is made "happy" by Eumaios's kindly reception. The servant "exalts the heart" of his disguised "master" when he offers him the choice cut (14.438). Odysseus twice tests Eumaios's hospitality, once by begging for an extra blanket and then by prompting Eumaios to invite him to stay (14.457–61; 15.304–6). Odysseus surely desires the welcome, the meal, the blanket, and the invitation, but his thoughts are directed to what this generosity implies about his servant and not to the gratification of his physical needs. Thus, for example, when Odysseus requests an extra blanket, the narrator describes him as "trying it out on the swineherd, to see if he might take off his mantle and give it to him, or tell one of his men to do it, since he [Eumaios] cared for him so greatly" (14.459–61).[16]

In a similar fashion Odysseus seems more focused on building a relationship with Telemachos than with the advantage of an ally in the coming battle. When Odysseus reveals himself to "beloved" Telemachos at Athena's command, he is overcome with emotion and kisses his son (16.167–91). Although Odysseus was "until now, . . . always unyielding," the two are overcome with emotion and "weep like birds that have lost their young" (16.216–19). The poignancy of this scene, as well as its importance within the narrative created by the combination of the *Iliad* and the *Odyssey*, derives in part from an earlier embrace between father and son, the embrace between Hektor and his baby son. Twenty years after leaving his own infant son at home, Odysseus experiences that which Hektor never will: the growth of his son into a man who may surpass himself and who lightens the heart of his mother.

Tellingly, it is Telemachos who turns the conversation from expressions of joy to question his father about strategy (16.220–24). In the books that follow, father and son work together, and Odysseus gives thought before the final battle to how Telemachos should conduct himself to avoid shame (24.506–9). But Odysseus does not ponder or discuss, not even with Penelope or Athena, his son's prospects for the crown or for glory. Odysseus's strongest desires for his son, as he voices them to Athena in book 13, are that the gods keep him secure and preserve him from wandering.[17] Far from being focused on his utility or his son's glory, Odysseus is overwhelmed with joy to embrace him and wishes him a safe and quiet—albeit shame-avoiding—future.

Similar to the emotional attachment he feels for his son and servant, Odysseus exhibits love for some of the nonhuman aspects of his home. This is most evident in the pleasure that he feels at the sight of his actual, physical house and the dog that he left behind as a pup. When he first comes within view of the house, he comments to Eumaios on the quality of its workmanship and points out that "one part is joined on to another, and the courtyard is worked on with wall and copings, and the doors have been well made, with double panels. Nobody could belittle this house" (17.264–68).[18] Moments later, Argos, a decrepit dog who can bring him no advantage, causes Odysseus to pause with pity and shed a carefully concealed tear (17.305). While some might argue that Odysseus's comment about the quality of his home is mock wonder intended to further his disguise as a beggar, Odysseus's concealed response to seeing Argos can have no strategic advantage. The genuine nature of his feeling for Argos is corroborated by the effort that he makes to conceal his tear.

Of course, Odysseus's affectionate response to his servant, son, home, and dog do not preclude consideration of how to achieve the deaths of the suitors.[19] Indeed, once Odysseus arrives in his home, his thoughts return to this problem frequently. After the feast has disbanded on the evening of his arrival, "Odysseus still remained in the hall, pondering how, with the help of Athene, he would murder the suitors" (19.1–2, 51–52).[20] Later that night, as he tosses and turns in his bedding, Odysseus devises "evils in his heart for the suitors" as he considers "how, though he was alone against many, he could lay hands on the shameless suitors" (20.5–30). Such thoughts demonstrate that Odysseus is applying his already established excellence in strategy to fulfilling the goddess's command, but other passages suggest that he has reservations about the feasibility, wisdom, and bloodiness of her plan.

To be clear, Odysseus does endorse Athena's premise that the suitors must be punished (20.169), but this is distinguishable from her desire for bloodshed, great violence, and the death of *all* the suitors. He questions Athena about how it will be possible for him to fulfill her command, cautioning the goddess that the suitors' deaths will create an even more difficult problem for him in Ithaka: "And here is a still bigger problem that my heart is pondering. Even if, by grace of Zeus and yourself, I kill them, how shall I make my escape? It is what I would have you think on" (20.41–43). After the goddess insists and he assents, Odysseus makes another small effort to undermine the thoroughness of Athena's plan by attempting to persuade Amphinomos, the best of the suitors, to leave his house before the vengeance begins (18.119–55). Odysseus obeys Athena, but in the process he takes several small steps to moderate the goddess's plan.

Athena's Wrath and Odysseus's Actions

Notwithstanding his desire to punish the suitors and his intent to fulfill Athena's command, Odysseus's emotional turmoil continues to point consistently toward the love that he feels for that which is his own. He does not daydream about the joy of vaunting over the defeated, nor does he think about the burial, renown, or glory associated with defeating his enemies. He does not think about or mention his crown, rule, or power. Odysseus's moments of happiness and his moments of distress during this period before he publicly announces his return indicate that his family and household rouse his greatest passions. The happiness that he experiences with Eumaios and with Telemachos is unrivaled until Penelope embraces him in private. By the same token, the difficulty with which he hides his pity for his dying dog and for Penelope's tears point consistently to the object of his love.

Odysseus chafes at maintaining his disguise, struggling to moderate his desire to proclaim his return imprudently. Together, Athena and Homer provide ample opportunity for Odysseus to exhibit his newfound ability to restrain himself from immoderately declaring his identity. Soon after Odysseus's arrival in his home, Athena instigates the insolence of

Eurymachos with the intent of ensuring that "still more grief would invade the heart of Odysseus" (18.347–48). Eurymachos ends the ensuing string of insults by hurling a footstool at the agile hero's head (18.346–405). In response, Odysseus remains silent and, whatever his emotional reaction, the poet does not find it worthy of report. Later, shortly before the contest of the bow begins, Athena "would not altogether permit the arrogant suitors to keep from heart-hurting outrage, so to make greater the anguish in the heart of Odysseus" (20.284–86). The goddess's interference results in an insult and an ox hoof hurled at Odysseus. This time, after Odysseus avoids the missile, he "smiled in his anger a very sardonic smile" (20.299–302). Even when Antinoos successfully hits Odysseus, the poet reports that the hurled footstool did not "shake him, but he shook his head in silence, deeply devising evils" (17.462–65). Despite his spirited impulses (established by Homer in earlier episodes) and Athena's attempts to rile him, Odysseus now remains coolly self-possessed when taunted by the suitors.

But when members of his household insult and threaten him, Odysseus struggles to control his inner turmoil and barely manages to maintain his self-restraint. Odysseus, outwardly patient but inwardly struggling, indulges in bloody mental images of gratifying violent impulses. When he first encounters Melanthios, his goatherd commences with a string of taunts and insults, concluding with a blow to Odysseus (17.204–34).[21] Avoiding the blow, Odysseus ponders whether to retain his disguise, considering "whether to go for him with his cudgel, and take the life from him, or pick him up like a jug and break his head on the ground. Yet still he stood it, and kept it all inside him" (17.234–38).[22] Later, Odysseus is "shamefully scolded" by Melantho (18.320–36). Odysseus responds with a dark look and violent threats, but he does not reveal himself (18.337–39). The two have a second exchange in which Melantho threatens to throw a torch at him, and Odysseus again contents himself with dark looks and threats (19.65–88).

In the most pronounced example, Homer provides a detailed description of the impulses that vie within Odysseus as he grapples with the desire for immediate action. Inspired by a sense of protectiveness, he wishes to rid his household of the women who sided with the suitors, betrayed his wife, and impiously scorned the beggar in their house. Before falling asleep after his conversation with Penelope in book 19, Odysseus hears the serving women laughing as they leave the house to meet the suitors. Odysseus is stirred to the breaking point as he lies pondering, "in the division of mind and spirit, whether to spring on them and kill each one, or rather to let them lie this one more time with the insolent suitors" (20.9–13). With Odysseus's heart "growling," Homer provides a provocative, nurturing image of the murderous Odysseus: "And as a bitch, facing an unknown man, stands over her callow puppies, and growls and rages to fight, so Odysseus' heart was growling inside him" (20.14–16). Odysseus's rage, perhaps partially fueled by an inference that the women meeting the suitors were the same ones who had betrayed Penelope's weaving, comes from a desire to protect. Like a mother dog with her puppies, he recognizes these women, among whom Melantho seems foremost, as a threat to his family.

Giving no outward indication of his inner turmoil, Odysseus moderates his impulse for immediate violence against the women.

> He struck himself on the chest and spoke to his heart and
>   scolded it:
> "Bear up, my heart. You have had worse to endure before this
> on that day when the irresistible Cyclops ate up
> my strong companions, but you endured it until intelligence
> got you out of the cave, though you expected to perish."
> So he spoke, addressing his own dear heart within him;
> and the heart in great obedience endured it and stood it
> without complaint, but the man himself was twisting and
>   turning. (20.17–24)

Here and in the numerous short exchanges between Odysseus and his servants and between Odysseus and the suitors, Homer reveals not only the strength of Odysseus's desire to reclaim his home but also his newfound ability to moderate his impulses toward immediate action. Through Odysseus's reference to his self-restraint when trapped by Polyphemos, these lines remind the audience of the growth of Odysseus's self-possession. Through the implicit reminder of Odysseus's imprudent self-identification to Polyphemos, these lines remind the reader of the extent to which Odysseus's self-possession has strengthened in the intervening ten years.

When Odysseus finally attacks the suitors, he does so in a controlled manner and in accord with a previously agreed-upon plan. Neither his spirit nor his anger is roused. Instead, he is methodical. Homer's description of the ease and matter-of-fact motions with which he strings the bow as he is about to kill the suitors is representative of the scene that follows.

> Once he had taken up the great bow and looked it all over,
> as when a man, who well understands the lyre and singing,
> easily, holding it on either side, pulls the strongly twisted
> cord of sheep's gut, so as to slip it over a new peg,
> so, without any strain, Odysseus strung the great bow.
> Then plucking it in his right hand he tested the bowstring,
> and it gave him back an excellent sound like the voice of
>   a swallow. (21.405–11)

As the scene proceeds, as he proclaims his return and battles with the suitors, Odysseus's emotions are barely mentioned. After Odysseus strings his bow, Zeus sends thunder, and "hearing this, long-suffering great Odysseus was happy" at the divine signal (21.414). During the battle, when he sees Athena, "Odysseus was happy when he saw her, and hailed her, saying: 'Mentor, help me from hurt, and remember me'" (22.207–8).[23] Once, when the suitors manage to find armor, Odysseus is filled with fear. These are the only references to his thoughts and feelings from the moment that he strings his bow until after the completion of the cleansing of his home.

Only once does Odysseus even mention glory: before killing the first suitor, he prays, "Now I shall shoot at another mark, one that no man yet has struck, if I can hit it and Apollo grants me the glory" (22.5–7). Never again in the course of the fight or its aftermath does he mention his own honor or that of his house, his reputation, fame, power, or the title of king. In other words, he never vaunts like a hero on the plains of Troy. Even when he explains the reason for his actions and publicly proclaims his identity for the first time in Ithaka—as he rejects the suitors' offer of wealth in exchange for their lives—he references the wrongs that the suitors have committed against the gods and himself without describing any emotional or spirited response to the wrongs.

> You dogs, you never thought that I would any more come back
> from the land of Troy, and because of that you despoiled my household,

and forcibly took my serving women to sleep beside you,
and sought to win my wife while I was still alive, fearing
neither the immortal gods who hold the wide heaven,
nor any resentment sprung from men to be yours in the
  future.
Now upon all of you the terms of destruction are fastened.[24]
  (22.35–41)

If Odysseus looked forward to winning glory, renown, or burial honors, like Ajax before his duel with Menelaus, this speech would be the appropriate place to say so. If he were consumed with rage, like Achilles hunting down Hektor, this speech should express his wrath and desire for vengeance. But Odysseus is not thinking in these terms.[25] Instead, Odysseus frames the suitors' wrongdoing in terms of impiety and encroachment.[26] He coolly tells them that their "terms of destruction are fastened" (22.41). True to his word, he completes Athena's assignment to the letter, killing each suitor and only sparing retainers of the suitors for whom Telemachos is willing to vouch.[27]

This passionless approach explains why Athena is unimpressed by Odysseus's manner of executing her commands. She taunts him that he lacks the vigor that he had at Troy, asking him, "How is it now, when you have come back to your own possessions and house, you complain, instead of standing up to the suitors?" (22.224–35).[28] Her taunt seems odd, given the fact that for a time the "floor was smoking with blood, and the horrible cries rose up as [the suitors'] heads were broken" (22.308–9). And yet, for all the bloodshed, the angry—as Homer describes her—goddess has a point. Odysseus is not consumed with hate, nor does he taunt those he has killed or is about to kill with speeches comparing their relative fame, glory, burials, or prominence.[29] In other words, he gives no speeches reminiscent of the vaunting or vengeance-bent heroes of the *Iliad*.

Odysseus's focus on the private, domestic aspects of his actions is again marked after the battle. The last suitor apparently slain, Odysseus first methodically searches the gore to be certain that Athena's command has been completed to the last man, but he gives no victory speech. Focused on the purification of his house, he proceeds directly to command the suitors' spared bard and his herald outside "so that I can do in the house the work that I have to" (22.371–77). His childhood nurse,

Eurykleia, finds "Odysseus among the slaughtered dead men, spattered over with gore and battle filth, like a lion . . . covered with blood, all his chest and his flanks on either side bloody, a terrible thing to look in the face" (22.401–5). She starts to vaunt, but Odysseus checks her gleeful boasting and seems to minimize his own role in the slaughter.

> [B]ut Odysseus checked her and held her, for all her eagerness,
> and spoke to her and addressed her in winged words, saying:
> "Keep your joy in your heart, old dame; stop, do not raise up
> the cry. It is not piety to glory so over slain men.
> These were destroyed by the doom of the gods and their
>   own hard actions,
> for these men paid no attention at all to any man on earth
> who came their way, no matter if he were base or noble.
> So by their own recklessness they have found a shameful
> death." (22.409–17)

In contrast to this calm at the end of the battle, when purification of his house is complete and the loyal serving women are invited in, Odysseus is finally overcome with emotion. The restoration of order in his domestic sphere triggers his relief and joy. As the serving women embrace and kiss him, he weeps for the first time since his first embrace of Telemachos. Having disavowed glory in the victory (and even quieted this sense in others), union with the household servants causes "sweet longing for lamentation and tears" to take "hold of him" (22.500–1).

As when his identity was still secret, Odysseus's disloyal servants prove better able to weaken his moderation than the suitors. The betrayal of his household servants provokes more brutality than did the actions of the suitors.[30] When the goatherd Melanthios retrieves armor for the suitors, Odysseus "thought it was monstrous treason" (22.144–52). Later, after Melanthios is captured (at the suggestion of one of the loyal servants), Odysseus commands torture for the only time (22.170–77).[31] Melanthios is hanged so that, in Odysseus's words, "while he still stays alive, he will suffer harsh torment" (22.177). Similarly, Odysseus commands Eurykleia to bring the serving women "who have been shameful in their devisings" to him (22.431–32).[32] He directs Telemachos to have the women clean the house of the battle gore and then to inflict a quick death so that they "forget Aphrodite, the goddess they had with them when they lay secretly with the suitors" (22.433–45).[33] While his attention is directed elsewhere, Telemachos and Odysseus's otherwise faithful servants (Eumaios and Philoitios) disobey, intentionally inflicting slow deaths on the women.

These are the most horrific moments of Odysseus's return. Even if the execution of the disloyal servants might be justified, the manner cannot be. Odysseus's decision to torture Melanthios—his only physically cruel act in the *Odyssey*—reveals the weakest spot in his otherwise reigning moderation. Remaining passionless, Odysseus had killed *all* the suitors at least in part because Athena commanded it. By contrast, it is Odysseus who chooses to kill and in one case torture his disloyal servants.[34] It is Odysseus who is responsible for these actions, and indeed we have no idea whether Athena and Zeus think that they are necessary, justified, or reprehensible.[35] Although the extent of Odysseus's wrath never approaches that of Achilles, the feelings and actions that he directs at disloyal servants come closest to paralleling Achilles's wrath at Hektor and the Trojan army.

As opposed to Athena, whose designs for bloody vengeance are centered on the suitors, Odysseus's most intentional infliction of suffering—without any prompting from Athena—is directed at his disloyal servant. Likewise, his most poorly justified and carelessly executed death sentences—again, without Athena's direction—are directed against the maids. Insofar as Odysseus explains his violence against the suitors, he speaks of outrages against the gods and the protection of his wealth, household, and Penelope. He never speaks, acts, or thinks directly with regard to political power or glory. Instead, his focus is directed to setting his house to rights, and his joy results from reunion with his wife, family, and household members.

Odysseus Minding His Own Business

After the battle, with Athena's commands fulfilled, Odysseus remains concerned about his family's (and his own) precarious situation, but he does not indicate any relish for the need to further assert himself in Ithaka. For the first time since his encounter with Athena on his first morning in Ithaka, Odysseus selects and prioritizes his own actions free of divine direction. First he purifies his house from the bloodshed, and next he turns to reunion with Penelope. Reunion with his father follows.[36] He turns his attention to defending against the anticipated response to the suitors' deaths then and only after each of his important relationships has been reestablished. If loves can be discerned from the way in which individuals choose to spend their time when necessity is not urgent, then—in the wake of the death of the suitors—Odysseus indicates that he loves his family more than his public position in Ithaka.

He spends the evening with Penelope, forgoing the potential tactical advantages that could have been gained overnight through preparing for the next day's conflict. First, however, as he bids Telemachos goodnight, he instructs his son to give thought to how best to handle the complications that will arise from fulfilling Athena's command.

> For when one has killed only one man in a community,
> and then there are not many avengers to follow, even
> so, he flees into exile, leaving kinsmen and country.
> But we have killed what held the city together, the finest
> young men in Ithaka. (23.118–22)

Were he set on glory or focused on regaining control of Ithaka in the coming conflict, Odysseus could have couched his instructions in such terms. Indeed, it would seem natural to speak to the young prince in terms of how best to secure their kingdom or the glory to be won. But Odysseus does not do this. Instead, as the returning warrior prepares to use precious hours reuniting with his wife, his last strategic thoughts concern the pressing necessity of survival and not the eventual implications to the longevity of his name.

In the morning Odysseus tells Penelope his plans. Speaking in more detail with her than he has or will to anyone else, he explains his plan to restore their wealth by raiding the neighboring islands.[37] First, however, he tells Penelope that he will visit his father and handle the response to the death of the suitors (23.354–60). Once again, Odysseus couches their situation in terms of danger and not in terms of a desire for power or prominence.

> Presently, when the sun rises, there will be a rumor
> about the men who courted you, whom I killed in our
>   palace.
> Then go to the upper chamber with your attendant
>   women,
> and sit still, looking at no one, and do not ask any questions. (23.362–65)

Odysseus's focus—at least insofar as he indicates to Penelope—is upon their wealth, his family relationships, and his family's security.

When he arrives at the farm where Laertes resides, Odysseus's pity for his father once again highlights the strength of his love for his family. Standing alone, watching his wretched father from a short distance, Odysseus weeps. He determines to "question him first about everything, and make trial of him" (24.238). Faced with his father's pain, Odysseus cannot maintain his test for long. Laertes's nearly mad misery quickly provokes pity: "The spirit rose up in Odysseus, and now in his nostrils there was a shock of bitter force as he looked on his father. He sprang to him and embraced and kissed" (24.318–26). This is the only time in Ithaka when an impulse—rather than a plan or an order from Athena—causes Odysseus to reveal his identity. Odysseus's reunion with his father reminds the audience of the destruction of private relationships that occurred in the *Iliad*. Odysseus comes home to support and comfort his aging father, but Peleus will find no such solace in his son Achilles.

Reunion with wife and father complete, Odysseus refocuses his attention on survival and thus on public matters. Odysseus, Laertes, Telemachos, and some loyal servants gather for a meal before the battle. Meanwhile, the story shifts to the gods.[38] At Athena's query, Zeus decrees peace, reconciliation, and Odysseus's kingship (24.482–86).[39] Thus, when Odysseus and his band of family and supporters (now twelve strong) prepare to face the approaching army of bereaved men, Athena (disguised as Mentor) joins them (24.487–503). Odysseus is understandably happy to see the goddess join them (24.504). In an indication that he has not lost all thought for honor, Odysseus warns Telemachos about the ramifications of poor performance: "You must be certain not to shame the blood of your fathers, for we in time past all across the world have surpassed in manhood and valor" (24.506–9). He does not prod Telemachos to increase the glory of his name or indicate desire for further accumulation of acclaim. Given Odysseus's past, this seems a gentle reminder of what is at stake in the fight that he thinks is to come.

When Athena incites the battle, Odysseus and Telemachos stand at the forefront. Ahrensdorf interprets Odysseus's behavior in this scene as bloodthirsty and exceeding Achilles's wrath after the death of Patroklos.[40] But although Odysseus exhibits willingness to lead the defense of his small group, he exhibits no eagerness or joy at the prospect of the battle. Much less does Homer indicate that he harbors any ill will against those who attack. As Zeus had ordained, Athena calls a halt, and all are afraid except Odysseus. Athena then speaks directly to Odysseus, warning him to stop lest he incur Zeus's wrath. With the gods' will clarified, Odysseus obeys "with happy heart" (24.545). The closing lines of the *Odyssey* recount that "pledges for the days to come, sworn to by both sides, were settled" by Athena in the guise of Mentor (24.545–48). Odysseus is happy when the opportunity to win glory ends and peace—and the opportunity to spend time with his newly reunited family—begins.

Although the peace settlement brings the *Odyssey* to a close, Odysseus will leave Ithaka again. In addition to plans to leave in order to restore wealth by raiding, Odysseus must fulfill Teiresias's prophecy by journeying inland until he meets someone who mistakes an oar for a winnowing fan. Far from indicating that he wishes to abandon his home, Odysseus expresses dismay at the prospect of renewed labors far from Ithaka (23.249). He is grieved about leaving, and both Odysseus and Penelope take comfort in the prophecy's promise that this voyage will secure a better, longer homecoming.[41] In his only conversation about the necessity of a final voyage, he tells Penelope that he is not "happy" at the thought of these further travels: "Dear wife, we have not yet come to the limit of all our trials. There is unmeasured labor left for the future, both difficult and great, and all of it I must accomplish" (23.248–50, 266–67). According to Teiresias, the successful completion of this journey will win Odysseus a permanent homecoming, a peaceful old age in Ithaka, and a death surrounded by prosperity.

> Death will come to me from the sea, in
> some altogether unwarlike way, and it will end me
> in the ebbing time of a sleek old age. My people
> about me will prosper. (23.264–84)[42]

Odysseus has ample reason to take this journey for the sake of that which is his own—for the sake of that which he has been so focused on in the second half of the *Odyssey*.

Conclusion

At the end of the *Odyssey*, Odysseus has temporarily left the sphere of public accomplishment and honor to rejoin a private life that Homer depicts as politically important *and* as a venue for excellence and friendship. Homer's epic does not portray private life as a realm of necessity and mere animal existence. Contrary to Arendt's representations of Homer and ancient Greek thought, Homer's *Odyssey* tells the story of a man who struggles to reclaim his family and then finds his greatest moments of happiness in reunion with his wife, a wife who is at least as notable for her mind as for any other quality. Penelope proves the key, not only to understanding the relationship of the private with the public, but also to understanding the potential human value of the private sphere in ancient epic. But Odysseus clearly has many additional reasons to prefer his private life in Ithaka: son, father, servants, dog, wealth, and home.

At the close of the *Odyssey*, Odysseus retains a public role and intends to engage in raiding. While the importance of Odysseus's role as "king" in Ithaka is easy to overstate, it nevertheless appears that he will continue to engage in public life. To the extent that this is true, however, it underscores (rather than undermines) the case for Odysseus's preference for private life. His determination to mind his own business leads him back into the public sphere—as a leader in Ithaka, to raid his neighbors, and to travel to lands unknown—for the sake of maintaining the security and wealth of his private sphere and ultimately to spend a peaceful old age surrounded by those he loves.

Few would argue that Odysseus is less than thorough in his manner of reclaiming his position in Ithaka. Yet evidence is lacking that his actions are driven by desire for the crown (for himself or Telemachos) or for glory or even by anger. By contrast, Odysseus's expressions of concern and joy in his family and household relationships are consistently powerful. Arising from the same source, his punishment of the disloyal element in his household leads to his greatest act of cruelty. Although his domestic relationships have political implications because of his public position, Odysseus's prioritization of these relationships and the narrator's account of his emotions indicate that his love of family and household is greater than his concern for political power and any related honors that he might win. Moreover, reference back to the events of the *Iliad* (in which he at least pondered his own desire for glory) and earlier portions of the *Odyssey* (in which he could not control his imprudent impulse to spread the glory of his own name) provide evidence that he now loves his own more deeply than in the past.

In Ithaka Odysseus can be seen to have overcome his love of honor in favor of the many strong attachments that dominate his private life. In other words, he seems to have overcome whatever similarity to Ajax and Agamemnon that he displayed in battle and in his struggle with the Cyclops. Within the Myth of Er, Socrates underscores the excellence—even the specifically human excellence—of Odysseus's choice of reincarnation. Socrates thus uses Odysseus as an example of the preference for a private life of minding one's own business, specifically explaining that this is made possible by overcoming the love of honor and by the ability to make choices deliberately rather than by following initial impulses. For Arendt, if Odysseus is thus understood, he cannot be fully human or excellent. Yet, for Socrates, Odysseus makes the best choice and—baring Atlanta and the tyrant—the only choice to be a *human* man. It seems that, at least in contrast to Agamemnon and Ajax, Socrates sees something praiseworthy and specifically human about Odysseus's choice of private life and rejection of public life in pursuit of honor. Homer's portrait of Odysseus as courageous, intelligent, and self-restrained explains this praise.

And yet, as embodied in Odysseus, the justice of the private man who minds his own business does not prove to resemble what one might expect based on the Myth of Er, or at least this characterization proves less unequivocally positive than one might think. Odysseus's justice, while clearly superior to the animal reference points provided by Arendt and Socrates, resembles the justice of a thief who helps his friends and hurts his enemies. A desire for wealth that stems from his love of his own, rather than desire for a famous name, drives him to injustice. Indeed, like a thief who hurts his enemies and helps his friends, Odysseus demonstrates both the positive and negative aspects of love for the private sphere. He surpasses honor-loving heroes in moderation, in recognition of the excellence possible within a household, and in ability to resolve conflicts with speech. But he plans to continue to be a thief, and he exhibits cruelty and carelessness in his actions against his disloyal servants. Yet, comparing Odysseus's injustices to the effects of the love of honor felt in the Trojan War, Odysseus's injustice appears relatively paltry.

In Odysseus's final choices, Homer's narrative of the origins and problems of politics unfolds. Politics arise, not only from the desire for an immortal name (as in the *Iliad*), but also through the love of one's own as illustrated by both Achilles and Odysseus. Odysseus's love for that which is his own and the resulting prioritization of private life motivate him to reenter the public sphere and thus illustrate a second potential origin of politics. Homer does not present the politics that arise out of love of private life as completely satisfactory. To the contrary, the *Odyssey* has an undercurrent that consistently demonstrates the injustices that may arise because of the love of one's own. Nonetheless, Homer does show over the course of his epics that the love of private life is, in many respects, superior to the love of honor. Consistent with Aristotle's description within the *Politics*, the household proves the starting point from which politics—and hence opportunities for greater virtue and justice—emerge.

Conclusion

Homer's Hero

The *Iliad* and the *Odyssey* each cast the dominant love of the other into relief, so that in a sense neither story can be fully told without the other. In the *Iliad* the dominant love is for honor: men strive for excellence, risking their lives for the chance of a brilliance that will shine through the ages to come. With Homer's help, Ajax, Agamemnon, Diomedes, Hector, and many of their peers win the immortal honor for which they compete, suffer, and in some cases die. Their feats are breathtaking, and the services that they perform prove necessary to the continued survival of their armies. The advantages of love of honor become particularly evident in times when the dangers, the corresponding sacrifices, and the resulting honors are all great.

    This passion suffices to motivate men to give their lives to a common cause in exchange for the memory of their names, but Homer mixes his praise of the love of honor with a harsh and multifaceted critique. Throughout the *Iliad* honor pits those working toward a common goal against one another, eroding moderation, nurturing wrath, and ultimately undermining political stability. The love that drives warriors to exchange their lives for immortal names also drives them beyond productive rivalry. The love of honor, according to the war epic that it animates, is a powerful but volatile political tool.

    A less obvious price of the love of honor lurks behind the leadership decisions that perpetuate the Trojan War. Agamemnon considers abandoning the Trojan War, and twice he determines to persevere because he is reminded of the glory that he will gain if he can defeat the Trojans. As Homer shows on numerous occasions, moreover, Agamemnon commands the obedience of those who follow him through his promises to gratify their desire for honor. Were it not for Agamemnon's desire for honor and the corresponding passion of the lords he commands, the war could not continue. However tenuous or sound the initial Achaian claim to justice in their campaign may have been, within the *Iliad* Agamemnon and his army fight, suffer, and inflict suffering primarily motivated by their desire for honor.

Particularly when read in light of the *Odyssey*, the *Iliad* indicates an additional casualty of the love of honor. Once their love of honor has propelled them to victory, the Achaians enslave defenseless women and kill children to demonstrate the dishonor of the defeated and enhance the honor of the victors. Homer depicts this in the greatest detail with Briseis and Chryseis, whom the Achaians allocate as prizes to mark the honor of the men who possess them. The same fate hangs over Andromache, and a related death waits for baby Astyanax. Countless other women are mentioned only as items in the catalogs of prizes—alongside cuts of meat, cups of wine, pieces of gold, and oxen—to denote the honor of the warriors to whom they are given. These women appropriately remain nameless in the epic in which the passion that dominates leads to their seeming disappearance from the ranks of humanity.

Based on the *Iliad* alone, one might argue that Homer is indifferent to the fate of Briseis, Chryseis, Andromache, and the nameless women and their invisible doomed children. It might be argued that Homer depicts and refers to their suffering solely to illustrate how their possession affects their possessors. But—even if the *Iliad*'s treatment of Hector and Andromache's marriage did not suffice to make the point— the *Odyssey*'s confirmation of the humanity of women and excellence in private life precludes this conclusion. If Odysseus's waiting wife and child qualify as human, then so too do the wives and children of his enemies—as Odysseus himself seems to feel in the moments before his departure from Phaiakia for home.

In sum, Homer's war epic reveals at least three objections to the love of honor. The love of honor pits companions against one another in their struggle for preeminence, undermining their moderation and nurturing their tendency to justice-disregarding wrath. Because war offers more opportunities to win glory than peace, the love of honor predisposes those dominated by it to perpetuate war without regard to justice, suffering, or prudence. Finally, those who emerge victorious in the contest for honor kill the children of their enemies and seize the surviving women, transforming powerless humanity into symbols to communicate the degree of the victors' public honor.

When the labor-worn hero returns home in the *Odyssey*, the advantages of the love of one's own are finally confirmed. The happiness that Odysseus finds in reunion with that which is his own arises from an excellence in his household that has relation to neither its comparative preeminence nor the poet's immortalization of their excellence. Homer's description of the private and political consequences of the love of one's own reveals much that is praiseworthy. Odysseus has learned to moderate his spirited impulses, and he no longer vaunts over the fallen. Homer's hero displays self-restraint, employs crafty intelligence, and commands great skill with speech. Depending on a mutual relationship with a household that Homer also portrays as excellent in many regards, Odysseus's excellence is not his alone. His virtue is intertwined with the excellence of the members of his household, most notably Penelope, Eumaios, and the potential of young Telemachos.

In the poem of homecoming, love of one's own facilitates recognition of the excellence and individuality of both men and women. Both Penelope and Odysseus emerge as mutually respecting models of intelligence, courage, and moderation. Sharing a genuine friendship based on their similarity and shared goals, they find happiness in speech, plan together for their future, and successfully defend their domestic sphere through joint action. In the private realm, with those whom he loves both because they are his own and because they are excellent, Odysseus has a value without reference to the prominence of his household, the wealth of Ithaka, or his performance in the war. Disguised and changed though he may be, Odysseus and only Odysseus can take his place within his bed, marriage, family, and household. Homer presents the marriage of virtuous and like-minded individuals as powerful: it nurtures virtue, proves politically salutary, and transforms the domestic sphere into an opportunity for friendship.

Homer does not hide notable blemishes in the hero of homecoming. In war the consequences of Odysseus's lesser love of honor were ambiguous: he excelled in counsel, strategy, and moderation, but he also failed to distinguish himself in either battlefield excellence or a willingness to risk his life for victory. Although Odysseus outpaces his Homeric peers in counsel in the *Iliad*, in the *Odyssey* he fails as a leader to bring his army safely home to Ithaka. Odysseus's love of wealth and the related raiding that he plans, as well as the cruelty and carelessness with which he punishes the disloyal elements of his household, highlight two avenues to injustice lurking within Homer's generally positive portrayal. Homer's praise of Odysseus's homecoming and the excellence of the life that this hero wishes to resume are qualified and should not be mistaken for a complete resolution of the problem of justice. He presents the love of one's own as a superior (if flawed) option—the benefits of which are most evident when they are compared with the heavy costs of love of honor in wartime.

The qualifications in Homer's praise of Odysseus, and more generally for love of one's own, are underscored by consideration of the final wrath and loss of self-restraint of Achilles. Like Odysseus, Achilles's love for the particular—his friend Patroklos—proves stronger than his love for public honor. But when shared life with his particular friend is irrevocably denied him, Achilles's wrath exceeds even that of the honor-loving warriors. He challenges the very gods, and the height of his hatred for his enemies is unmatched by that of any other Homeric character. Achilles's wrath underscores a weakness within the excellence and happiness found at the end of the *Odyssey*: without the ability to preserve that which is his own, Odysseus's self-restraint—like Achilles's—would be vulnerable or perhaps vanish altogether. This vulnerability of the excellence arising from the love of one's own points to the need of private life for peace and for protection—for politics based on speech.

Homer provides an account of the origins of politics in which two opposing human desires lead toward political action for different individuals. Most of the heroes of the *Iliad* prefer public action to private life because of the opportunity to win an immortal name that it offers them. But Odysseus prefers his own home and those who inhabit it, leaving the center of his life only for the sake of protecting or improving that which is his own. When Odysseus emerges from his household at the end of the *Odyssey* to respond to threats to the safety of his family, he engages in political action that results from his love of his own. For Odysseus, politics is thus subordinate to private life, resulting from the hero's desire to care for that which is his own. Ultimately, Homer gives his audience reason to believe that neither of the two sources of politics leads to justice or a completely satisfactory political outcome. The worldviews at the heart of these sources of political action may at times be compatible—as when Odysseus proves a valuable resource to his honor-loving companions in the *Iliad*—but their measures of human excellence and a life well spent remain in tension with one another.

Offering no blueprint, Homer has instead detailed the complex problem of divergent human desires and pointed his readers to the passion—love of one's own—that he finds most likely to lead to a just politics.

The Excellence of the Homeric Hero

Odysseus is devoted to that which is his own, entering the public sphere because it is necessary for the sake of that which he loves most. In other words, he represents the inverse of what Arendt presents as the exclusive vision of human life in ancient Greece and a plausible fit for Socrates's description of his soul's selection for his next life. As Arendt characterizes the world of Odysseus, Plato, Socrates, and Aristotle, there could be no action, no speech, and no humanity—let alone excellence—in private.[1] But for Odysseus the most important and characteristic act is reclaiming his home from within. His desire to accomplish this feat, moreover, is the impetus for his growth into a more deliberate and self-restrained individual who can truly master his own considerable courage and intellect. A strange epic, indeed, if its hero, the hero's greatest friends, and indeed all that which the hero most loves fails to register in the realm of humanity.

Not only does Odysseus love and prioritize what Arendt argues that—given his cultural context—he should rank as subhuman, but what Odysseus prizes is that which she claims is of value only insofar as it makes possible the political life that is the threshold of action and humanity.[2] It is true that Odysseus leaves Penelope after their night together to quell the angry neighbors and that he will leave her again to fulfill Teiresias's prophecy. He does this not for the sake of political or enduring achievements but in order to return again and in the hope of growing old with his wife and family in their well-built home. Similarly, twice he insists that his greatest wish for Telemachos is for his son to live out his days in relatively rustic Ithaka, thus in Arendt's terms cursing his son with a smaller field of potential action and emergence into the human realm than Telemachos might otherwise have within the broader Greek world.

In perhaps her boldest claim, Arendt finds intimacy altogether lacking in ancient Greece, crediting its first discovery to Rousseau and tying this discovery to the subsequent popularity of the novel.[3] But Homer shows us intimacy and the literary origins of the novel in the tender exchanges and emotions between Odysseus and Penelope and between Odysseus and Telemachos. The *Odyssey*, through its survival and prominence in the ancient world, shows that ancient Greece cannot have been as wholly innocent of the knowledge of love and affection between a man and his wife, family, and household as Arendt claims. The drama of the reunion between Odysseus and Penelope, to say nothing of the allocation of so much of the poem to their relationship, would be utterly absurd were she correct. Even the poet's choice of how to frame the story—starting with Odysseus distraught in his despair of returning to his home and family—serves to emphasize the importance of Odysseus's desire for his home and wife within the epic as a whole.

Scholars who ponder the *Odyssey*'s claim to the title of first novel do so because of qualities that Arendt claims are lacking in the epic's entire culture: intimacy between lovers, tenderness in family attachments, and prominence of struggle internal to individuals within the story as a whole. While it may be admitted that Homer's focus on the importance of marriage is less than one expects in the novels of Jane Austen, that institution nevertheless remains a critical, plot-driving aspect of the *Odyssey*.[4] The success of the hero is not imaginable without the success of his relationship with his wife. And Homer clearly defines the success of this relationship in terms of more than the couple's political function or physical reunion. The rekindling of their friendship—the reestablishment of a friendship founded on similarity in virtue—is carefully woven into the poem. Their reunion is dependent, moreover, on Odysseus's preference for his home and Penelope over mere security and superior physical beauty and on Penelope's ability to recognize the identity and individuality of Odysseus. The couple falls asleep side by side at the epic's climax only when they have finished speaking with one another.

Arendt argues that the "public realm, in other words, was reserved for individuality; it was the only place where men could show who they really and inexchangeably were."[5] To the contrary, only Odysseus can take his place within his bed, marriage, family, and household. Only after he is home does Odysseus have a value without reference to the prominence of his household, the wealth of Ithaka, or his performance in the war. The *Iliad* suggests the same truths about the value of speech and the individual within the private sphere. Andromache's public mourning for the loss of her husband's final words spoken to her alone and Hektor's distress over the suffering of Andromache make sense only if private life has human value. The same is true of Achilles's grief for his father and Priam's grief for the best of his sons. By Arendt's account these epic moments can be dismissed as private and subhuman. By her logic, Achilles's wrath over the loss of a long, wealthy life enjoyed with a wife of his own choosing and the companionship of his particular friend, Patroklos, would animate the basest moments of the hero of the *Iliad*. Much less could we make sense of his statement, spoken from Hades, that he would prefer a life as a slave to existence as lord of the dead.

Within the *Odyssey* Homer underscores the value of private life through the excellence of Odysseus's servant Eumaios. Arendt draws our attention to this slave for his famous statement that a man loses half his excellence on the day that he becomes a slave.[6] She fails to observe, however, that Eumaios is in fact excellent. For all the evident disadvantages of a life of slavery and labor, he demonstrates through his piety, loyalty, and intelligence that even in such circumstances a man may attain excellence utterly deprived of any public dimension in his life. Indeed, both Eumaios and Penelope, because of their excellence within the private realm and their salutary effects upon their political contexts, emerge as important counterpoints to Arendt's generalizations against the sum total of their limited, nonpublic spheres of action. Homer presents a vision of human life in which virtue exists in the household, influencing the political environment outside the private sphere.

Arendt argues that for the ancient Greeks isolated life, like domestic life, was essentially private and therefore less than human.[7] But the *Odyssey* is the story of a hero who passes countless hours by himself at sea, on beaches, and among monsters. The work opens not with the wrath of an honor-deprived hero but with a man alone and weeping. Those of his companions who witness most of his feats before he returns to Ithaka die before they can share his exploits in the public world of enduring action. Arguably, Odysseus's greatest struggles are the internal struggles that take place in his breast as heart and mind battle with one another. These struggles may not take place in isolation, but they surely are not political, action, or human in any form that Arendt would recognize. Odysseus does not, as Ajax does, combat his enemy's greatest hero in broad daylight in the midst of war between two great political powers. He undergoes hardships—and many labors—and does battle with his own spirit. It is hard to imagine how a conflict could be more private.

Similarly, many of Odysseus's joys are private insofar as human bodies are private. Arendt claims that private joys could only be comprehended as the absence of pain.[8] Yet Odysseus is famous (some would say infamous) for his acknowledgment of the power of the belly. Consider his curiously large number of baths (occurring almost as often as his feasts). These baths, among them the only bath in the *Iliad*, are described by Homer as bringing about refreshment of spirit (and you can almost see Odysseus, emerging from his bath, sighing, and commenting, "I feel human again"); they illustrate, in Homer's vision of Odysseus, the humanity in this private experience. Odysseus is—as Arendt accuses moderns of being—happy in the "small things."[9]

He also loves other elements of the private and "necessary" world that Arendt catalogs as utterly subhuman. He loves his house and sheds a tear for his dog. He describes with pride the bed that he labored with his own hands to make. His reunion with the women of his household reduces him to tears. Nor can we imagine that Odysseus loves these for the sake of their glory, as might perhaps be the case if he lived in the most glorious of homes in the most glorious of kingdoms. Telemachos's wonder at the riches of Nestor and Menelaus (as well as Odysseus's similar reaction in Phaiakia) suggest that "rugged Ithaka" has little to boast in comparison to the glory of its neighbors. Arendt has argued that, while the ancient Greeks relied on domestic contrivance, such arrangements were not esteemed or valued as good. Not only slaves but all that is relegated to the necessary and private realm, she argues, was subhuman for Homer's audience. Its only value, according to Arendt, was its ability to provide for the necessities of life (including the future of the species) so that the heads of households might emerge into the free and human world—the public arena of the potentially remembered and thus enduring act.

The *Odyssey* cannot be reconciled with this view. Odysseus's excellence results from his desire and ability to return to, protect, and rejoin his family. A hero of renowned deeds at Troy, he was noteworthy but not among the most exceptional. In his return and in his desire to return, he is preeminent relative to his peers. Arendt overlooks another essential element to the *Odyssey*: as much as the strength of Odysseus's desire and the excellence of his ability (partially through interior struggles) to claim his home is integral to the *Odyssey*, the value of that for which he strives is critical. Odysseus would be a Don Quixote (or worse, insofar as he is a true warrior) if Penelope, Telemachos, his house, his dog, and his servants were valueless. But they are not. The story is a drama, rather than a comedy, because a man with the qualities necessary to earn glory at Troy chooses to forsake glory for the sake of what is his own *and* it is worth it.

Homer shows us that Odysseus finds happiness in private, but he places at least equal emphasis on the value of that which Odysseus loves. This can be observed in the moment in which Odysseus recognizes the wiles of Penelope's mind, his outraged description of the skill with which he constructed his own bed, and his description of how well joined his house is. The excellence of all that which is his own is integral to the value of his homecoming. Having seen the wonders of the world and earned an immortal name, Odysseus does not come home to find Ithaka smaller, his wife shorter, and his house decrepit. Rather, he finds a rugged land in which he wishes his son to spend his days, a wife whose mind delights him, and a house and bed that are excellent because they are well built. Homer shows us a hero who is right to be happy in his homecoming. The temporal limitation of this happiness, moreover, does not arise from an unmet desire or deficiency felt by Odysseus. Necessity calls, and Odysseus will reluctantly reenter the public realm so that he can return to find his happiness again.

Odysseus's plan to depart—the storm cloud on the horizon at the end of the poem—intensifies the reader's appreciation for that which is good within the *Odyssey*. And Odysseus's unhappiness about the final voyage serves to demonstrate the hero's conscious preference for the excellence of his private life. The portrait of human happiness and human excellence at the end of the story is that of a life spent with one's own, a life that includes a good prospect for the continued thriving of what is one's own. As Odysseus might articulate it, it is a harmonious marriage (far more likely with a sensible woman) that brings joy to friends and harm to enemies. It is enough wealth for ten generations and time spent both with an aging father and in mentoring a son who will be permitted by the gods to live out his days in humble Ithaka (and who is thus more fortunate than oneself). This portrait bears a strong resemblance to the lives that Hektor and Achilles would have chosen had the war—a war perpetuated by the love of honor—not foreclosed their potential for happiness derived from intimate relationships with family and particular friends. The core of human life and its happiest fulfillment is harmony and unity with that which is one's own and the prospect for this happy state to continue insofar as humanly possible. A degree of virtue is necessary among the members of such a household (improving its chances for survival and success) and intensifies the happiness and friendship that its members find in one another.

In sum, within the *Odyssey* nothing is more desired and nothing is more satisfying than the various aspects of Odysseus's reunion with, in Arendt's terminology, his private life. The tapestry of human excellence that Homer weaves is dependent on Odysseus's rejoining that which is his own and on the excellence that he finds in his own private life. The moments of private happiness found in the *Odyssey* portray the side of human desire and excellence that is absent from Arendt's summation of ancient Greek humanity. The love of one's own is the heart of the *Odyssey*.

When Odysseus takes leave of Penelope to prepare for his confrontation with the suitors' families, he reemerges—in Arendt's framing of the issue—into the realm of human action. For Odysseus, political action emerges from his love of his own, rather than standing in opposition to it. Far from constituting an ascension to human life, Odysseus views his own return to public action as an interruption from the continued enjoyment of what he desires most. He undertakes this public task for the sake of protecting that which is his own—that which he prizes.

Homer's Odysseus is the antithesis of Arendt's summation of "human essence." The human essence, she claims, is most exemplified by Achilles and "can come into being only when life departs, leaving behind nothing but a story."[10] Thus she contends that Achilles's humanity and greatness are dependent on both his early death and Homer's preservation of the meaning of that act.[11] Whereas Agamemnon and Ajax can be seen to pursue the greatness she so vividly describes, this produces mixed results in terms of both excellence and political stability—let alone justice. Achilles himself, however, ultimately exhibits an understanding of human excellence and happiness far more similar to that of Odysseus than Arendt allows. In his greatest love and his resulting rage and utter loss of moderation after the death of Patroklos, Achilles simultaneously undermines Arendt's character portrait and forces reconsideration of the connection between Odysseus's desires and the growth of his self-restraint.

In the final analysis Arendt fails to take into account the counterpoint that Homer provided to the honor-loving culture that perpetuated the Trojan War. As much as many of the poet's war heroes are dependent on Homer for their greatness, Odysseus's life is independent of Homer for its meaning. Homer's greatest achievement may not be the elevation of the honor-loving warrior but rather the portrayal of a hero and his household whose humanity is independent of the poet's public art.

The Justice of the Homeric Hero

A related but far more difficult question than the nature of excellence in Homer's epics relates to the nature of justice and the origin of politics. In addition to engaging in political life to protect his family, home, and life, Odysseus plans to leave his home to steal from his neighbors. To put it bluntly, he is a thief. As with the immoderation and resulting injustice that Odysseus displayed in relationship to the disloyal household servants, his love of his own also motivates an immoderate love of wealth that in turn leads him to plan to raid his neighbors.[12] As he explains to Penelope in book 23, he intends to replenish their livestock: "As for my flocks, which the overbearing suitors have ruined, many I shall restore by raiding, others the Achaians shall give me until I have built my sheep folds" (23.356–58).[13] There is thus a fundamental disjunction between the love that Odysseus bears for his own family and household and his disregard for the corresponding relationships of others.

In the final analysis Odysseus minds his own business in a positive sense only: he protects and loves his own private and domestic sphere, but he does not refrain from interfering with the domestic spheres of others. He fails to recognize that, as much as he was right to reclaim and defend his own home and family, his future victims have the same rightful claim against him. Much less does he recognize the potential for his planned raiding to lead to a war with a similar catalyst to that of the Trojan War. To articulate this from Odysseus's perspective, minding his own business often requires (and, he might say, justifies) interfering with the business of others.

This aspect of Odysseus's character brings to mind a preliminary definition of justice from the *Republic*. Leading up to this formulation of justice, Socrates had questioned the implications of justice understood as "doing good to friends and harm to enemies" (332d6–7). Within the *Republic*, this topic leads to a discussion of the relationship of justice to guarding. From thence Socrates develops this understanding of justice with descriptions fitting Odysseus. Seeming to allude to the Night Raid, he asks his interlocutor whether "a good guardian of an army is the very same man who can also steal the enemy's plans and other dispositions" (333e9–334a1). When this is agreed to, Socrates prompts agreement to the conclusion that "of whatever man is a clever guardian, he is also a clever thief" (334a3–4). Within a few lines, Socrates's elaboration overtly connects to Odysseus.

> The just man, then, as it seems, has come to light as a kind of robber, and I'm afraid you learned this from Homer. For he admires Autolycus, Odysseus's grandfather on his mother's side, and says he surpassed all men "in stealing and in swearing oaths." Justice, then, seems, according to you and Homer and Simonides, to be a certain art of stealing, for the benefit, to be sure, of friends and the harm of enemies. (334a9–b3)

The resonance between Socrates's description of the justice of a clever thief and Odysseus is striking. Odysseus's actions demonstrate that he is a thief who does a fine job of aiding his friends and hurting his enemies (both in the Trojan War and as he reclaims his household). Odysseus himself articulates a partial version of Socrates's formulation, tellingly tying his formulation to happy domesticity rather than a definition of justice. When stranded in Phaiakia, he wishes the princess Nausikaa a harmonious marriage, which brings "much distress to the people who hate" her and "pleasure" to her "well-wishers" (6.184–85).[14]

In his focus on friends and enemies, as well as in his inclination toward theft, Odysseus is different—if not self-evidently better—than honor-loving Ajax and Agamemnon. Ajax and Agamemnon are most immoderate in pursuit of the glory of their own names. Odysseus's immoderation appears in his harshness against the disloyal servants and in his ready willingness to use violence to secure private wealth. His love of his own incites him to immoderate acts of violence both within and outside the home. For both those driven by love of their own and those driven by love of glory, the absence of moderation and the loss of self-possession result in serious injustice. In other words, it is no accident that Odysseus of the many baths is also the man who exhibits the least moderation in purifying his house and in plans for raiding his neighbors. A "harmonious marriage" (to use Odysseus's words) and a love of private life are the source of both his virtues and his failings.

However much these failings point to deficiencies in Odysseus (as well as in Socrates's formulation of justice in book 1 of the *Republic*), Odysseus's immoderation itself appears moderate when placed in light of the *Iliad*.[15] Odysseus's desire for household wealth does not inspire him to continue or start a war. His reckoning with the suitors leaves their corpses intact and freely returned to families. Even his merciless treatment of the disloyal household servants inspires neither public display nor intentional torture of the innocent. At a word from Athena, Odysseus's battle cry dies, and "with a happy heart" he obeys the goddess's decree of peace (24.545).

Homer (and goading Athena, too) do much to justify Odysseus as he harms his enemies and helps his friends. Far more than the Trojans—among whom only Alexandros seemed culpable (and even he was not unequivocally impious)—the suitors are presented as wrongdoers, impious, uncivilized, and contemptuous of others. The suitors have not just courted Odysseus's wife: they have menaced her. They have not just maneuvered to strip Telemachos of his inheritance and potential crown: they have attempted to murder him. They have not just taken advantage of Odysseus's absence and probable death: they have conspired to kill him should he return. Disgusting table manners and a general lack of courtesy aside, the suitors are wantonly impious in their manner of feasting and in their treatment of guests, prophets, beggars, and strangers.[16] As Athena does not wish Odysseus to waiver in the thoroughness of his violence, Homer does not wish his audience to shed tears over the deaths of the suitors.[17]

Not only does Homer depict suitors worthy of the category of enemies, but he also gives his audience reason to believe that Telemachos and Eumaios—on the whole—are well-chosen friends whose elevation will render Ithaka a better place. Eumaios's exemplary loyalty and prudence yield scrupulous care of Odysseus's estate and an observant ally for Penelope and Telemachos. Eumaios's superior character and fitness to take his place among the nobility is further demonstrated through his zealous respect of Zeus's rules of hospitality as he hosts the disguised Odysseus.[18] Telemachos too exhibits his superiority vis-à-vis the suitors by accepting a fleeing prophet as his suppliant, through the solicitude that he shows to beggars and strangers, and in his respect for Eumaios.

As the *Odyssey* closes, Odysseus is neither a paragon of virtue within his household nor entirely just in his politics. As much as one can critique this clever thief, Homer indicates that the love of his own that motivates him constitutes a superior—if inadequate—foundation for both virtue and justice relative to the love of honor that dominated in the *Iliad*.[19] Most evident are the distinctions in degree of the loss of moderation and the resulting violence and cruelty. But Odysseus's potential to use speech to resolve and prevent conflict and his friendship with his wife are important points of distinction as well. Without defending Odysseus's immoderation in search of wealth or in defense of his household, one may also note that Homer's hero chooses his friends and enemies well. Yet, because Odysseus sees no distinction between his own private life, the public sphere, and the private lives of others—or perhaps because no such distinction exists in his world—he is doomed to future acts of injustice. His love of his own has fostered both virtue and positive political outcomes for himself, but it ultimately undermines a satisfactory solution to the problem of justice and threatens to provide the basis for a new war.

This is all the more disappointing because Homer at least implicitly shows that the hero who is most strongly motivated by a love of his own could be an invaluable asset to a polis based on deliberation and respect for the common good. Without offering a developed solution, Homer indicates that justice will find the firmest foundation in Odysseus and Penelope's excellence. Homer intimates what Odysseus does not realize: that the virtue fostered in private and protected by the love of one's own does not contain the same intrinsic flaws as love of honor. Compared to his honor-driven peers, Odysseus has no inherent desire for the conflict created by war as a venue in which to demonstrate his superiority.[20] On the contrary, because he loves his own home, family, and physical well-being more than the memory of his name, Odysseus has an intrinsic motivation for limiting strife, warfare, and—ultimately—injustice. And his moderation and superiority in speech, negotiation, and persuasion—which he demonstrated during the Trojan War—would prove particularly well suited to politics based on consensus, deliberation, and discussion. Unfortunately, because Odysseus does not identify the flaws in his own virtues, he cannot identify the need for either justice or politics oriented toward the common good.

Homer's portrayal of Odysseus's inadequate excellence—of the virtues and limitations arising out of the love of one's own—bears a resemblance to the role of the household as described by Aristotle in his *Politics*. Aristotle defines the household as "by nature a community set up for the needs of the day" (1252b9).[21] This community entails more than mere survival: within the household, justice and speech raise human life above the animal experience.

> But speech serves to make plain what is advantageous and harmful and so also what is just and unjust. For it is a peculiarity of humans, in contrast to the other animals, to have perception of good and bad, just and unjust, and the like;

and community in these things makes a household and a city. (1253a7)

As Aristotle describes it, within the household, relations between husband and wife are political rather than despotic. The husband's rule over the family is monarchical (1252b15; 1255b16).

In addition to justice, political rule, and perception of the distinctions between good and bad, virtue and therefore friendship too have a place within the household.[22] Both child and wife, Aristotle reasons, "must have a share in virtue" (1260a2). Noting that the virtue of women is in tension with the justice of the rule of men over their families, Aristotle concludes that a woman's moderation differs from a man's in that it "is not in control" and that her courage differs in that it is only "assisting courage" (1260a2–24).[23] Despite inferiority, the virtues of women prove politically salient, as demonstrated by Aristotle's assertion of the importance of the virtues and education of women within the regime as a whole (1260b8).[24] The virtue of women contributes directly to the polis, and excellence in both marriage partners—as with Penelope and Odysseus—creates the conditions necessary for friendship in the household.[25] As Salkever has noted in critiques of readings of Aristotle that overstate the philosopher's position on the superiority of masculine excellence, the household thus aims "at that virtue or excellence which is distinctively human."[26]

Aristotle's description of the humanity and excellence possible within a household includes at least some slaves. As he explains in the *Politics*, slaves are human: a slave is one who, "while being human, is a possession" (1254a13). Although he defends the enslavement of those who are naturally slaves, Aristotle notes that some who are in fact enslaved have superior natures to natural slaves. Whether slavery is just depends upon the slave's degree of virtue: the more virtuous the slave, the more evident that he is not a slave by nature (1255a3–b4).[27] The humanity and virtue of one like Eumaios, who was abducted and made a slave while a small child, is not in question within this framework. Rather, prior to Odysseus's decision to free him, it is the justice of his rule by Odysseus that Aristotle brings into question.

Despite the humanity and virtue possible therein, Aristotle—like Homer—shows the household to be limited. Villages develop from households, and a city emerges from the combination of villages (1252b7).

Although the city originated "for the sake of staying alive," the new community—the polis—"exists for the sake of living well" (1252b7). The desire to live in a polis exists in everyone because the perfection of each human is most possible when living in such a community.

> The reason is that injustice is most difficult to deal with when furnished with weapons, and the weapons a human being has are meant by nature to go along with prudence and virtue, but it is only too possible to turn them to contrary uses. Consequently, if a human being lacks virtue, he is a most unholy savage thing, and when it comes to sex and food, the worst. But justice is something political, for right is the arrangement of a political community, and right is discrimination of what is just. (1253a29)

Hence, life in a polis is desirable because it improves the potential for virtue and justice (not because polis life is the only condition in which any degree of virtue or justice is possible). Without detracting from the more complete virtue and justice that Aristotle links to the city, it is important to remember that the household—from which the greater community grows—has at least a share in these benefits of the city.

This transition from household into the kind of polis that Aristotle is referring to never takes place within Homer's *Odyssey*. Rather, as the epic draws to a close, Homer leaves his audience with recognition of what is good in Odysseus, Penelope, and their household and a yearning for conditions under which their prospects for peace and justice would be better. Like Odysseus, Homer's audience can appreciate the excellence possible within private life and the virtues nurtured by love of one's own. But unlike Odysseus, Homer's audience can perceive the injustice that originates from this love and work to establish a polity in which minding one's own business has a more limited meaning and encompasses the corresponding rights of others. In other words, by teaching his audience to love what is good about Odysseus and Penelope (and therefore also to wish Telemachos a bright future), Homer instills his audience with a desire for a more complete good than his characters can envision.

Leaving his readers without a clear path, Homer offers an intimation based on his poetic comparison of the love of one's own and the love of honor and their respective consequences. Because the love of one's own fosters superior virtues and leads to less human suffering, future architects of justice would do well to incorporate the loves and virtues of Odysseus and Penelope.

Conclusion

Throughout both epics Odysseus, "like Zeus in counsel," has been and increasingly is the hero most likely to stifle his initial impulse and ponder the best action or speech for a specific moment. This quality, which I have often referred to as his self-restraint or moderation, can be observed as early as his strategic choice of where to join the battle in book IV of the *Iliad*, and it becomes an evident aspect of his character during the Night Raid with Diomedes. As many as are his failings during his voyage home, his self-control is the only reason why he ever emerges from Polyphemos's cave, and it is his self-control that enables him to be the only man not to eat the cattle of Helios. It is this quality that Athena gives for her preference for Odysseus when she compliments him for avoiding Agamemnon's blunder in his return to his home: "Always you are the same, and such is the mind within you . . . you are fluent, and reason closely, and keep your head always" (13.330–32).

As Athena also indicates, Odysseus's use of speech rather than force in many situations is closely related to both his intelligence and his self-restraint. His skillful use of speech is the source of his singular role in the *Iliad* and is central to the storytelling component of the *Odyssey*. It is his skill in speech that indicates that Odysseus, although capable of using force, has the potential to develop political relationships with his neighbors such as Agamemnon could neither envision nor maintain. Lacking the inherent need for conflict as a source of glory, capable of using speech to negotiate and coordinate, and practiced in self-restraint, Odysseus as revealed in Homer's closing portrait is a hero ignorant of his own superior preparation for politics based on speech and justice.

Homer's epics portray human love as a powerful factor in the development of virtue and politics. The *Iliad* commences with a quarrel over honor and chronicles the loss of moderation and suffering that follows. The *Odyssey* begins with a man—a courageous and singularly crafty speaker—who wants to get home; the epic then chronicles the imperfect inner struggles through which he develops the self-restraint that eventually makes possible his arrival home and that prepares him to endure the labor of reclaiming his home and family.[28] Of course, this is not the whole story. There are moments of intimacy in the *Iliad*, and Odysseus's failings as a leader are many. He fails to bring his army home safely, and he brutally punishes the disloyal elements of home and kingdom (albeit at Athena's command). His plans to depart to enrich his household (and to fulfill Teiresias's prophecy) demonstrate the potential for future suffering: his departure will lead to injustice and will leave his home and family vulnerable again. Telemachos, Eumaios, and Philoitios, although their cruelty should give us pause, may form the beginnings of a stable new order in Ithaka, but it is not clear how well this will end.

Homer's insights about the political implications of love might seem hopelessly romantic in an age that has adopted reasonableness as its public standard and universal human rights as its battle cry. To the contrary, Homer's poems provide a rich resource in an age with blind spots resulting from its own beliefs. Taking a respite from the modern perspective, if only briefly, and reviewing the human landscape through a Homeric lens reveals undercurrents that contemporary paradigms do not fully explain. Taken together, Homer's epics challenge their readers to choose between visions of human excellence, each of which presents a different dominant love as superior. While we are not on the brink of denying the title of humanity to anyone based on his or her preference for public honor or for that which is his or her own, our culture often assigns status as important, serious, or excellent based on a corresponding distinction. One has only to pick up a history textbook or a newspaper to see this. In the popular imagination serious individuals devote the preponderance of their time to public matters. Similarly, public accomplishment (whether political or not) and the height of human greatness are frequently equated with one another. In mass media and scholarship alike, politics dominates the spotlight on the stage of human action.

In competition with this view of the centrality of public achievement is the prioritization of private life, family, marriage, and household excellence. From this perspective the core of human existence lies in choosing a well-matched and virtuous mate, raising well-educated and excellent children, and caring for (and sometimes enriching) the household itself. Participation in politics, from this perspective, may be necessary, but it is also a loss of time that would otherwise be better spent with one's own. This preference—to use a decidedly modern term for the dichotomy—has its champions, but far more than its rival it suffers from the accusation of marginal importance on the scale of human excellence.

In truth, the cultural predisposition against love of one's own does not necessarily result from the numbers of individuals who prefer their own or honor. Rather, this predisposition arises from the self-selection of those who pursue honor for positions of power and influence, whether in government, science, business, media, education, or philosophy. Those who love their own more than honor are less likely to compete for such positions, and when they do compete, they (like Odysseus on the battlefield) are willing to sacrifice less because they have less to gain through the competition. Meanwhile, their honor-loving peers, having little else to lose or gain, push forward to ever-greater heights of glory, affecting those about them like Ajax cheering on and protecting his fellow warriors. Of course, Ajax proved an essential asset to his allies, and one would be rash to conclude that the love that drove a man to such excellence should or could be scorned. The problem, however, lies in the leadership decisions that such individuals make and how their decisions inflame the passion for honor and inflict suffering within the private realm that they discount. And yet, the love of honor being what it is, the individuals most dominated by it are similarly those most likely to wield a disproportionate amount of influence and power.

The controlling question between these competing views is over the source of human happiness: what is a good life? If accumulating public accomplishments for the sake of building one's legacy is the answer, then politics and the love of honor claim the first prize for a life well spent. If this is the case, then private life will always be—no matter how adamantly political actors defend human rights or society explores the possibility of a "balanced life" that facilitates the simultaneous pursuit of honor and of one's own—a secondary or lesser choice. Rather than creating a dichotomy between human and subhuman endeavors in our society, this results in a hierarchy of choices for how to devote one's life. Because in the aggregate (and almost by definition) those in the most influential positions love honor more, those who have the most power in establishing cultural definitions value the pursuit of public achievement over a life devoted to one's own.

As Agamemnon's choices reveal, the agenda of such leaders—in politics and in popular opinion—is not neutral. In the aggregate they prioritize the pursuit and accumulation of honor while marginalizing private interests and dismissing both the individual and the political value of the love of one's own. From within this perspective the search for the best mate, the dynamics of the household, and the care of the young are appropriate uses of time for individuals with less excellence. We live in a culture in which all concur on the universality of humanity, but simultaneously the competitive and honor-driven aspect of our culture equates failing to compete for a place of public importance with an inadequacy for any "higher" calling.

And yet, as Homer noted, the pursuit of virtue and excellence within private life has a salutary effect on the whole precisely because such a pursuit escapes the relentless competitiveness (and resulting lack of moderation) of the public sphere. Within a private realm dominated by the love of one's own, political and public accomplishments take on importance insofar as they are necessary to support and protect the private sphere and the friendships enjoyed therein. Excellence—as well as happiness—within the private realm relates to how well matched the individuals at the heart of the family are and to how well they are able to protect and to inculcate virtue in one another, in their offspring, and in those around them. Do they help their friends and hurt their enemies?

Notes

Introduction

1. There are, of course, a multiplicity of approaches and goals within Homeric scholarship. I postpone a broader discussion of this question to the close of this introduction.

2. MacIntyre, *After Virtue: A Study in Moral Theory*, 3rd ed. (Notre Dame: University of Notre Dame Press, 2007).

3. MacIntyre, *After Virtue*, 122–23. MacIntyre's reading is strongly influenced by Arthur Adkins's claim that successful completion of social function is central to the ancient Greek concept of virtue. Adkins, *Merit and Responsibility: A Study in Greek Values* (London: Oxford University Press, 1960), 32–34.

4. MacIntyre, *After Virtue*, 122–23; Adkins, *Merit and Responsibility*, 32–34.

5. MacIntyre, *After Virtue*, 122–23, 180; Adkins, *Merit and Responsibility*, 32–34.

6. Arendt, *The Human Condition* (Chicago: University of Chicago Press, 1998).

7. Arendt, *Human Condition*, 13.

8. Arendt, *Human Condition*, 13.

9. Arendt, *Human Condition*, 19.

10. Arendt, *Human Condition*, 19.

11. Arendt, *Human Condition*, 24.

12. Arendt, *Human Condition*, 24.

13. Arendt, *Human Condition*, 49.

14. Arendt, *Human Condition*, 101.

15. Arendt, *Human Condition*, 112. Although she does not give the issue much attention, Arendt includes the "pain of giving birth" in the meaning of labor. Arendt, *Human Condition*, 121.

16. "Hidden away were the laborers who with their bodies minister to the bodily needs of life, and the women who with their bodies guarantee the physical survival of the species. Women and slaves belonged to the same

category and were hidden away not only because they were somebody else's property but because their life was laborious, devoted to the bodily functions." Arendt, *Human Condition*, 72. For an overview of the relationship between contemporary feminism and Arendt's public/private dichotomy, see Benhabib, "Feminist Theory and Hannah Arendt's Concept of Public Space," *History of the Human Sciences* 6, no. 2 (1993): 97–114. For a broader history of feminist reactions to Arendt, see Dietz, *Turning Operations: Feminism, Arendt, and Politics* (New York: Routledge, 2002). Some readings have interpreted Arendt's work as more amenable to mainstream contemporary thought, including Benhabib's "The Pariah and Her Shadow: Hannah Arendt's Biography of Rachel Varnhagen," in *Feminist Interpretations of Hannah Arendt*, ed. Bonnie Honig (University Park: Pennsylvania State University Press, 1995), 83–104.

17. Arendt, *Human Condition*, 64.

18. The sharpness of Arendt's "unwavering" distinction between public and private has been noted. Kohn, "Freedom: The Priority of the Political," in *The Cambridge Companion to Hannah Arendt*, ed. Dana Villa (Cambridge: Cambridge University Press, 2000), 113–29, 116, 125. For discussion of the meaning and content of Arendt's use of "politics," see Kateb, "Political Action: Its Nature and Advantages," in *The Cambridge Companion to Hannah Arendt*, ed. Dana Villa (Cambridge: Cambridge University Press, 2000), 130–50.

19. Arendt, *Human Condition*, 24.
20. Arendt, *Human Condition*, 25, 176–77.
21. Arendt, *Human Condition*, 106.
22. Arendt, *Human Condition*, 26–28.
23. Arendt, *Human Condition*, 30.
24. Arendt, *Human Condition*, 36.
25. Arendt, *Human Condition*, 36.
26. Arendt, *Human Condition*, 41.
27. Arendt, *Human Condition*, 50–51.
28. Arendt, *Human Condition*, 55.
29. Arendt, *Human Condition*, 56.
30. Arendt, *Human Condition*, 179.
31. Arendt, *Human Condition*, 182–83.
32. Arendt, *Human Condition*, 184.
33. Arendt, *Human Condition*, 188.
34. Arendt, *Human Condition*, 193.
35. Arendt, *Human Condition*, 194.
36. Arendt, *Human Condition*, 197.

37. Arendt, *Human Condition*, 194. Benhabib aptly notes that "one of the curious aspects of Arendt's account of the agonal space of the polis is that she subdues and, yes, 'domesticates' the Homeric warrior-hero to yield the Aristotelian deliberative citizen." "Feminist Theory," 103.

38. Arendt, *Human Condition*, 33.

39. Arendt, *Human Condition*, 37.
40. Arendt, *Human Condition*, 37.
41. Arendt argues that this dichotomy—the dichotomy we moderns have lost—formed part of the very foundation of an "ancient political thought" that rested on it "as self-evident and axiomatic." *Human Condition*, 28.
42. Arendt, *Human Condition*, 38.
43. Arendt, *Human Condition*, 39.
44. This transformation into a household resulted in the "rebellious reaction against society during which Rousseau and the Romantics discovered intimacy." Arendt, *Human Condition*, 39.
45. Arendt, *Human Condition*, 40.
46. For example, Katz chronicles a systematic scholarly blind spot to women in ancient Greece that is due, she argues, to classical liberal norms about the private nature of the domestic sphere. "Women and Democracy in Ancient Greece," in *Contextualizing Classics: Ideology, Performance, Dialogue—Essays in Honor of John J. Peradotto*, ed. Thomas Falkner, Nancy Felson, and David Konstan (Lanham: Rowman & Littlefield, 1999), 41–68. For direct discussion of the relationship between Arendt and the classical liberal distinction between public and private, see Zaretsky, "Hannah Arendt and the Meaning of the Public/Private Distinction," in *Hannah Arendt and the Meaning of Politics*, ed. Craig Calhoun and John McGowan, 207–31 (Minneapolis: University of Minnesota Press, 1997), 211–14, and Hansen, *Hannah Arendt: Politics, History, and Citizenship* (Stanford: Stanford University Press, 1993), 83–88.
47. Wolin, "On Hannah Arendt: Democracy and the Political," *Salmagundi* 60 (1983) 3–19, 7; Euben, "Arendt's Hellenism," in *The Cambridge Companion to Hannah Arendt*, ed. Dana Villa (Cambridge: Cambridge University Press, 2000), 152; see also Elshtain, *Public Man, Private Woman: Women in Social and Political Thought* (Princeton: Princeton University Press, 1981), 346.
48. Salkever, *Finding the Mean: Theory and Practice in Aristotelian Political Philosophy* (Princeton: Princeton University Press, 1990); Swanson, *The Public and the Private in Aristotle's Political Philosophy* (Ithaca: Cornell University Press, 1992); see also Levy, "Does Aristotle Exclude Women from Politics?" *Review of Politics* 52, no. 3 (1990): 397–416.
49. Salkever concludes, for example, that Aristotle and Plato worked to "subvert the prevailing conception of the best human life. . . . and to replace it by a novel, more complex, and surely less masculine one." "Women, Soldiers, Citizens: Plato and Aristotle on the Politics of Virility," *Polity* 19, no. 2 (1986): 252; see also Salkever, *Finding the Mean*.
50. As witnessed in an ever-growing body of literature, Arendt's sharp distinction between private and public results in a correspondingly harsh elimination of numerous states of being from participation in human life. Topper, "Arendt and Bourdieu between Word and Deed," *Political Theory* 39, no. 3 (2011): 354; Klausen, "Hannah Arendt's Antiprimitivism," *Political Theory* 38,

no. 3 (2010): 396; Marso, "Simone de Beauvoir and Hannah Arendt: Judgments in Dark Times," *Political Theory* 40, no. 2 (2012): 180; Locke, "Little Rock's Social Question: Reading Arendt on School Desegregation and Social Climbing," *Political Theory* 41, no. 4 (2013): 537; Hyvonen, "Tentative Lessons of Experience: Arendt, Essayism, and 'The Social' Reconsidered," *Political Theory* 42, no. 5 (2014): 572; Bickford, "Constructing Inequality: City Spaces and the Architecture of Citizenship," *Political Theory* 28, no. 3 (2000); Elshtain, "Political Children: Reflections on Hannah Arendt's Distinction between Public and Private Life," in *Reconstructing Political Theory: Feminist Perspectives*, ed. Mary Lyndon Shanley and Narayan Uma (University Park: Pennsylvania State University Press, 1997), 109–43.

51. Hammer, *The "Iliad" as Politics: The Performance of Political Thought* (Norman: University of Oklahoma Press, 2002), 11–18; Hammer, "The Politics of the *Iliad*," *Classical Journal* 94, no. 1 (1998): 11–14, 19. In a different context, Euben observed the threat posed by Arendt's misinterpretation of ancient Greek thought: "This seeming perversity has led even Arendt's sympathetic critics to seek ways of marginalizing or softening her Hellenism, and less sympathetic ones to dismiss her because of her Hellenism and dismiss ancient political thought because of Arendt." "Arendt's Hellenism," 151–52. This threat is particularly acute with regard to the androcentric worldview that results from Arendt's interpretation. As Saxonhouse has noted generally with regard to the androcentric study of the history of political thought, the authors of the past "do not make the error of defining the human being as only male, though much scholarship has made the mistake of assuming they did." *Women in the History of Political Thought: Ancient Greece to Machiavelli* (Westport: Praeger, 1985), vii. When the perceived androcentrism of the ancients does not cause us to dismiss their wisdom altogether, a second threat lurks in the possibility that contemporary scholars—as they often seem to do—will study the Greeks but preemptively ignore their teachings on private life and gender. This option poses two risks: (1) it impoverishes contemporary study by foreclosing the possibility of learning about these subjects, and (2) it runs the risk of misconstruing ancient teachings in the aggregate by effectively "deleting" portions with complex interrelationships to the theoretical whole. This second risk can be perceived in Elshtain's optimistic explanation of the project of editing Aristotle's teachings to support contemporary feminist views: "The key is to assay what one can drop without so eroding the overall structure of the theory that one's favored alternatives are dropped as particular dimensions of explanation are rejected." *Public Man, Private Woman*, 53.

52. Arendt, *Human Condition*, 58.

53. Plato, *The Republic of Plato*, 260. I have consulted the original Greek in the Cambridge University Press editions edited by James Adam, but all citations to the *Republic* refer to Allan Bloom's translation. Plato, *The Republic of*

Plato, ed. and trans. James Adam, 2 vols. (Cambridge: Cambridge University Press, 2009); Plato, *The Republic of Plato*, trans. Allan Bloom, 2nd ed. (New York: Basic Books, 1991).

54. Plato, *Republic*, 620b.

55. In his critique of poetry early in the *Republic*, Socrates indicates that because Achilles is the son of a goddess he ought not to be portrayed behaving poorly (388a, 391b–c). It follows that if Socrates did not have anything positive to attribute to Achilles, he might remain silent on the subject of Achilles's choice of reincarnation.

56. Plato, *Republic*, 620c.

57. Reeve recently remarked on Socrates's generally favorable portrayal of Odysseus's choice of reincarnation, noting that Odysseus's care in the selection of his next life is similar to that of a philosopher. *Blindness and Reorientation: Problems in Plato's "Republic"* (Oxford: Oxford University Press, 2013), 35, 45–47.

58. MacIntyre, *After Virtue*, 123; see also Adkins, *Merit and Responsibility*, 34–37.

59. MacIntyre, *After Virtue*, 123.

60. MacIntyre, *After Virtue*, 127; see also Adkins, *Merit and Responsibility*, 35, 40.

61. MacIntyre, *After Virtue*, 123.

62. I follow the standard practice in textual references and citations to Homer, referring to the books of the *Iliad* by roman numerals and the books of the *Odyssey* by arabic numerals. The titles to these two works are therefore omitted from citations. I quote Lattimore's translations throughout, except where relevant corrections, based upon the Oxford Classical Texts edited by Allen and Munro, have been noted. Homer, *Homeri Opera*, ed. David B. Munro and Thomas W. Allen, vols. 1–2 (Oxford: Oxford University Press, 1920); Homer, *Homeri Opera*, ed. Thomas W. Allen, vols. 3–4 (Oxford: Oxford University Press, 1922); Homer, *The Iliad*, trans. Richmond Lattimore (Chicago: University of Chicago Press, 1961); Homer, *The Odyssey of Homer*, trans. Richmond Lattimore (New York: Harper Perennial Modern Classics, 2007).

63. Ahrensdorf, *Homer on the Gods and Human Virtue: Creating the Foundations of Classical Civilization* (New York: Cambridge University Press, 2014), 218–19, 252–53.

64. Horkheimer and Adorno, *Dialectic of Enlightenment: Philosophical Fragments* (Stanford: Stanford University Press, 2002), 45; see also Held, *Introduction to Critical Theory: Horkheimer to Habermas* (Berkeley: University of California Press, 1980) ("Odysseus is a prototype of the bourgeois individual").

65. Benardete, *The Bow and the Lyre: A Platonic Reading of the "Odyssey"* (Lanham: Rowman & Littlefield, 2008).

66. Deneen, *The Odyssey of Political Theory: The Politics of Departure and Return* (Lanham: Rowman & Littlefield, 2003).

67. Howland, *The Republic: The Odyssey of Philosophy* (Philadelphia: Paul Dry Books, 2004); Clay, *The Wrath of Athena: Gods and Men in the "Odyssey"* (Princeton: Princeton University Press, 1983).

68. Donlan, "Kin-Groups in the Homeric Epics," *Classical World* 101, no. 1 (2007): 29–39, 29.

69. For example, Donlan's scholarship examines gift economies and historical use of reciprocity in political rule. "Reciprocities in Homer," *Classical World* 75, no. 3 (1982): 137–75; Donlan, "The Unequal Exchange between Glaucus and Diomedes in Light of the Homeric Gift-Economy," *Phoenix* 43, no. 1 (1989): 1–15. Hammer relies on Homer's description of the role of the people in Homer's Ithaka as evidence of the people's role in archaic Greece. "Plebiscitary Politics in Archaic Greece," *Historia: Zeitschrift für Alte Geschichte* 54, no. 2 (2005): 107–31. Burkert uses Homer throughout as evidence for his analysis—not of Homer—but of myth more generally. *Structure and History in Greek Mythology and Ritual* (Los Angeles: University of California Press, 1979).

70. Until the eighteenth century, there was virtual unanimity on the question of how the *Odyssey* and the *Iliad* had been composed. It was taken for granted that some*one*—or possibly two some*ones*—had *written* the poems. Knox, Introduction, in *The Iliad*, trans. Robert Fagles (Penguin Classics Deluxe ed., London: Penguin Books, 1998), 7; Finley, *The World of Odysseus* (New York: New York Review of Books, 1954), 6. Since the eighteenth century, various theories have come to the fore: Homer's ability to write, as well as the number and gender of the person(s) responsible for the poems, have been questioned. Perhaps, some have suggested, the poems were created over the course of centuries through a collective, cultural process, so that we ought to consider them authored by the Greek people. Knox, Introduction, 8; Deneen, *Odyssey of Political Theory*, 30. Or did a man or a set of men merely edit and compile the works of various bards who predated writing in ancient Greek? Knox, Introduction, 8. Does the *Odyssey* bear the indications of a female author who wrote herself into the poem as the lovely and intelligent Nausikaa?

After centuries of analysis tending in these directions, scholars are returning to the historic understanding of Homer. When linguistic, metrical, and historical analysis could not agree upon sources or fault lines in the poems, scholarly opinion began "to concentrate on the qualities of the poem itself, to stress the unity of the main action rather than the digressions and inconsistencies, above all to explore the elaborate correspondences of structure that often link scene to scene." Knox, Introduction, 14. For an overview of the history of scholarly theories of multiple authorship and their attempts to delineate the fault lines in the *Odyssey*, see Clay, *Wrath of Athena*, 3–7. After these swings in opinion, there seem today to be (1) an acceptance that we cannot know the answer to this question with any degree of certainty and (2) a tentative preference for the conclusion that one or two poets were responsible for writing the *Iliad* and the

Odyssey—the major remaining question being whether each epic had its own author or whether they were written by the same person. Knox, Introduction, 22; Finley, *World of Odysseus*, 6.

It is important to ask what bearing the conclusion to the Homer question has upon this study. Plato, Aristotle, and their contemporaries treated Homer as if he was one man, author of both the *Iliad* and the *Odyssey*. In the *Republic*, for example, many Homeric references appear alongside parallel citations to other poets on the same point, in which Socrates can be seen to reference Homer in the same fashion as any other individual author (for example, see Plato, *Republic*, 363a8, 468d–469a, 600d, and 612b). For example, when he lists poets, Homer's name simply appears in the list: "The ones Hesiod and Homer told us, and the other poets too" (Plato, *Republic*, 377d3–4). Similarly, Aristotle's *Poetics*, which devotes considerable attention to the *Iliad* and the *Odyssey*, refers to Homer as if he were one male poet.

71. John Foley, who admits that we cannot know the precise relationship of the texts of the *Iliad* and the *Odyssey* to their oral poetic predecessors and who concedes the continued relevance of a literary approach, reads Homer's poems in the context of the now-lost traditional art that he reconstructs. *Homer's Traditional Art* (University Park: Pennsylvania State University Press, 1999), xiii–xiv. See also John Foley, "Guslar and Aoidos: Traditional Register in South Slavic and Homeric Epic," *Transactions of the American Philological Association* 126 (1996): 11–41; Elmer, "*Kita* and *Kosmos*: The Poetics of Ornamentation in Bosniac and Homeric Epic," *Journal of American Folklore* 123, no. 489 (2010): 276–303; Graziosi, *Homer* (Oxford: Oxford University Press, 2016), 15–27. In this approach to studying the epics, the definition of "writing" itself has become a debated issue. Elmer, "Helen Epigrammatopoios," *Classical Antiquity* 24, no. 1 (2005): 1–39; John Foley, "'Reading' Homer through Oral Tradition," *College Literature* 34, no. 2 (2007): 1–28; John Foley, "Signs, Texts, and Oral Tradition," *Journal of Folklore Research* 33, no. 1 (1996): 21–29.

72. Redfield, "The Proem of the Iliad: Homer's Art," *Classical Philology* 74, no. 2 (1979): 95–110, 95. Raaflaub argues that epic language is "dynamic and flexible and must have given the poet much freedom to expand, condense, and vary any component of his story." "Homer, the Trojan War, and History," *Classical World* 91, no. 5 (1998): 386–403, 395. Oral composition does not imply primitive art, and Homer's greatness—compared to the greatness of Milton or Dante—is found in the text of his poem as a result of the employment of the narrative tools available. MacLeod, *Homer Iliad Book XXIV* (New York: Cambridge University Press, 1982), 38–40.

73. Donlan, "Character Structure in Homer's *Iliad*," *Journal of General Education* 21, no. 4 (1970): 259–69, 259; Friedrich and Redfield, "Contra Messing," *Language* 57, no. 4 (1981): 901–3, 903 (arguing that, although the *Iliad* was probably orally composed, "it contrasts with the oral tradition because of

its scale and aspiration to create a single permanent work of art. This is the hypothesis of the 'monumental author or composer'").

74. Donlan, "Character Structure," 259 ("It is by means of character that Homer makes his most sublime observations on the human condition"); Donlan, "Homer's Agamemnon," *Classical World* 65, no. 4 (1971), 109–15; Graziosi and Haubold, *Homer Iliad Book VI* (Cambridge: Cambridge University Press, 2010), 18–21; Redfield and Friedrich, "Speech as a Personality Symbol: The Case of Achilles," *Language* 54, no. 2 (1978): 263–88.

75. "An epithet must not be considered a useless relic: each contains a real part of the *Iliad*." Benardete, *Achilles and Hector: The Homeric Hero* (South Bend: St. Augustine Press, 2005), 10. Benardete argues that epithets are a tool for drawing attention to both the common and unique characteristics of characters. See also Saïd, *Homer and the "Odyssey"* (Oxford: Oxford University Press, 2011), 51–53 ("Epithets are not simply used to fill out the line and . . . their presence cannot be justified entirely by metrical concerns. Instead, they can also contribute to the meaning of the poem"); Scully, *Homer and the Sacred City* (Ithaca: Cornell University Press, 1990), 4.

Chapter 1

1. Ajax, still angry over his loss of Achilles's armor to Odysseus during Achilles's funeral games, shunned humankind and opted for a lion's life (620b). Agamemnon, also hating humankind, determined to become an eagle (620b3–5).

2. If there is one battle skill in which Ajax surpasses the otherwise peerless Achilles, this is it. Ajax's contributions to the battles of the *Iliad* cannot be fairly measured in terms of the men whom he slays himself; one must also count the men slain by those with whom he fights in tandem, by those he directs in the minute details of battle tactics, and by those he inspires with courage.

3. Only nine contingents numbered twelve ships or fewer. By comparison, seventeen contingents included forty ships or more, including four of eighty to one hundred ships (II.494–759).

4. There are a few lines in the text that, at least by implication, question Ajax's inferiority to Achilles (see, for example, VII.113–14; XIII.321–25).

5. It appears that his immense size is the most obvious thing that sets him apart. When Helen and Priam observe the Achaian hosts together, Ajax is one of three whose appearance catches Priam's eye, prompting him to ask, "Who then is this other Achaian of power and stature towering above the Argives by head and broad shoulders" (III.226–27). Helen responds with Ajax's epithet, "That one is gigantic Aias, wall of the Achaians" (III.229).

6. Clay convincingly demonstrates the coherence of the spatial layout and the battle sequences in the *Iliad*. Clay, *Homer's Trojan Theater: Space, Vision,*

and Memory in the "Iliad" (Cambridge: Cambridge University Press, 2011). Sections devoted to books XII–XVII demonstrate this coherence with painstaking detail, tracking Ajax's movement through the battle and the consequences of his decisions about where to face the Trojans.

7. Initially, Menelaus alone takes up Hektor's challenge. When Agamemnon objects, Nestor taunts the leaders until nine, including Ajax, volunteer (VII.92–180).

8. Before Agamemnon takes Briseis from Achilles, he threatens to take the prize woman of one of his leaders, mentioning Ajax and Odysseus as possible candidates—indicating that Ajax's prize and thus Ajax too must have been among the most honored of the Achaians (I.137–39). Later, in book II, Ajax is among a handful of elite warriors selected to attend Agamemnon's prebattle sacrifice and prayer (II.406).

9. In books XII and XIII Ajax engages with Sarpedon and Hektor and then leaves the defense of his own ships to others to hold the Achaian line in more critical portions of the battle (XII.265–66, 364–77). In book XIV Ajax again engages Hektor and is prevented from killing Hektor only by the overwhelming efforts of the Trojans to protect their leader (XIV.401–32). By book XV Ajax is defending from the prows of the ships against a direct onslaught by Hektor. Hektor is unable to set the ships afire, but Ajax cannot drive Hektor back. Credit for this defense of the ships is particularly due to Ajax; this is evident not only through the focus put upon him by the text but also because by this point in the battle many leading Achaian warriors (including Diomedes, Agamemnon, Odysseus, and Nestor) are wounded and no longer fighting.

10. Or, as Clay describes Ajax's retreat: "Zeus forces Ajax, who has been manning the center, to retreat, which he does with great reluctance and asinine stubbornness." *Homer's Trojan Theater*, 60. There are two additional instances in which Ajax retreats, both times because of a sign from Zeus (VIII.78–79; XI.544–74).

11. Menelaus initially spots Patroklos's fall and pushes his way through the fight to defend the body and Achilles's armor. Menelaus despairs of being able to protect the body by himself but believes that if Ajax will come to his assistance, they will be able to drag the body back together (XVII.89–105). Ajax does come to his assistance and, for a while, they are able to hold the Trojans back (XVII.113–236). But as the Trojans surge forward in greater numbers— goaded and promised rewards by Hektor—Ajax speaks in fear for both their lives to Menelaus (XVII.238–43). Ajax and Menelaus redouble their efforts, rallying others to help them (and, in turn, defending those that they have called to defend the body).

12. Powell argues that half siblings were generally portrayed as antagonistic toward one another in ancient Greece. *The Greek World* (London: Routledge, 1995), 219–24. If this general observation is correct, the teamwork between

Ajax and Teukros may be all the more exceptional because of their family relationship.

13. Lesser Ajax, if less physically imposing, is prominent in his own right. As explained in the catalog of ships, Lesser Ajax excels in speed and surpasses all Achaians with the throwing spear (II.527–30). Later, Lesser Ajax outfights Greater Ajax in one scene because "there was none like him in the speed of his feet to go after men who ran, once Zeus had driven the terror upon them" (XIV.520–22).

14. Eurypylos is introduced in the catalog of ships as third in charge of Diomedes's contingent and the son of a king (II.565–66).

15. This is in striking contrast to the usual relationship of the lesser soldiers to the leaders, in which the leaders merely use their followers for protection when wounded or bested. For example, compare Ajax's tactic in this scene to wounded Agamemnon's removal from the battle (XI.280–83) and Hektor's retreat behind friendly lines (XIV.421–33). For a discussion of the relative importance of the leading warriors in comparison to the nameless soldiers who supported them and fought by their sides in Homer's account of the Trojan War, see Powell, *Greek World*, 166–69.

16. "Now with the son of Telamon many people and brave ones followed him as companions, and took over the great shield from him whenever the sweat and weariness came over his body" (XIII.709–11).

17. The *Iliad* does not provide any indications of Ajax's age, making it difficult to guess whether he is likely to have his own wife and children at home. Though he is doubtless younger than Nestor, the text does not indicate whether he is part of the younger generation (like Nestor's sons and Diomedes) or the middle-aged set of warriors (like Agamemnon, Menelaus, and Odysseus).

18. The degree of Ajax's anger over the loss of the arms to Odysseus leads Brann to conclude that Ajax is "emotionally fragile" when it comes to the loss of public distinctions. *Homeric Moments: Clues to Delight in Reading the "Odyssey,"* 71 (Philadelphia: Paul Dry Books, 2001).

19. Agamemnon had refused to ransom Chryseis because, as he stated, he wanted to take her home to work the loom and share his bed (I.26–32).

20. Donlan, "Homer's Agamemnon," 111 (chronicling the conflict between Agamemnon's concern for his army and his personal dignity).

21. Although the issue is never broached, Agamemnon's lack of affection for Klytaimestra does not preclude a concern with her faithfulness linked to the legitimacy of his children and the potential for the acquisition of honor through future deeds of his descendants.

22. "In an atmosphere of fierce competition among men, women were viewed symbolically and literally as properties—the prizes of contests and the spoils of conquest—and dominion over them increased the male's prestige." Pomeroy, *Goddesses, Whores, Wives, and Slaves: Women in Classical Antiquity* (New York: Schocken Books, 1975), 25; see also Finley, *World of Odysseus*, 123–26.

23. Hammer chronicles the vulnerability caused by Agamemnon's focus on his own honor and the resulting rift with Achilles. "'Who Shall Readily Obey?' Authority and Politics in the *Iliad*," *Phoenix* 51, no. 1 (1997): 1–24; Hammer, *"Iliad" as Politics*, 80–92.

24. An alternative interpretation of Agamemnon's courage in these books would be that he begins to put himself at risk for the first time to try to disprove Achilles's accusation of cowardice. In either case, he puts his own life at risk to win honor through battle.

25. I postpone discussion of Agamemnon's disingenuous statement of intent to sail home in book II. Even in this instance, Agamemnon clearly associates leaving without victory with shame. He claims, lying, that Zeus commands him back to Argos "in dishonour" and complains that "this shall be a thing of shame for the men hereafter to be told, that so strong, so great a host of Achaians carried on and fought in vain a war that was useless" (II.114–15, 119–22).

26. Zanker, *The Heart of Achilles: Characterization and Personal Ethics in the "Iliad"* (Ann Arbor: University of Michigan Press, 1996), 5.

27. Donlan, "Reciprocities in Homer," 161–64 (on the social utility of gift-giving).

28. When Ajax takes on Hektor in single combat, Agamemnon honors him with the choice cut at the feast that follows (VII.321–22). Noticing a particularly daring bowman (Ajax's illegitimate brother Teukros), Agamemnon offers him rich recompense and explicitly notes the link between the prize offered and the honor that it denotes. He promises the daring warrior, if they win the war, "[F]irst after myself I will put into your hands some great gift of honour; a tripod, or two horses and the chariot with them, or else a woman, who will go up into the same bed with you" (VIII.286–91).

29. Agamemnon's offer includes seven new tripods, ten bars of gold, twenty cauldrons, a dozen stallions, seven women (skilled in handiwork) who had been his own prizes, the return of Briseis (with an oath that he has not touched her), and also—if they take Troy—as much gold and bronze to fill his ship as his heart desires, twenty women (second only to Helen in beauty), and the hand of any one of his own daughters in marriage (along with a portion of his kingdom). Schein notes that these gifts are in accord with "the normal value system of the poem, which defines such honor in terms of women, land, and other tangible possessions that Agamemnon offers." *The Mortal Hero: An Introduction to Homer's "Iliad"* (Berkeley: University of California Press, 1984), 105.

30. There are also situations in which Agamemnon simply reminds his men of the shame of cowardice (see, for instance, IV.242–49).

31. When Agamemnon is concerned that the army may not follow his commands (after Achilles's rejection of his offer of gifts for his return to the battle), Agamemnon reminds Menelaus that they cannot afford to be haughty toward the men who follow them (X.65–71).

32. There is a final proof of the persistence of Agamemnon's love of honor. In the penultimate book, during Patroklos's funeral games, Agamemnon steps forward to take part in the spear-throwing competition (XXIII.884–88). The inappropriateness of the army's commander taking part in the competition is evident from Achilles's reaction. Achilles stops the competition, awards Agamemnon the highest prize, and brings out an extra prize for the competitor who has lost the opportunity to compete for a prize (XXIII.889–94).

33. Brann reminds readers of Homer that Agamemnon is significantly more sympathetic in Homer's epics than in Aeschylus's plays because the Agamemnon of Homer never sacrificed his own daughter to obtain favorable winds. *Homeric Moments*, 199.

34. As Howland remarks of the love of honor in the *Iliad*, this work "is essentially an exploration of precisely this issue." *Odyssey of Philosophy*, 8; see also MacIntyre, *After Virtue*, 123–28; Finley, *World of Odysseus*, 20; Flaumenhaft, "The Undercover Hero: Odysseus from Dark to Daylight," *Interpretation* 10, no. 1 (1982): 9–42, 10 ("They wish to be excellent, and also to be recognized for their excellence, to have others behold and identify them in their gleaming armour").

35. Stoneman, "The 'Theban Eagle,'" *Classical Quarterly* 26, no. 2 (1976): 188–97, 189; Vermeule, "Greek Funerary Animals," *American Journal of Archaeology* 76, no. 1 (1972): 49–59, 51, 55, 59; see also Hobbs, *Plato and the Hero: Courage, Manliness and the Impersonal Good* (Cambridge: Cambridge University Press, 2000), 25 ("It is no accident that the lion is a favourite epithet in Homer for the proudly egotistic and volatile warrior").

36. Graziosi and Haubold note both the hypermasculinity and the problematization of the corresponding lack of self-restraint in the Homeric hero. "Homeric Masculinity: ἠνορέη and αγηνορίη," *Journal of Hellenic Studies* 123 (2003): 60–76.

37. Salkever, *Finding the Mean*, 174.

38. As Ahrensdorf notes, Agamemnon is unjust. *Homer on the Gods*, 138.

Chapter 2

1. Arendt, *Human Condition*, 194.

2. This is not to say that—particularly in relation to Achilles—a healthy debate over the nature and extent of their excellence has not occurred. As Lutz notes, "Among the most problematic figures in Homeric poetry is Achilles, who is called by his companions the 'best of the Achaians' and who was taken as a model of excellence by men such as Alexander the Great but who often appears to modern readers as a model of self-absorption, vindictiveness, and brutality." "Wrath and Justice in Homer's Achilles," *Interpretation* 33, no. 2 (2006): 111; see also Nagy, *The Best of the Achaeans: Concepts of the Hero in Archaic Greek Poetry*,

rev. ed. (Baltimore: Johns Hopkins University Press, 1999), 26–41 (defending the superlative excellence of Achilles); Ahrensdorf, *Homer on the Gods*, 186, 197 (arguing for Achilles as the best and most just of the Achaians).

3. Winn argues that the *Iliad* simultaneously elicits grieving for the warriors who die and lauding of the bravery of heroes. *The Poetry of War* (New York: Cambridge University Press, 2008), 11, 49. Evidence of the psychological trauma caused by war has also been observed in the *Iliad*. Raaflaub, "Conceptualizing and Theorizing Peace in Ancient Greece," *Transactions of the American Philological Association* 139, no. 2 (2009): 225–50, 227–30; Shay, *Achilles in Vietnam: Combat Trauma and the Undoing of Character* (New York: Scribner, 1994).

4. Weil, *The "Iliad" or the Poem of Force*, ed. James P. Holoka (New York: Peter Lang, 2003), 45–46; see also Simonsuuri, "Simone Weil's Interpretation of Homer," *French Studies* 39, no. 2 (1895): 166–77. Rachel Bespaloff, also writing in the context of World War II, similarly highlights the suffering that Homer brings to light in his poem, arguing that the ancient poet meant to demonstrate that "war takes everything away from us." Weil and Bespaloff, *War and the "Iliad"* (New York: New York Review of Books, 2005), 50, 72.

5. Oswald, *Memorial: A Version of Homer's "Iliad"* (New York: W. W. Norton, 2013), 66; see also Graziosi and Haubold, who point to the omnipresence of weeping women, *Homer Iliad Book VI*, 31.

6. Many scholars have focused on the questions of justice that Achilles raises in his wrath, arguing that his degree of wrath can best be explained by an outraged sense of justice. Ahrensdorf, for example, focuses on Achilles's assessment of Agamemnon's justice and Achilles's resulting estimation of the role of the gods in ensuring human justice. *Homer on the Gods*, 138. Saxonhouse describes Achilles's "*thymos* in defense of justice" as a "spirited insistence on what is owed as the guardian of justice for men who cannot rely on the gods." "Thymos, Justice, and Moderation of Anger in the Story of Achilles," in *Understanding the Political Spirit: Philosophical Investigations from Socrates to Nietzsche*, ed. Catherine H. Zuckert (New Haven: Yale University Press, 1988), 30. Similarly, Lutz reads Achilles as grappling with justice, which Achilles initially understands as distributing "goods and honors that are commensurate with the excellence or virtue displayed by each individual" to a later understanding of justice as "helping one's friends and harming one's enemies." Lutz, "Wrath and Justice," 113, 118. For further discussion of Achilles's complexity, character development, and role within the *Iliad*, see Cain and Nichols, "Aristotle's Nod to Homer," in *Socrates and Dionysus: Philosophy and Art in Dialogue*, ed. Ann Ward (Newcastle, UK: Cambridge Scholars Publishing, 2013), and Holway, "Achilles, Socrates, and Democracy," *Political Theory* 22, no. 4 (1994): 561–90.

7. Hammer, "Who Shall Readily Obey?," 12–13.

8. See Schein, *Mortal Hero*, 109 ("Since he himself no longer is interested in fighting Hektor and winning honor and glory, he will go home with

the possessions he still has left now that Agamemnon has taken his special gift of honor"); Lutz, "Wrath and Justice," 115 ("But having come to doubt the worth of honor, Achilles does not believe that the community of warriors at Troy possesses anything that could compensate him for the cost of his life").

9. Patroklos too feels the power of friendship (or at least pity) causing him to stop to assist a wounded companion rather than return directly to Achilles. When he finally returns to Achilles as the Trojans begin to set the Achaian ships ablaze, Patroklos fears for the Achaian army (not himself) and repeats to himself Nestor's admonition that he may prevail on Achilles where no other supplicant could "since the persuasion of a friend is a strong thing" (XI.792; XV.390–404).

10. Zanker, *Heart of Achilles*; MacLeod, *Collected Essays* (Oxford: Clarendon Press, 1983).

11. Schein notes the thematic importance of death from this point forward and details its presence in Homer's use of language. *Mortal Hero*, 129–30. The strength of the death theme in these final passages, however, also serves to underscore the strength of the passion that motivates Achilles. Ahrensdorf points out that Achilles's sorrow following the death of Patroklos has made him suicidal and that Achilles feels that "the deaths of his father and son would not have affected him more deeply than the death of his beloved companion." *Homer on the Gods*, 68, 83.

12. There are other references to Achilles's glory in these passages, but they are conclusions of fact (Achilles is winning honor) and not conclusions about his desire (Achilles wants honor) that are either made by a god (XXI.293–97; XXII.217) or the narrator (XX.493). Hobbs argues that Achilles has now regained his desire for honor "as a defiant means of compensation" for his own death. *Plato and the Hero*, 213. This conclusion does not seem to account for Achilles's relatively small number of references to glory, compared to desires stemming from Achilles's grief over the death of his friend.

13. Even when sleeping, Achilles dreams of Patroklos (XXIII.61–107); see also Schein, *Mortal Hero*, 155.

14. Lutz notes that Achilles's pity for Priam is aroused by "feelings for familial love" when Achilles begins to see "the old man as a father." "Wrath and Justice," 123.

15. In the second of these two glimpses, Achilles's speech is entirely devoted to expressing sympathy for Agamemnon's unhappy homecoming. It thus provides very little insight into Achilles's assessment of his own life or desires (XXIV.15–34).

16. Nagy concurs, explaining that Achilles would give up his glory for a safe return home. *Best of the Achaeans*, 35.

17. Only once is Hektor eclipsed by his father in the field: when Priam descends to make the sacrifices, prayers, and vows necessary before Alexandros's

and Menelaus's duel, Hektor takes second place. Once Priam has performed the ritual words and deeds, he returns to Troy, leaving Hektor to coordinate with Odysseus about the logistics of the impending fight (III.310–19).

18. Scully and Redfield helpfully explore the complex interrelationships among Hektor's roles as warrior, defender, future king, father, son, husband, and brother. Scully, *Homer and Sacred City*, 123; Redfield, *Nature and Culture in the "Iliad": The Tragedy of Hector* (Durham: Duke University Press, 1994), 55, 60–63, 119. Hektor is portrayed in more family relationships (son, father, brother, brother-in-law, and husband) than any other Homeric character.

19. Cairns's study of shame confirms that reference to shame implies concern with one's personal honor. *Aidos: The Psychology and Ethics of Honour and Shame in Ancient Greek Literature* (Oxford: Clarendon Press, 1993), 68–71, 95–100.

20. Alexandros is commonly known as Paris. Homer refers to him as both Alexandros and Paris but uses Alexandros far more frequently.

21. Brann also notes Hektor's mindfulness of the Trojan families. *Homeric Moments*, 95.

22. For a discussion of gender-related spatial demarcations within Homer, see Saxonhouse, *Women in Political Thought*, 21–22. Andromache's name, related to the Greek word for "man," may also indicate an unusually manly aspect.

23. This is Hektor's only smile. Graziosi and Haubold, *Homer Iliad Book VI*, 45.

24. Achilles killed her father and seven brothers, and her mother died soon after being ransomed from Achilles (VI.409–28).

25. While some scholars focus on Hektor's tender affection for his family, others conclude that feelings of shame or love of glory eclipse any love of family he might feel. Schein, *Mortal Hero*, 177–79; Crotty, *The Poetics of Supplication: Homer's "Iliad" and "Odyssey"* (Ithaca: Cornell University Press, 1994), 29 ("Far more important to the warrior than results is the conspicuousness of his fighting: Hektor insists on being seen in the front ranks, whether or not that leads to his death and the downfall of Troy, because that is what the warrior code demands"). Ahrensdorf highlights how Hektor fights both out of the fear of shame and for his family. *Homer on the Gods*, 104, 127, 128.

26. "Homer includes in Book VI of the *Iliad* a tender, indeed romantic, scene between Hector and Andromache. Love and concern are expressed by each." Saxonhouse, *Women in Political Thought*, 21; see also Brann, *Homeric Moments*, 95; and Graziosi and Haubold, "Homeric Masculinity," 69.

27. More than any other warrior in the *Iliad*, Hektor is spurred on to courageous feats in battle over the loss of a companion whom he loves or is related to.

28. The confrontation prompted by Hektor's response to his brother's death does not end Hektor's life because Apollo protects Hektor from harm one last time (XX.438–51).

29. Ahrensdorf describes Hektor as a "peacemaker who only continues fighting in order to save his people from destruction." *Homer on the Gods*, 86.

30. Even if he escapes death in the possible destruction of Troy, his life will be hard and lonely without a father to protect and provide for him (XXII.487–507).

31. Andromache plans to burn the now-useless linens (XXII.508–14).

32. Crotty observes one such moment when he describes Achilles's mourning at the end of the epic as like the sympathy of Homer, "who describes the deaths even of unimportant soldiers in a way that underscores their pathos—the grief inflicted by the death on father or wife, or the sadness of youth cut down in all its beauty." *Poetics of Supplication*, 99.

33. See IV.473–81; V.151–58; XI.241–45.

34. See IV.482–89; V.553–60; VIII.306–8; XIV.493–500; XVII.50–60; XIII.177–82; XIII.384–91.

Chapter 3

1. "[O]ne of his chief qualities, as Homer portrayed him, was adaptability." Stanford, *The Ulysses Theme* (Dallas: Spring Publications, 1963), 7; see also Steiner and Fagles, eds., in *Homer: A Collection of Critical Essays* (Englewood Cliffs: Prentice-Hall, 1962), 9. "Odysseus, a very different sort of man, is the protagonist par excellence of the shadows. While he may show well from time to time in the daylight battles, it is in embassy, ambush, and council that he proves most valuable." Flaumenhaft, "Undercover Hero," 9.

2. Redfield and Friedrich, "Speech as a Personality Symbol," 275–77.

3. Achilles may make a harsher judgment on Odysseus's use of speech in book IX: "As I detest the doorways of Death, I detest that man, who hides one thing in the depths of his heart, and speaks forth another" (IX.312–13). The target of this accusation is not completely clear because Achilles is also defending the directness of his own speech and possibly attacking Agamemnon's offer of peace.

4. Helen makes a less flattering reference to Odysseus's mental abilities, describing him as "resourceful Odysseus, who grew up in the country, rough though it be, of Ithaka, to know every manner of shiftiness and crafty counsels" (III.200–2).

5. Elmer, *Poetics of Consent: Collective Decision Making and the "Iliad"* (Baltimore: Johns Hopkins University Press, 2013), 100–4.

6. Lattimore translates πολύμητις as both "resourceful" and "of the many designs." For an exploration of the implications of Odysseus's most frequent epithet, see Detienne and Vernant, *Les ruses de l'intelligence: La mètis des Grecs* (Paris: Flammarion, 1974).

7. Given the paltry army that Odysseus commands (and its utter lack of noteworthy warriors), it seems that Agamemnon and Menelaus must have been primarily concerned to recruit Odysseus himself. Neither Agamemnon nor Menelaus bothered to recruit Achilles (and his fifty ships) personally: they delegated that task to Nestor and Odysseus (XI.764–73).

8. Odysseus, like Ajax, Achilles, and Nestor, has been awarded a prize woman. There is only one mention of Odysseus's prize woman. She is never named, neither narrator nor Odysseus ever give an indication of Odysseus's regard for or attachment to her, and she is mentioned only once in passing (I.145). Agamemnon calls Odysseus, along with six other noblemen, to his sacrifice before battle in book II (II.402–18).

9. Nestor publicly names Phoinix, an old companion of and father figure to Achilles, as the group's leader, but Homer indicates that Nestor places his highest hopes for the success of the mission on Odysseus. As he gives them instructions, Nestor looks "eagerly at each, and most of all at Odysseus, to try hard, so that they might win over the blameless" Achilles (IX.179–81). Odysseus's prominence is discernable throughout the mission. Not only does he take the lead as they come and go, but Odysseus communicates Agamemnon's proffered gifts to Achilles and, upon their return, reports their failure (IX.262–99, 676–92).

10. Odysseus's assessment that Hektor would be unlikely to let the Achaians run away is probably correct. Hektor has been careful not to let the Achaians flee at night because he wants to send his enemy home "in such a way that a man of them at home will still nurse his wound, the place where he has been hit with an arrow or a sharp spear springing into his ship; so that another may shrink hereafter from bringing down fearful war on the Trojans, breakers of horses" (VIII.513–16).

11. "With characteristic rhetorical skill, Odysseus confirms the transition of power which has taken place." Haubold, *Homer's People: Epic Poetry and Social Formation* (Cambridge: Cambridge University Press, 2000), 82.

12. One other passage notes that Odysseus is not among the younger Achaians (XXXIII.787–92). Some might suggest Odysseus's greater age as an explanation for his self-restraint and skill with speech. The text however provides no reason to believe that Odysseus is any older than Agamemnon and Menelaus (both of whom already have grown children at the time when the Trojan War starts), let alone anywhere near as old as Nester or Idomeneus. It seems thus that this factor cannot sufficiently account for Odysseus's unique set of characteristics.

13. Donlan, "Unequal Exchange," 6; Hammer, "Achilles as Vagabond: The Culture of Autonomy in the 'Iliad,'" *Classical World* 90, no. 5 (1997): 341–66, 358–59.

14. Schein also notes the dual function of Odysseus's persuasion in this scene. *Mortal Hero*, 139.

15. Flaumenhaft calls Odysseus's speeches during the Trojan War "prudential, as opposed to heroic." "Undercover Hero," 20–22.

16. In addition to the encounters discussed, Odysseus appears briefly twice more in this battle. Once, as he fights alongside the Ajaxes and Diomedes, Odysseus is described by Homer as fearlessly urging the army forward (V.519–26). Later, he earns a one-line mention for his deadly use of his spear (VI.30–31).

17. Stanford, *Ulysses Theme*, 72. Stanford argues that "the crucial verb is open to two interpretations. It was left open to Odysseus's defenders in post-Homeric controversies to argue that Odysseus had simply not heard Diomedes cry for help. Homer's own intention is hidden in the ambiguity." I find less convincing Stanford's argument that one should presume, based upon the fact that none of the other "heroes attached any blame to Odysseus for his conduct," that Odysseus did not in fact hear Diomedes. The text is also equally open to the interpretation that either the confusion of battle obscured Odysseus's action or that collective guilt over their flight might have kept others from mentioning the particular circumstances of Odysseus's flight.

18. One additional reference arguably suggests Odysseus's cowardice. After the initial retreat to their ships (the Achaians are pushed back to the ships once early in the book and again at its conclusion), Diomedes and Agamemnon rally the army. Diomedes then leads the army and eight additional named warriors back into the fight (VIII.261–68). Though we are not explicitly told that Odysseus is absent from this sally, his name is not mentioned among those following Diomedes back to defend the ships (nor is his name mentioned again in the book). It is plausible that Odysseus is not mentioned though present in this sally, but the more likely interpretation is that Odysseus (who is nearly always among those warriors explicitly named) did not reenter the battle after his flight. For whatever reason—and the text gives no clue—it appears that Odysseus did not choose to rejoin the fight.

19. Flaumenhaft aptly describes this quality of Odysseus's approach to battle: "Though he does not lack hearty spirit (*thumos*) in battle, still we sense that his heart is not fully in it." "Undercover Hero," 18.

20. Athena protects Odysseus's vitals, preventing the stroke from being fatal.

21. Odysseus reenters battle briefly once but only to help direct the army (XIV.27–134).

22. In fairness it should be noted that Odysseus's next epithet is "sacker of cities" (X.363).

23. Because these horses are newly arrived at the war, they are not yet accustomed to—and therefore more easily spooked by—corpses.

24. Stanford notes Odysseus's relative disinterest in glory for his own role in the Dolonia: "He is eager to get to work without any flourish of trumpets, and when his work has been well done, to go to rest without such fulsome congratulations as Nestor offers." *Ulysses Theme*, 28.

25. With little time remaining before dawn, the lack of public feast is arguably unremarkable because of the late hour. The detailed description of their bath, however, is less easy to explain.

26. In the *Iliad*—and perhaps also in the *Odyssey*—Homer both links and distinguishes Hektor and Odysseus poetically through his references to their bathing, an act both intensely private and yet carrying public significance. Odysseus, his family many miles and a ten-year voyage away, enjoys the only bath that occurs in the *Iliad*. Like the Night Raid that precedes it, this bath is thus a unique event in the *Iliad*. No other bath is actually taken, and only two other baths are mentioned. Both of these baths would have been Hektor's, but neither actually occurs. When Hektor falls at Achilles's hands—in the moment that his homecoming becomes impossible—Andromache is preparing a bath for him that he will never take. Hektor also mentions bathing during his book VI return to Troy, when he tells his mother that he cannot stop to take wine and make a sacrifice because he has no time to wash away the battle grime.

27. "Like the great combats, the ambush of Book Ten involves warriors in bodily conflict with the enemy. Courage, speed, and power are necessary here as on the battlefield. But success now requires, in addition, special qualities of mind: wit (*noos*) and craft (*metis*) (X.226), and an extraordinary sense of timing, virtues shared by spies, ambassadors, and counselors." Flaumenhaft, "Undercover Hero," 13.

28. Hammer, "Who Shall Readily Obey?," 14.

29. During the wrestling match "resourceful" Odysseus, "who was versed in every advantage," manages to reach a draw with the "huge Telamonian Ajax" (XXIII.708–9). The wrestling match drags on, with the champions matched: "Neither Odysseus was able to bring Aias down or throw him to the ground, nor could Aias, but the great strength of Odysseus held out against him" (XXIII.718–20). Ajax becomes impatient, giving Odysseus's craft a momentary advantage, but no winner is in sight when Achilles calls the match to a halt for fear that one of them will be hurt (XXIII.721–34). Immediately following the wrestling, Odysseus takes first place in the foot race, beating Lesser Ajax and Antiochus. Although Lesser Ajax had pulled into the lead, Odysseus "overhauled him close, as near as to the breast of a woman fair-girdled is the rod she pulls in her hands carefully as she draws the spool out and along the warp, and holds it close to her chest" (XXXIII.760–63). After Odysseus prays to Athena, the goddess makes Odysseus's limbs light and guides Lesser Ajax to slip. Odysseus, "great and much enduring," takes first prize (XXXIII.763–79).

30. Similarly, after Achilles's death, Odysseus wins Achilles's divine armor in a competition with Ajax (11.543–67).

31. Some might wonder whether Odysseus is motivated by greed. This possibility is strengthened by an insult that Agamemnon directs at Odysseus before the first battle of the *Iliad*: "you with your mind forever on profit." If one

applies this explanation to the prizes won by Odysseus, however, it seems fair to ask why it ought not to apply to Ajax, Agamemnon, and the rest of the soldiers involved in the Trojan War. Ajax battles Hektor, perhaps, not for the glory to be won but instead for the long cut of filet mignon to be bestowed. Likewise, if one accepts this logic, Agamemnon is motivated by the Trojan wives that he will drag away from Troy rather than by the honor accorded to the supreme commander of the victorious army in the Trojan War. Such an argument proves too much, and the glory-filled speeches of Ajax, Agamemnon, and Diomedes all demonstrate that honor and glory are the primary goal, with the things that denote it serving as markers of the distinction they have won. In principle, there is no reason why Odysseus could not differ from them in terms of desiring the prizes, not for the honor with which they are associated, but from greed. But without textual support beyond one insult, this theory remains tenuous.

32. Wrestling with Ajax can hardly be understood, even under the most amicable of circumstances, to be a risk-free endeavor. Achilles's concern that the contestants will injure one another and his decision to stop the match confirm this (XXIII.721–34).

33. Stanford notes Odysseus's "unique expression" and suggests that it indicates that "father of Telemachos" is the title that is "nearest to [Odysseus's] heart." *Ulysses Theme*, 44.

34. In the book IV reference it could be argued that "Telemachos's beloved father," denoting the boy's love rather than his father's, is an equally valid translation. Given the fact that the boy was a baby when he last saw his father, however, it seems more logical to allocate the love to the father who remembers his son.

35. Flaumenhaft explains how distinct this is to the practice of the other Achaian lords: "Odysseus is further distinguished from his peers by not sharing their attitudes towards their forbears. Others envision themselves in the eyes of their glorious fathers, as well as their glorious contemporaries. Whether revering them or competing with them, they somehow define themselves by them. . . . In the *Iliad* [Odysseus] does not boast of his ancestors, and on the voyage home he disguises himself under different family names. Other warriors address Odysseus as 'son of Laertes,' but in the *Iliad* neither he nor Homer uses the patronymic." "Undercover Hero," 25–26.

36. As mentioned in chapter 2, Achilles refers to Briseis as "bride of my heart" and continues on to describe the love that men bear their wives as the love that he bears for Briseis: "Since any who is a good man, and careful, loves her who is his own and cares for her, even as I now loved this one from my heart, though it was my spear that won her" (IX.336–43).

37. Stanford argues that Odysseus describes his own longing for home in this speech: "Here Odysseus speaks from his own heart, though with an admirable avoidance of egoism." *Ulysses Theme*, 44.

38. Odysseus's desire to be with his family is also a possible explanation for the difficulty that Agamemnon encounters in recruiting Odysseus. Agamemnon hints at this difficulty in his Hades encounter with the deceased suitor Amphimedon: "Or do you not remember when I came into your house there, together with godlike Menelaos, to rouse up Odysseus so he would go to Ilion on the well-benched vessels with us? And we were a whole month crossing over the wide sea, having hardly persuaded Odysseus, sacker of cities" (24.115–19).

Chapter 4

1. Unfortunately, a similar straightening of the geography of the story is not possible. Finley, *World of Odysseus*, 26 ("This is not to say that the travels of Odysseus in Never-Never-Land can be retraced on a map. All attempts to do just that, and they have been numerous from ancient times on, have foundered").

2. Benardete, *Bow and Lyre*, 99.

3. Benardete, *Bow and Lyre*, 13, 34–35. Benardete argues instead that Odysseus's homecoming can last for no more than a month, is blemished by unconquerable political upheaval, and leads to a voyage from which Benardete does not seem to find return a serious prospect. *Bow and Lyre*, 3; see also 103 ("For all his impatience to get home, it is not obvious that he will be at home once he is home; and this alienation is not due solely to the necessity he is under to ship out again"). Rather than loving his private life, Odysseus "cannot resist the enchantment of omniscience" cast by the Sirens. *Bow and Lyre*, 99. Benardete's focus on Odysseus's interest in knowledge is echoed, if in varying permutations, by others. Ahrensdorf, *Homer on the Gods*, 227 (noting that Odysseus has curiosity and longs to learn about "the strange and distant lands he visits and their strange inhabitants"); Ruderman, "Odysseus and the Possibility of Enlightenment," *American Journal of Political Science* 43, no. 1 (1999): 143 (arguing that Odysseus seeks enlightenment rather than homecoming).

4. Deneen argues that Odysseus has a strong love of home and wife and acts meaningfully in giving up immortality for them. *Odyssey of Political Theory*, 115 ("Odysseus leaves Kalypso's island because of an understanding of his limitations, his bonds to humanity, and his desire for homecoming"). In this Deneen stands apart from Benardete, who discounts Odysseus's desire for home to almost nothing.

5. Deneen, *Odyssey of Political Theory*, 19–20. Deneen views Odysseus's love of home as remaining in tension with both the hero's desire for immortality and his desire for knowledge: "Odysseus—having heard the Sirens, descended to Hades, tasted the moly plant, slept with Kalypso—will never be wholly content with the limits of the human condition, even if . . . he continues to view his choice as correct." *Odyssey of Political Theory*, 228–29. "As the Sirens

episode reminds us, humans may successfully resist the temptations of knowledge, the cosmopolitan gaze, the transcendent opportunity of divine sight; but the temptation nevertheless remains and, above all, it is a *temptation*, constant, irking, never fully overcome. There is something *desirable* about transcendence, a longing that even our eros for particular people cannot overcome." Deneen, *Odyssey of Political Theory*, 227 (emphasis in original).

6. Howland, *Odyssey of Philosophy*, 47. In Howland's account, Odysseus's voyage to Hades, with its various tales of death and pursuit of an immortal name, is pivotal to his development. Similarly, his many close calls associated with sleep and darkness, which Howland associates with death, are crucial to Odysseus's embrace of life.

7. Howland, *Odyssey of Philosophy*, 50.

8. Howland, *Odyssey of Philosophy*, 50.

9. Clay, *Wrath of Athena*, 152, 214, 152. Thus, for Clay, Odysseus's preference for home and family is an important motivating force that increases in strength over the course of the poem. Unlike Benardete, Clay credits the prophecy of Teiresias with offering Odysseus the genuine promise of an eventual peaceful death at home.

10. Clay, *Wrath of Athena*, 111.

11. Unfortunately, neither the *Iliad* nor the *Odyssey* answers the question as to why Odysseus chose to go to war in the first place. The only reference to this issue in either epic comes from Agamemnon in Hades, who incidentally mentions to one of the deceased suitors that recruiting Odysseus was difficult. Even this passage is ambiguous and might be interpreted to mean simply that Odysseus was difficult to reach geographically because of Ithaka's location (24.114–19).

12. For a detailed overview of the *Odyssey's* narrators, see Saïd, *Homer and the "Odyssey,"* 116–31. More than half the lines in Homer's epics consist of narration by his characters. Griffin, "The Speeches," in *The Cambridge Companion to Homer*, ed. Robert Fowler (New York: Cambridge University Press, 2004), 156.

13. Odysseus's use of speech supports the continuity of his character between the *Iliad* and the *Odyssey*. As Ahrensdorf observes, Odysseus uses speech effectively, both as a source of wisdom and "as an instrument—to gain the assistance of the Phaiacians and Eumaeus, for example, or to win glory." *Homer on the Gods*, 254; see also Griffin, "Speeches," 161 (noting the effectiveness of Odysseus as an orator); Nagy, *Best of the Achaeans*, 19–20 (noting that Odysseus's tale is "monumental" in scale compared to Demodokos's own song). Odysseus's storytelling has prompted some scholars to remark that he shares the qualities of a bard. Segal, *"Kleos* and Its Ironies in the *Odyssey,"* in *Reading the "Odyssey": Selected Interpretive Essays*, ed. Seth L. Schein (Princeton: Princeton University Press, 1996), 202–5; Ahrensdorf, *Homer on the Gods*, 202 (noting that Odysseus is "a singer of the deeds of men," including his own deeds); Saïd,

Homer and the "Odyssey," 116, 150 (noting that Odysseus's "words are said to provoke the same effects as those of the bard").

14. A wary reader observes that Odysseus has been "shown over and over again to be an accomplished liar." Saïd, *Homer and the "Odyssey,"* 151; see also Crotty, *Poetics of Supplication,* 161 ("Odysseus' speech might be expected to invite skepticism about its truth and, ultimately, about its value"); Ahrensdorf, *Homer on the Gods,* 202 (Odysseus is seen "repeatedly concocting fictitious tales about himself").

15. King Alkinoos does claim the reverse (11.362–69).

16. Saïd confirms that Homer warns the audience when Odysseus lies. *Homer and the "Odyssey,"* 184.

17. Another example is Odysseus's initial conversation with Polyphemos. When Odysseus shifts from giving vague answers to the Cyclops's questions to outright lying, he describes himself as starting to use "crafty" speech (9.282). This example, however, may be less dispositive than his interactions in Ithaka because Odysseus narrates the conversation with Polyphemos.

18. "They were destroyed by their own wild recklessness, fools, who devoured the oxen of Helios, the Sun God, and he took away their day of homecoming."

19. "But when in the circling years that very year came in which the gods had spun for him his time of homecoming to Ithaka, not even then was he free of his trials nor among his own people."

20. This question has produced some disagreement among scholars. Saïd confirms that the "story Odysseus addresses to Penelope of his adventures in Book 23 retells in indirect discourse the stories that he told to Alcinous, summing them up in little more than thirty lines." *Homer and the "Odyssey,"* 121. Benardete, who fails to note that the lines in book 23 are only an indirect summary of what Odysseus tells Penelope, disagrees: he concludes that Odysseus does not tell Penelope his entire adventure. *Bow and Lyre,* 96–99, 150.

21. At 1.13 (νόστου κεχρημένον ἠδὲ γυναικός). It bears noting that the operative verb for "longing" (χράω) can be translated with equal fidelity but increased intensity as any of the following: "having his heart set upon," "needing," or "wishing/desiring to possess." Lattimore opts for one of the least dramatic interpretations of Odysseus's desire that the Greek permits.

22. For a more detailed breakdown of both the chronology and the geography of Odysseus's voyage, see Saïd, *Homer and the "Odyssey,"* 100–8.

23. This subject is examined in greater detail in the subsequent chapter.

24. Arguably, Odysseus should have had the wisdom and the authority to forbid his men from landfall at Thrinakia. But, once landfall was made, the five weeks they were stranded were necessitated by the driving winds that made departure impossible. The loss of this time may indicate Odysseus's lack of wisdom, but it hardly seems indicative of a lack of desire to reach home.

25. Dobbs observes that Odysseus shows a new sense of moderation after his trip to Hades. In his interpretation, however, the incidents on Thrinakia point to Odysseus's newfound moderation of his spirited, honor-seeking tendencies rather than an overcoming of his physical desires. "Reckless Rationalism and Heroic Reverence in Homer's *Odyssey*," *American Political Science Review* 81, no. 2 (1987).

26. "I sacked their city and killed their people, and out of their city taking their wives and many possessions we shared them out, so none might go cheated of his proper portion."

27. "There I was for the light foot and escaping, and urged it, but they were greatly foolish and would not listen."

28. "And now I would have come home unscathed to the land of my fathers, but as I turned the hook of Maleia, the sea and current and the North Wind beat me off course, and drove me on past."

29. It seems that the king kept his visitors answering questions until Odysseus specifically requested to leave: Odysseus explained, "a whole month he entertained me and asked me everything."

30. Ahrensdorf observes that Odysseus's failures as a commander "lead to disaster for [his men] and for himself." *Homer on the Gods*, 214. Although Odysseus and his men seem to alternate in their imprudence during the voyage home, the underlying issue of Odysseus's failures in leadership (and consequent loss of the army that constitutes a generation of Ithaka's men) looms in the first half of the *Odyssey*. As in the decision to land on Thrinakia and Odysseus's subsequent ill-timed sleep, which permits his men to eat the cattle of Helios, Odysseus's prudence and leadership in this episode are highly questionable. I concede that the allegations against his leadership are serious, but the scope of this work forces me to focus on the equally complex issue of Odysseus's desire for homecoming. Therefore, I distinguish between the underlying desire exhibited by Odysseus and the prudence and leadership ability with which he pursues it.

31. At first, Odysseus seems to be motivated by curiosity, desire for a guest gift, or a combination of the two. Clay points to Odysseus's losses to Polyphemos as the key lesson that instills his curiosity with a moderating sense of caution. *Wrath of Athena*, 113. Odysseus's initial description of why they explore seems more motivated by the search for knowledge: "I, with my own ship and companions that are in it, [will] go and find out about these people, and learn what they are, whether they are savage and violent, and without justice, or hospitable to strangers and with minds that are godly" (9.173–76). His initial speech to Polyphemos, invoking guest rights, seems motivated by the desire for a gift but is perhaps better understood as attempting to procure the safety inherent in status as a guest (9.256–71). Clay argues that Odysseus's strong interest in guest gifts should be understood as related to international relations. *Wrath of Athena*, 116. At any rate, his inquisitiveness and desire for a gift lead him to this situa-

tion, but it is his eventual glory-driven announcement of his name that dooms Odysseus to a long journey and his men to death en route.

32. Odysseus's tendency to be overcome by his passions and spiritedness has been observed and even emphasized by some scholarship. Ahrensdorf claims that, despite his thoughtfulness, Odysseus is often "in the grip of the passions and especially in the grip of anger." *Homer on the Gods*, 23. Ruderman argues that Odysseus fails to reach enlightenment because he is unable to control his *thymos*. "Possibility of Enlightenment," 142. On the other hand, because he controls himself until he reaches the relative safety of his own ships, Clay highlights Odysseus's interaction with Polyphemos as an example of his ability to moderate his initial impulses through imperfect but growing self-restraint. *Wrath of Athena*, 123–24.

33. Arguably the language "and the seasons changed" could be read to mean that, after the first year, Odysseus remained for anywhere from one to three seasons. As the text gives no indications of which, for the sake of simplicity I am approximating this length of time to a year and a half, with the understanding that the precise time may have been a few months more or less.

34. Odysseus specifically warns his men of the weakness that accompanies hunger: "Come then, while there is something to eat and drink by the fast ship, let us think of our food and not be worn out with hunger."

35. "A grave housekeeper . . . told us to eat, but nothing pleased my mind, and I sat there thinking of something else, mind full of evil imaginings."

36. When Odysseus's companion Eurylochos warns him not to return to Circe's house, Odysseus becomes violently angry. His men restrain him, and he consents to permit Eurylochos to guard the ship. When the rest of the crew follows Odysseus back to Circe's house, Eurylochos accompanies them for fear of Odysseus's reproach.

37. Circe seems to have realized that Odysseus's labors have worn down his spirit. Indeed, the wording of her invitation reveals that she has spotted Odysseus's specific weakness: he accepts her offer of refreshment (and eventually forgetfulness) because his labors have brought him to a spiritless emotional state in which he despairs of return (10.460–65). Odysseus accepts the offer of refreshment at her table, but there is no indication that he rejoins her in her bed.

Chapter 5

1. Horkheimer and Adorno, *Dialectic of Enlightenment*, 45.
2. Horkheimer and Adorno, *Dialectic of Enlightenment*, 45.
3. Ahrensdorf, *Homer on the Gods*, 23, 217–23.
4. Lattimore's description of Odysseus's condition during his entrapment by Kalypso opts for a moderate rendering in English among the possibilities in

Greek: "strong" pain could be translated as "overpowering," "overmastering," or "overbearing" pain, any of which provides a more dramatic image of Odysseus being held in sway by his suffering, rather than merely experiencing a strong sensation.

5. Benardete, although he generally places weight on incidents in proportion to the length of the passages dedicated to their telling (*Bow and Lyre*, 45, 103), disagrees with this interpretation of the poem's emphasis. Rather, he argues that the narrative places more emphasis on the encounter with Circe because she is the middle of the nine adventures chronicled by Odysseus to the Phaiakians. *Bow and Lyre*, 63.

6. Benardete argues that the phrase "no longer pleasing" demonstrates that there was a time when Odysseus did not wish to leave Ogygia. *Bow and Lyre*, 36–37. However, there are multiple passages supporting Odysseus's longstanding unhappiness to be on Ogygia, and this is the only phrase that is even arguably open to interpretation that Odysseus's desire to leave is a new development. Moreover, the period referred to in the phrase "no longer pleasing" more consistently refers to the night before and not to the early years of Odysseus's time with Kalypso. In other words, this passage is most naturally understood to refer to the fact that, although by night the goddess pleases Odysseus (even though "it is against his will"), in the morning she is "no longer pleasing" when he returns to the beach to think of Ithaka.

7. Even Benardete admits that Odysseus "prefers Penelope to Kalypso." *Achilles and Hector*, 67; see also Deneen, *Odyssey of Political Theory*, 54 (concluding that Odysseus left Kalypso because "of his connections to other human beings, his love of family and home"); Howland, *Odyssey of Philosophy*, 48. Scholars have also posited a variety of other reasons why Kalypso's offer of immortality may not be appealing. Vernant argues that Odysseus rejects immortality because life with Kalypso creates only an "obscure, anonymous immortality." "The Refusal of Odysseus," in *Reading the "Odyssey": Selected Interpretive Essays*, ed. Seth L. Schein (Princeton: Princeton University Press, 1996), 188; see also Howland, *Odyssey of Philosophy*, 48 (describing life with Kalypso as life "not worth living—an eternity of anonymous isolation on Calypso's depressing island"); Deneen, *Odyssey of Political Theory*, 53 (describing immortality with Kalypso as "inglorious and uninteresting").

8. See also 8.457.

9. From the time they met outside the city, Nausikaa was struck with the possibility of taking Odysseus as a husband (6.244–45). She betrays her interest to Odysseus by slyly giving him instructions as to how to enter the city without causing gossip (6.255–89). Once Odysseus meets the king, it becomes apparent that Nausikaa's father would welcome Odysseus as a son-in-law (7.311–14). King Alkinoos mentions that, though he will not detain Odysseus against his

will, if he wished to marry Nausikaa, he would dower him "with a house and properties, if you stayed by your own good will" (7.314–15).

10. For example, Odysseus insists upon focusing on his dinner without interruption when King Alkinoos gently probes about his origin (7.215), and he welcomes sleep in the beautifully arranged bed prepared for him by Queen Arete's maids (7.334–43).

11. Odysseus wonders at the city as he makes his way to the palace (7.43–45), examines the king's house as he enters (7.81–135), and observes the inhabitants' excellence in dance (8.264–65, 381–84).

12. In both the *Iliad* and the *Odyssey* Odysseus emphasizes his limitations as a mortal, consistently emphasizing the superiority of the gods. Crotty correctly connects Odysseus's emphasis on his mortality with his recurrent admissions of the demands of his belly: Odysseus is "rooted in the vulgar and unremitting demands of the body." *Poetics of Supplication*, 135–37. Whether this is a positive aspect of his character is a matter of debate. Odysseus's acceptance of his mortal limitations—his failure to ask "the most far-reaching questions concerning justice, happiness, and the gods"—provides the basis for Ahrensdorf's critique of Odysseus's excellence. *Homer on the Gods*, 23. For Deneen, the uneasy acceptance of mortal limitations is an integral and positive aspect of Odysseus's character. *Odyssey of Political Theory*, 45.

13. Odysseus's vaunting continues for nearly another thirty lines. Even here, however, there is a note of moderation: he admits that Achilles's son, Philoktetes, surpasses him, and he exempts from his claim of supremacy both immortals and those mortals who rival the gods (8.207–33).

14. The "ironic assimilation of the victor to the vanquished in the comparison of the tears shed by Odysseus when he hears Demodokos singing of the sack of Troy with the tears of the captive woman about to be taken away as a slave as she weeps over the body of her husband is unparalleled." Saïd, *Homer and the "Odyssey*," 73.

15. Indeed, Odysseus's first encounter in Hades (with the recently deceased Elpenor) suggests that Odysseus is known among his companions for a strong attachment to his family. Elpenor asks Odysseus for burial and, presumably requesting the oath that he believes Odysseus will find most compelling, importunes Odysseus to assent and swear "by those you have yet to see, who are not here, by your wife, and by your father, who reared you when you were little, and by Telemachos whom you left alone in your palace" (11.66–68).

16. Segal too notes the relatively keen interest that Odysseus expresses in conversation with his mother in comparison to hearing about his own fate. "The Phaecians and the Symbolism of Odysseus's Return," *Arion* 1, no. 4 (1962): 41 ("Striking, however, is his calm acceptance of his death [as told him by the prophet] in his eagerness to speak with his mother").

17. Alkinoos surmises that Odysseus has a wife waiting for him at home (8.243; see also the speech of Euryalos, another Phaiakian who makes a similar guess, at 8.410–11).

18. The delicacy and graciousness of Odysseus's treatment of Nausikaa exceeds what is necessary to secure his gifts and return to Ithaka and thus speaks of a genuine appreciation of her qualities of stature, beauty, and judgment. Nor does it seem that his appreciation of Nausikaa stems merely from her physical attractiveness. The princess's good judgment, for example, in driving the horses as he walks beside her (6.319–20), is evident, and Odysseus comments to her parents on this quality: "It was as you could never have hoped for a young person, so confronted, to act, for always the younger people are careless" (7.293–94); see also Stanford, *Ulysses Theme*, 55. Stanford argues that Odysseus's disinclination toward entanglement with the princess lends credibility to Odysseus's claim to have been an unwilling intimate of Circe and Kalypso.

19. Stanford makes a related point when he distinguishes the development of the Odysseus of Homer from the many future reincarnations of the character: the latter "are outward bound, centrifugal, while in the *Odyssey* the force of Odysseus's heart and mind is essentially homeward bound, centripetal, towards Ithaka and Penelope." *Ulysses Theme*, 89. Benardete, no champion of Odysseus's desire for homecoming, admits that "Odysseus, no matter how much he might have profited from his travels, did not welcome them." *Achilles and Hector*, 134.

Chapter 6

1. To say nothing of female monsters and goddesses, the women that Homer describes run quite the spectrum, from the aged and regal Hecuba to the weakest of Odysseus's servant women, nameless but recorded as she labors and prays to Zeus for Odysseus's return (20.105–21). Even the servant women can prove useful allies or dangerous enemies. Both Eurykleia, the faithful nurse, and Melantho, the treacherous servant, prove powerful actors in the drama of Odysseus's potential for a successful homecoming. It is due in part to this quality of the *Odyssey* that Samuel Butler suggested (although the suggestion has gained little traction) that the *Odyssey* was written by a woman. For a concise discussion of the reception of his work, *The Authoress of the "Odyssey"* (Chicago: University of Chicago Press, 1967), see Winkler, *The Constraints of Desire: The Anthropology of Sex and Gender in Ancient Greece* (New York: Routledge, 1990), 129–30.

2. To point to only the most famous of examples, both Herodotus and Thucydides virtually scoff at the importance of the role that Homer ascribes to Helen in the Trojan War.

3. In comparison with surviving ancient Greek literature, Homer provides a relatively positive view of both the moral excellence and the importance of women.

Arthur, "Early Greece: The Origins of the Western Attitude towards Women," in *Women in the Ancient World: The Arethusa Papers*, ed. John Peradotto and J. P. Sullivan (Albany: State University of New York Press, 1984), 8–15; Powell, *Greek World*, 94; but see Finley, *World of Odysseus*, 25. Of course, comparison to other surviving ancient Greek literature is a low bar, and the "dramatic importance and emotional influence of women should not at all be mistaken for evidence of their equality." Pomeroy, *Goddesses, Whores*, 18, 30–31. Moreover, the indirect and dominantly masculine perspective, to say nothing of the gender injustice of the society as a whole from which it comes, provides a problematic vantage point from which to analyze these characters. A fuller discussion of these dynamics can be found in McClure, "Introduction," in *Making Silence Speak: Women's Voices in Greek Literature and Society*, ed. Andre Lardinois and Laura McClure (Princeton: Princeton University Press, 2001), 3–16; and O'Gorman, "A Woman's History of Warfare," in *Laughing with Medusa: Classical Myth and Feminist Thought*, ed. Vanda Zajko and Miriam Leonard (Oxford: Oxford University Press, 2006), 189–207.

4. Helen Foley underscores the importance of the role that Penelope takes in questioning visitors, overseeing the fulfillment of obligations as host, and managing communications among the powerful actors in Ithaka. She also notes that Homer at least suggests that the kingship will be transferred with Penelope, should she remarry. "'Reverse Similes' and Sex Roles in the *Odyssey*," in *Women in the Ancient World: The Arethusa Papers*, ed. John Peradotto and J. P. Sullivan (Albany: State University of New York Press, 1984), 62; see also Vetter, *"Women's Work" as Political Art* (Lanham: Lexington Books, 2005), 45. But Finley dismisses Penelope as inconsequential in both political power and even in the transfer of the kingship. *World of Odysseus*, 86–89. Saïd notes Mentor's commission as an indication of the limitation of Penelope's political authority. *Homer and the "Odyssey,"* 280. Heitman focuses on the role of Penelope's speech to epic as a story, arguing that her words are important for an understanding of "the plot, the characters, and the theme of the *Odyssey*." *Taking Her Seriously* (Ann Arbor: University of Michigan Press, 2008), 10.

5. Some have suggested that, with the cessation of such activity, Penelope should be viewed less as wielding a political office and more as managing a large household. Helen Foley, "'Reverse Similes,'" 62–66; Vetter, "Women's Work," 45. Whatever her official role, Penelope holds only a partially successful command in Ithaka and over the household servants. The people and some of the nobles support her, but clearly the suitors do not obey her. Within the household some of the servants are disloyal, and Telemachos has begun to assert himself in his relationship to his mother.

6. It should be noted that the Klytaimestra of Homer is not the Klytaimestra of the ancient Greek plays. Agamemnon has not murdered any of their children, and thus Klytaimestra lacks some of the justification for rage and disloyalty of the later reincarnations of her character.

7. Zeus and Athena condemn Aigisthos (Klytaimestra's new husband) for his courtship of Klytaimestra and his subsequent murder of Agamemnon (1.28–47). But Zeus does not directly condemn Klytaimestra, leaving open the question of whether he considers her an accomplice to her new husband's crimes or merely weak. Nestor and Athena (disguised as Mentes) mention to Telemachos Orestes's vengeance on his father's murderer (1.298–300). The story also surfaces, if only implicitly, when the bard Phemois begins to sing of "the Achaians' bitter homecoming from Troy" (1.326–27). Menelaus provides a brief account, but his version does not mention the queen's role (4.512–50). Agamemnon tells the story of his wife's betrayal to Odysseus in Hades (11.385–466).

8. Saïd notes both the obvious parallel between Klytaimestra and Penelope and the "uncertainty" surrounding Klytaimestra's motivations. *Homer and the "Odyssey,"* 123–25, 273–75; see also Vetter, "Women's Work," 41.

9. There is no completely satisfactory explanation of how Penelope controls her decision to marry. Finley, *World of Odysseus*, 89. Such freedom does not accord with known ancient Greek practices. Finley plausibly suggests that the suitors planning to usurp Odysseus's crown hope that through Penelope's voluntary choice the winner might gain "some shadow of legitimacy, however dim and fictitious." *World of Odysseus*, 89. The poem seems to portray a fluid system, within which Penelope could be pressured into marriage but is at least unlikely to be openly forced even by her "own grown son or parent" (1.249–51, 274–78; 2.130–37). It appears that, even if her son or parents had the authority or power to force remarriage, there would be some shame associated with using coercion. The suitors may also be reluctant to use force in order to avoid bloodshed among themselves. Permitting Penelope the authority to choose her husband seems akin to appointing a mediator to settle the dispute.

10. The suitor Antinoos refers to Penelope as "greatly resourceful" (2.88). He describes her as devious: she "holds out hope to all . . . but her mind has other intentions," and she uses her wiles to "torment the sons of the Achaians, since she is so dowered with the wisdom bestowed by Athene, to be expert in beautiful work, to have good character and cleverness, such as we are not told of even in the ancient queens" (2.91–92, 115–19). None have thoughts "so wise as those Penelope knew," and with them "she is winning a great name for herself" (2.121–26).

11. Helen Foley, "Penelope as Moral Agent," in *The Distaff Side: Representing the Female in Homer's "Odyssey,"* ed. Beth Cohen (New York: Oxford University Press, 1995), 104; Helen Foley, "'Reverse Similes,'" 61; see also Saïd, *Homer and the "Odyssey,"* 278; Brann, *Homeric Moments*, 257–59.

12. Murnagham, *Disguise and Recognition in the "Odyssey"* (Lanham: Rowman & Littlefield, 2011), 104 ("There is an underlying analogy between what Helen actually did and what Penelope feared she might be doing"); see also Brann, *Homeric Moments*, 154–55.

13. Helen is the source of her claims to have been tricked into leaving her husband, leaving room to question Helen's veracity. It seems reasonable to conclude that "in the end the poem leaves the question of Helen's moral responsibility and even the moral status of adultery open and in doubt." Schein, "Female Representations and Interpreting the *Odyssey*," in *The Distaff Side: Representing the Female in Homer's "Odyssey,"* ed. Beth Cohen (New York: Oxford University Press, 1995), 25; see also Worman, "This Voice Which Is Not One: Helen's Verbal Guises in Homeric Epic," in *Making Silence Speak: Women's Voices in Greek Literature and Society*, ed. Andre Lardinois and Laura McClure (Princeton: Princeton University Press, 2001), 20; Saïd, *Homer and the "Odyssey,"* 266 ("Helen remains enigmatic").

14. Scholars have filled volumes debating when Penelope knows, suspects, intuits, or feels Odysseus's presence and whether (and why) she delays in openly acknowledging him. Saïd, *Homer and the "Odyssey,"* 285–314; Katz, *Penelope's Renown: Meaning and Indeterminacy* (Princeton: Princeton University Press, 1991), 76–154; Murnagham, *Disguise and Recognition*, xi–xii, 87–108; Zeitlin, "Figuring Fidelity in Homer's *Odyssey*," in *The Distaff Side: Representing the Female in Homer's "Odyssey,"* ed. Beth Cohen (New York: Oxford University Press, 1995), 138–39; Winkler, *Constraints of Desire*, 155; Brann, *Homeric Moments*, 274–84; Austin, *Archery at the Dark of the Moon* (Berkeley: University of California Press, 1975), 200–38. Homer masterfully keeps her speeches, thoughts, and actions ambiguous, thus holding his audience in suspense about Penelope's knowledge. My reading is that she recognizes him, if not when she first hears his voice, at least quite quickly during their conversation in book 19. But Penelope has two reasons to keep her identification of Odysseus to herself. First, there are spies among the maidservants, who hear every word, and she does not wish to betray him to their enemies. Second (and this is what accounts for her continued reticence after he kills the suitors), I take Penelope at her word when she claims to fear that the man she recognizes as Odysseus might be a god who could trick her senses. Because detailed defense of this interpretation is not feasible here, I limit myself to the following observation: Penelope's recognition and certainty does not matter for the purposes of the claims of this chapter. Whether one interprets Penelope (1) as nearly certain of Odysseus's identity but silent, or (2) as unsuspecting and plotting with the aid of a stranger whose good sense she recognizes (independent of his identity), the outcome is the same. In either scenario her caution and attention to verifying Odysseus's identity set her apart from Helen.

15. This relates to the question of whether Penelope's excellence points to a view of human and female excellence that supports equality or difference feminism or perhaps points to an alternative. Michelle M. Kundmueller, "On the Importance of Penelope: Transcending Gender-Based Models of Private Virtue and Political Efficacy," *Polity* 50, no. 1 (2018): 43–71. Initially, it might appear that weaving Penelope could only accord with a difference-focused understanding

of female excellence, related to that found in Gilligan's *In a Different Voice: Psychological Theory and Women's Development* (Cambridge: Harvard University Press, 1982) or Tronto's *Moral Boundaries: A Political Argument for an Ethic of Care* (New York: Routledge, 1993). Indeed, Nagler has pointed to Penelope as a "generic woman" whose occasional "manliness" deforms her. "Penelope's Male Hand: Gender and Violence in the *Odyssey*," *Colby Quarterly* 29, no. 3 (1993): 252. If, as I argue, Penelope transcends cultural gender benchmarks in a positive way, the question that follows is whether Penelope then emerges "as a variant of the old man." Elshtain, "The Mothers of the Disappeared: An Encounter with Antigone's Daughters," in *Finding a New Feminism: Rethinking the Woman Question for Liberal Democracy*, ed. Pamela Grande Jansen (Lanham: Rowman & Littlefield, 1996), 135; see also, Elshtain, *Public Man, Private Woman*. The answer, I think, is "no," at least insofar as one also notes that Odysseus too emerges changed: he is not the "old man." I conclude by observing that "feminism's inability to reconcile its aspirations toward equality and its desire for distinction may reflect an insurmountable conflict within liberalism." Nichols, "Toward a New—and Old—Feminism for Liberal Democracy," in *Finding a New Feminism: Rethinking the Woman Question for Liberal Democracy*, ed. Pamela Grande Jansen (Lanham: Rowman & Littlefield, 1996), 171; see also Saxonhouse, "Political Women: Ancient Comedies and Modern Dilemmas," in *Finding a New Feminism: Rethinking the Woman Question for Liberal Democracy*, ed. Pamela Grande Jansen (Lanham: Rowman & Littlefield, 1996), 161 ("the liberal focus on rights and the individual can obscure the complexity of the issue, ignoring the private world's need of the public and the public world's need of the private").

16. Some scholars argue that the ruse of Laertes's shroud and fidelity remain Penelope's only claims to excellence. Accordingly, she should not be credited with protecting the household. Saïd, *Homer and the "Odyssey,"* 276–80; Finley, *World of Odysseus*, 86.

17. Brann, *Homeric Moments*, 261 ("They are alike in so many more ways, superficial as well as deep"); Murnagham, *Disguise and Recognition*, 103 ("When Odysseus and Penelope both finally give up their disguises, they recover a quality of *homophrosyne*, 'like-mindedness,' that is expressed in the text in a variety of ways"); Helen Foley, "'Reverse Similes,'" 69 (also observing their "mutual recognition of like-mindedness"). As Foley observes, "Numerous critics have commented on Odysseus's special ability to comprehend and respond to the female consciousness, on his 'non-masculine' heroism and on his and Penelope's special affinity with the androgynous Athena." "'Reverse Similes,'" 72. It also bears noting that Odysseus himself seems to come from a home that defies contemporary stereotypes about ancient Greek marriage and gender within the household: his father, Homer has explained, never slept with Odysseus's nurse from fear of his mother, and both of Odysseus's parents are emotionally distraught over their separation from one another at her death.

18. Penelope repeatedly ties her own reputation and glory to the continuation of her life with Odysseus, but she also expresses a keen awareness of how social behavior influences the reputation of individuals (18.254-55; 18.177-84; 19.123-28). She considers proper guest treatment crucial to reputation, as she explains to the disguised Odysseus: "For how, my friend, will you learn if I in any way surpass the rest of women, in mind and thoughtful good sense, if you must attend, badly dressed and unwashed, the feasting in the palace? . . . But when a man is blameless himself, and his thoughts are blameless, the friends he has entertained carry his fame widely to all mankind and many are they who call him excellent" (19.325-34). Proper behavior as a guest is also, according to Penelope, a matter of reputation (21.333).

19. Given the generally boorish behavior of the suitors, their willingness to wait—particularly as they are well fed in the interim—becomes more plausible when viewed as an accommodation of their own individual pursuits of honor rather than as a kindness to Penelope. "She takes on the feigned role of 'your future bride' to each suitor in turn." Winkler, *Constraints of Desire*, 141.

20. For an analysis of Telemachos's transition into adulthood, see Heitman, *Taking Her Seriously*, 50, 53, 62.

21. Odysseus has already been made sure of his wife's fidelity numerous times and by numerous sources, including Telemachos, Eumaios, and Athena.

22. A related but somewhat distinct common determination lies in the fact that Penelope and Odysseus identify the same goals for their joint protection: offspring and wealth. Odysseus displays one of his greatest moments of emotion in his reunion with Telemachos (16.190-221). Penelope is most often distracted from her grieving over Odysseus by her concern for Telemachos, and she expresses her heartfelt concern for her son frequently (4.703-5; 4.819; 17.38-42). Odysseus considers the wealth with which he returns home to be very important (as is demonstrated by his desire for gifts from the Cyclops and the Phaiakians and in his concern for preserving his wealth when he first arrives home in Ithaka). Penelope, for her part, worries about the dissipation of Telemachos's estate (4.686-87; 16.431-32; 17.532-38; 18.274-80; 19.130-33; 21.68-72).

23. Amphinomos is the suitor who "pleased Penelope more than others in talk, for he had good sense and discretion" (16.397-98). Odysseus (still disguised as a beggar), concurs that Amphinomos is "well spoken" and "prudent" (18.125-50). Odysseus singles Amphinomos out as the one suitor whom he tries to help escape before the "reckoning" (18.125-50).

24. The accord that emerges between Odysseus and Penelope at this stage does not depend upon her recognition of her husband. What matters in this scene (and in all Penelope's actions vis-à-vis Odysseus) is that the couple establishes mutual respect, sympathy, and coordination based on a recognition of the other's intelligence and suffering. This aspect of their negotiation is constant, whether Penelope (1) knows that she speaks with Odysseus and fears

that spying maids will overhear and betray them, (2) suspects that she may be speaking to Odysseus but fears that he may be a god in disguise, or (3) has no idea that the stranger is Odysseus but recognizes an individual of good sense with whom to plan.

25. Penelope says that she lacks *metis*—the very quality for which Odysseus is famous. *Metis*, the word for "crafty," "wily," "ingenious," "devious," or "clever," is at the root of more than seventy of Odysseus's epithets in the *Odyssey*. Saïd, *Homer and the "Odyssey,"* 228. Penelope tells Odysseus that she wishes to have a good reputation for *metis*: she wishes him to know that she surpasses "the rest of women, in mind and thoughtful good sense." As it is Penelope (and not Odysseus) who devises the plan of the bow, it seems that Penelope's claim to be without *metis* refers to a momentary lapse rather than a permanent dependence on Odysseus. Indeed, her reference to this quality emphasizes the couple's common reliance upon *metis*.

26. "The sympathy between them establishes a kind of emotional alliance, illustrating once again the deep similarity between them." Winkler, *Constraints of Desire*, 151. Winkler and others who support the contention that Penelope is already at least suspicious of Odysseus's identity point to the listening servant women (and other instances when something is heard from outside the room) as a partial explanation of why Odysseus and Penelope cannot openly discuss his claim to be Odysseus in this scene. *Constraints of Desire*, 149–51.

27. Odysseus seems even to plead this wealth as an excuse for the length of his absence (19.282–86) ("Odysseus would have been home a long time before this, but in his mind he thought it more profitable to go about and visit much country, collecting possessions. For Odysseus knew profitable ways beyond all other men who are mortal, no other man could rival him at it").

28. As Austin notes, their manner of reaching agreement under such difficult circumstances underscores the similarity of the couple. *Archery*, 231 ("Far from creating any confusion, what Penelope says [in book 19] is perfectly intelligible to Odysseus. The *homophrosyne* between the two has reached a remarkable level of cognizance").

29. "So I wish that they who have their homes in Olympus would make me vanish, or sweet-haired Artemis strike me, so that I could meet the Odysseus I long for, even under the hateful earth, and not have to please the mind of an inferior husband."

30. She continues her public accusations against Antinoos: "Now you eat up his [Odysseus's] house without payment, pay court to his wedded wife, try to murder his son, and do me great indignity. I tell you to stop it, and ask the others to do so likewise" (16.431–33).

31. Penelope explains that she has no desire to forsake "this house where I was a bride, a lovely place and full of good living. I think that even in my dreams I shall never forget it."

32. The gravity of this risk is communicated by the deliberate, mournful manner in which Penelope fetches the bow and prepares to announce the contest for which she is the prize (21.1–66).

33. Penelope's epithets and their translations are cataloged in Saïd, *Homer and the "Odyssey,"* 276.

34. For a discussion of Penelope's use of the metaphor of weaving and its relationship to her skillful use of questioning and deliberation as an effective political tool, see Vetter, "Women's Work," 31–61.

35. According to Heitman, both Odysseus and Penelope express "their deep-felt feelings" but neither ever allows "emotion to trump rationality." *Taking Her Seriously*, 107.

36. "No other woman, with spirit as stubborn as yours, would keep back as you are doing from her husband who, after much suffering, came at last in the twentieth year back to his own country. Come then, nurse, and make up my bed, so that I can use it here; for this woman has a heart of iron within her."

37. I have modified Lattimore's translation, omitting his nonliteral use of "virtue."

38. Stanford argues, "Homer always insisted that Odysseus's love of home was his dominant desire. . . . As Homer saw it Penelope was at the centre of Odysseus's affections." *Ulysses Theme*, 50. As Clay argues in support of considering the placement and focus of elements of the story as an interpretive aid, "[a] convincing interpretation of the *Odyssey* as a whole must at least attempt to take into account the proportions of the work as we have it." *Wrath of Athena*, 213–14.

39. As Saïd notes, similes "serve to establish a link between Odysseus and Penelope." *Homer and the "Odyssey,"* 73–74.

40. Griffin, "Speeches," 162 (commenting that in "the subtle psychology of this kind the epic comes close to the novel"); see also Doody, *The True Story of the Novel* (New Brunswick: Rutgers University Press, 1997), 3, 152 (relying frequently on the *Odyssey* to demonstrate the similarities between ancient fiction and the modern novel); Konstan, *Sexual Symmetry: Love in the Ancient Novel and Related Genres* (Princeton: Princeton University Press, 1994), 170–75.

41. Notable among such readers is Benardete, who argues that Odysseus does not long for Penelope during his journey and that the couple's reunion is not as honest, joyful, or complete as one might expect of husband and wife. *Bow and Lyre*, 63–65, 96–99, 143–50. Benardete is not alone: various scholars have argued that domestic life in Ithaka is not glory-inducing enough or that Penelope is too old, too boring, or too stupid to plausibly be the object of Odysseus's erotic desires. Finley, *World of Odysseus*, 25, 130–31; Block, "Odysseus Did Not Die in Ithaka," in *Homer: A Collection of Critical Essays*, ed. George Steiner and Robert Fagles (Englewood Cliffs: Prentice-Hall, 1962), 81; Bolotin, "The Concerns of Odysseus: An Introduction to the *Odyssey*," *Interpretation* 17, no. 1 (1989): 55.

42. "They then gladly went together to bed, and their old ritual"; see also 23.295–96 (mutual pleasure in conversation); 23.345–46 ("the heart of Odysseus had full contentment of the pleasure of resting in bed beside his wife, and of sleeping").

43. Apparent ambiguity in Homer's explanation of how completely Odysseus tells Penelope appears only in Lattimore's translation. I have modified his translation—usually beyond reproach—because it understates the completeness of the spouses' accounts. Lattimore omits the final "telling her all" that clearly appears in the original Greek lines (23.306–8).

44. Again, Homer's Greek is emphatic to the point of redundancy about the completeness of Odysseus's tale to Penelope. Lattimore's translation once again introduces an ambiguity that does not exist in the Greek, and I have therefore modified his translation. Homer used the verb καταλέγω, for which a primary meaning is to "recount, tell at length and in order," or "to tell a tale in full." Any of these alternate translations, particularly as the verb is followed by ἅπαντα (all), gives an accurate sense of the text's emphasis on the completeness of Odysseus's account. This translation and sense of the verb καταλέγω also comports better with Homer's general use. He tends to employ καταλέγω when one character asks another "for all the details" or "the whole story." The verb is heavily employed, for example, when characters ask each other about their experiences during Odysseus's trip to Hades. It is also the verb that King Alkinoos uses, near the end of book 8—and immediately before Odysseus speaks for four books—when he requests that Odysseus tell them his whole story. Saïd discusses some of the details of Homer's other uses of this verb, *Homer and the "Odyssey,"* 116–18.

45. Segal concurs that Odysseus gives Penelope an honest account of his adventures that corresponds to the story he tells the Phaiakians. "Phaeacians," 24 ("Yet on Ithaka he tells the full version of them only to Penelope, the person with whom his communication is fullest and most intimate, at the point of fulfillment of his return to humanity and his most important human relationship"); see also Murnagham, *Disguise and Recognition*, 127; but see Herzog, *Cunning* (Princeton: Princeton University Press, 2006), 29–30 (arguing that Odysseus deceives Penelope).

46. Odysseus is cognizant too of the possibility of more children with Penelope, as he shows when he accuses a fleeing suitor of wishing to have children with her (23.324–25).

Chapter 7

1. This discussion also relates to the extent to which Odysseus's family and household have direct public importance. This argument, then, has particular

importance vis-à-vis readers who remain unconvinced that Odysseus claimed his house for private reasons.

2. Donlan, "Reciprocities in Homer," 152–53; Raaflaub, *The Discovery of Freedom in Ancient Greece* (Chicago: University of Chicago Press, 1985), 32; see also Drews, *Basileus: The Evidence for Kingship in Geometric Greece* (New Haven: Yale University Press, 1983), 98–115.

3. How or why Laertes ceased to be king is never explained. Laertes is the only example of a living individual who is no longer king in either epic.

4. Further suggesting that Telemachos is not automatically heir to the crown is the implication that, should she remarry, Penelope's husband may claim the title. Why this is so, or whether this would be viewed as legitimate, is never explained. Do the suitors think the victor will have a claim to this title because marrying the queen legitimates a claim? Or perhaps the title flows to the wealthiest of Ithakans. It is also conceivable that the suitors envision that the one who prevails will be wealthy enough to amass military might such that others will be forced to acknowledge a new king.

5. Odysseus led the army from his region, but otherwise his duties or rights are not delineated. It is unclear whether Odysseus led the army because this was a part of his position or whether he was put in charge as the most able or the most popular. The likelihood of the latter conclusion is supported by the fact that the army that he led included neighboring areas outside Ithaka.

6. The opinion of the people is mentioned more than once in a manner that indicates that their leaning is a factor in Ithaka's politics. Haubold argues that political institutions in Ithaka lack permanency and structure: the people do not meet on their own accord, and it is easy for their institutions and "life among the *laoi*" to break down. *Homer's People*, 33; see also Hammer, "Plebiscitary Politics."

7. The plot of the last twelve books of the *Odyssey* is straightforward, but it contains many moving pieces. Slatkin agrees that "the narrative sequence of the remainder of the poem, though more strictly chronological, displays a complementary virtuosity of concentration, counterpointing discretion and disclosure in the actions of Odysseus and Penelope until the Odyssey's ultimate closure is achieved in the crucial convergence of events on a single day." She comments on the complexity of the interactions and relationship of Odysseus and Penelope but admits that chronologically the sequencing of the poem is direct. "Composition by Theme and the *Mētis* of the *Odyssey*," in *Reading the "Odyssey*," ed. Seth L. Schein (Princeton: Princeton University Press, 1996).

A brief recap of the sequence of events may facilitate analysis of Odysseus's desires in Ithaka. Upon arriving home in book 13, Odysseus does not recognize his homeland. Thinking himself still far from home, he weeps and then busies himself with protecting the treasure given to him by the Phaiakians. Athena soon comes to Odysseus, but he cautiously determines to keep his identity to himself. After she recognizes her favorite, Athena reveals Ithaka to Odysseus (to his great joy), helps him hide his treasure, and directs him about how to proceed. Before they part, Athena disguises the returning hero as an aged beggar.

Books 14 through 16 chronicle Odysseus's stay with the faithful servant Eumaios (who confirms and elaborates upon Athena's description of the suitors' position) and Odysseus's reunion with the newly returned Telemachos (13.392–440) (Telemachos, at Athena's prompting, has just returned from his voyage to seek information about Odysseus. When he returns, he goes first to Eumaios's house, where his reunion with Odysseus takes place). At Athena's bidding, Odysseus reveals himself to his son, and the two agree on the objective of ridding their home of the suitors. Book 16 ends with a series of short scenes preparing the plotlines that are about to collide in Penelope's house: Penelope receives word that her son has arrived home, the suitors plan Telemachos's death, Penelope chides her suitors, and Eumaios reports back to Telemachos on the situation in his house. After a second night with Eumaios, Odysseus returns (still disguised) to his own house in book 17. In the books that follow, Odysseus observes firsthand as the suitors, the household servants, and Penelope reveal their respective loyalty and virtue or betrayal and vice. Behind the scenes Athena incites the suitors to ever-greater levels of insolence.

By book 21, the straining plotlines are pulled to their utmost tension. At Athena's prompting, Penelope challenges the suitors to string Odysseus's bow and reenact her husband's trick shot to win her hand (22.1–79). Telemachos appears capable of stringing his father's bow, but at Odysseus's indication he steps aside. The suitors, unable even to string the bow, make increasingly desperate efforts (22.80–187, 245–72). Meanwhile, Odysseus reveals himself to Eumaios and his loyal oxherd, Philoitios, and they agree to help him defeat the suitors (21.188–244). When Odysseus finally takes up his bow, he strings it deftly and proceeds to shoot the target described by Penelope at the beginning of the contest (21.273–434).

In book 22, Odysseus first shoots the most insolent of the suitors, then proclaims his own return, and proceeds to purify his house of the suitors, their retainers, his disloyal servants, and the consequent bloodshed. After an emotional reunion with the household serving women, his prolonged reunion with Penelope follows in book 23. During this night Odysseus tells Penelope both that he must eventually depart to fulfill Teiresias's prophecy and that he intends to replenish their wealth through raiding.

Book 24 recounts Odysseus's response to the volatile situation that he has created at Athena's command. Having predicted the problem, Odysseus rejoins his father, Telemachos, and a few faithful servants and prepares to face the suitors' families. But the gods (who are at least partially responsible for the problem) intervene to set things right. Zeus and Athena agree that, the punishment of the suitors finished, Odysseus shall be king in peace, prosperity, and friendship (24.477–88). Accordingly, as the two factions commence battle, Athena intercedes: Odysseus obeys with a happy heart, and peace is established in Ithaka (24.489–548).

8. Earlier, when Athena (still disguised as a boy) tells him that he is home but has not yet lifted the mist for him to see this for himself, Odysseus is "happy, rejoicing in the land of his fathers" (13.250–52).

9. Before Odysseus wakes up, Athena has already planned Odysseus's punishment of the suitors and his use of a disguise (13.187–93).

10. Athena also suggests that he test Penelope (13.335–36). Debate surrounds the question of whether and to what extent Odysseus is dependent upon Athena with respect to the strategy and his disguise. Thus, for example, Benardete claims that Odysseus has no need of the goddess's divine disguise, but Clay insists that Athena's disguise is essential to avoiding discovery at an inopportune moment. Benardete, *Bow and Lyre*, 112; Clay, *Wrath of Athena*, 207. Ahrensdorf faults Odysseus for failing to reject the "comforting belief in divine providence." *Homer on the Gods*, 237. Finding fault with Odysseus's continued piety, which he contrasts with Achilles's passionate rejection of the injustices of divine providence, Ahrensdorf attributes some of Athena's commands to Odysseus. *Homer on the Gods*, 204 (killing all the suitors), 219 (keeping his identity secret from all family members).

11. Odysseus's initial decision to conceal his identity from Athena may make one question whether he was, as he claimed to be, in need of the goddess's warning not to rush home openly to meet a fate like that of Agamemnon (13.382–85). Without questioning the wisdom of Athena's exhortation, one may note that Odysseus seems unlikely to have revealed himself prematurely. His decision to test his father, even after all the suitors are slain, supports this conclusion. Clay notes that "Odysseus, we know, was not the kind of man to run home impulsively without first ascertaining what kind of welcome he might expect." *Wrath of Athena*, 205.

12. Kearns notes that Athena attempts to push Odysseus toward anger and violence against the suitors. She makes the suitors "more overbearing and arrogant" so that Odysseus's vengeance may be greater. "The Gods in the Homeric Epics," in *The Cambridge Companion to Homer*, ed. Robert Fowler (New York: Cambridge University Press, 2004), 69. Ahrensdorf, on the other hand, credits Odysseus's vengeance to a passion for glory and vengeance. *Homer on the Gods*, 223–27.

13. Deneen, also noting the intertwining of private and public in Ithaka, finds Odysseus more focused on the private aspects of his actions: "All of Odysseus's 'craftiness' does not go toward remaking ordinary raw materials into a piece of unnoticed furniture; rather, his work is the crowning achievement of his *oikos*, a place both private (familial), hence natural, yet also public, inasmuch as the fate of his *oikos* is also intimately bound up with the fate of the *polis* itself."

Odyssey of Political Theory, 39; see also 35, noting the entanglement of private and public in Telemachos's life.

14. In the meantime Athena goes to Sparta to prompt Telemachos's return.

15. As Fisher explains, "Slaves in Homer are not treated as mere property, or as beings beyond the moral system of reciprocal giving of honour, hospitality, and respect." Rather, slaves are "humans" with "admittedly lessened claims to status." Among Odysseus's slaves Eumaios "is the most notable of a number of exceptions in the poem to his own theory [that a slave has lost half his potential for virtue]; he is a *dmos*, a bought slave, who retains a remarkable capacity for displaying the proper *arête* of a trusted and relatively independent slave, and he will be rewarded for it at the end." "Hybris, Status, and Slavery," in *The Greek World*, ed. Anton Powell (London: Routledge, 1995), 54–55. The excellence of Eumaios (and sometimes also the oxherd Philoitios) is a rare subject of general agreement. Deneen, *Odyssey of Political Theory*, 62; Saïd, *Homer and the "Odyssey,"* 191–94. In particular, Eumaios excels in the virtues related to hospitality (and hence to piety), which the suitors lack.

16. Odysseus also takes great joy in Eumaios's loyalty to him, particularly with regard to the stewardship of Odysseus's herd of swine. At the close of his first day home in Ithaka, Odysseus drifts off to sleep as Eumaios heads into the stormy night to watch over the herd. Odysseus is, in the moment, "happy that his livelihood was so well cared for while he was absent" (14.523–33).

17. I therefore part company on this point from Benardete, who argues that the "narrowly political problem Odysseus faces is how to secure the throne for Telemachos." *Bow and Lyre*, 121. If this is an issue that Odysseus faces, it is only indirectly: neither Odysseus nor Penelope mentions the issue.

18. To be clear, Odysseus is not glorying in the wealth, magnificence, or strength of his house. Indeed, in comparison to other houses described in the *Odyssey*, "the reader is struck by its ordinariness." Saïd, *Homer and the "Odyssey,"* 197.

19. Scholarly opinion differs over the degree of culpability and vice of the suitors. On one end of the spectrum, Benardete (apparently dismissing their conspiracy on Telemachos's life and their intent to kill Odysseus if he returns) argues that their "series of apparently petty offences . . . do not add up to anything criminal enough to make the justice of their punishment self-evident." *Bow and Lyre*, 131. Attention to the details of their behavior, however, reveals that Homer portrays the vice of the suitors, not only in their implicit and explicit threats against Odysseus and his family but also in their manner of feasting and hosting strangers, beggars, and prophets. Their feasts, as Saïd details with great care, demonstrate their thorough lack of virtue: "By contrast [to other feasts described by Homer], the impiety of the suitors and their transgressions of the code of hospitality are revealed through the series of omissions, changes, and distortions of the normal literary presentation of the banquet that characterizes

the four accounts of their feasts." *Homer and the "Odyssey,"* 65; see also 122, 206–8, 367–72. It should also be noted that the suitors, though all participating in certain vices at certain moments, participate to various degrees.

20. This is not the first time that Odysseus has considered how to carry out Athena's command. He had quietly "devised evils for the suitors" while staying with Eumaios and discussed the plan with Telemachos during their reunion (14.111; 16.233–39).

21. Later, when Odysseus is insulted by the beggar Iros and the suitors arrange a fistfight between them, Odysseus has trouble determining whether to display more strength than would be congruent with his disguise (18.90–94). In any event, he restrains his full strength and manages to keep his disguise intact.

22. Before departing, Melanthios threatens to sell Eumaios into slavery and prays for the death of Telemachos, but still Odysseus keeps his exterior calm (17.238–58).

23. Athena takes the form of a bird during the fight.

24. Eurymachos responds to this speech with an apology and promises of restitution (and by trying to shift more of the blame to Antinoos), but Odysseus's response makes clear that no amount of payment will appease him until he has "taken revenge for all the suitors' transgression" (22.35–41, 22.60–67). Of course, in refusing the offer of Eurymachos, Odysseus does no more than what Athena has insisted upon.

25. The fact that Odysseus frames this as a domestic rather than public issue does not keep the suitors' actions from having both dimensions. I mean to highlight Odysseus's focus, not to argue that the suitors' actions weigh more heavily in one realm than the other.

26. Odysseus's response to one of the most sympathetic of the suitors, Leodes, provides a window on this mindset. Leodes is among the suitors who is happy to take a turn attempting to string Odysseus's bow. Indeed, he was the first to try. Yet Homer distinguishes this suitor by describing him as sitting "always in the corner beside the fine mixing bowl. To him alone their excesses were hateful, and he disapproved of all of the suitors" (21.143–47). Before slaying Leodes, Odysseus again frames the suitors' wrong as private rather than political, accusing Leodes of having prayed that "the completion of my sweet homecoming be far from me, that my dear wife would go off with you, and bear you children" (22.323–25).

27. Only two of those trapped are spared, and neither is a suitor (at Telemachos's indication of their innocence, the suitors' bard, Phemios, and Odysseus's herald, Medon, are spared).

28. Homer indicates that Athena "still was putting to proof the strength and courage alike of Odysseus and his glorious son" (22.236–38).

29. Flaumenhaft describes the distinction between Odysseus's battle to reclaim his home and the battles of the *Iliad*: "The battle is as dark and unheroic

as the attack on Rhesus [the victims of the Night Raid]: the smokey, tarnished weapons, unused for years, send forth no gleams; there is no boasting or exalting. This is a clean-up job. Odysseus expresses no regret—though some readers do—that Antinoos doesn't know who kills him. In a grim inversion, Odysseus is now compared to the sun, not sustaining life, but as the final killer (xxii.388)." "Undercover Hero," 39; see also Saïd, *Homer and the "Odyssey,"* 213–15; Segal, "*Kleos* and Its Ironies in the *Odyssey*," 201.

30. Ahrensdorf claims that Odysseus is in the grip of intense anger and violent passion, and he argues that Odysseus's passionate response arises from anger at the suitors and an intense love for glory. *Homer on the Gods*, 23, 203, 224, 252.

31. Later, however, when he orders the disloyal serving women killed, Odysseus gives an explicit command that it be done quickly "with the sword" (22.449–56).

32. Odysseus's order to Eurykleia is shockingly unclear. Odysseus wrongly believes that these women aided the suitors during the battle, and he knows that some of the serving women betrayed Penelope's nightly unraveling. But he does not attempt to verify the first. Nor does he do anything to be sure that the women whose deaths he has ordered are the same ones who betrayed Penelope. It is their nightly betrayal in the suitors' beds that he has foremost in mind as he commands their deaths, perhaps partially due to (if not excused by) the giddy manner in which they went out to meet the suitors on the prior night and the implication of complicity in this manner.

33. While Odysseus is absent, his son (filled with resentment against the maids) and the servants disobey, hanging the women, and then torture Melanthios as they kill him (22.461–76).

34. Deneen makes an apt comparison between Odysseus's wrath at the end of the *Odyssey* and Achilles's wrath at the end of the *Iliad*. He does not however note the distinction in scope and degree of the consequences of their wrath. My reading further differs from his in that he finds that Odysseus only regains his self-restraint with difficulty: according to Deneen, Odysseus is more immoderate at the end of the epic than at any other point in either poem. *Odyssey of Political Theory*, 64–65.

35. Stanford justifies Odysseus's violence against both suitors and servants via reference to cultural context: "As far as archaic ethics was concerned, usurpers and traitors were beyond the pale of kindness." *Ulysses Theme*, 32. Notwithstanding any truth in this comment, the epic nevertheless invites our evaluation of the justice of Odysseus's manner of reclaiming his home. At least insofar as the *Iliad* invites judgment on the evils of war, Odysseus's homecoming should not escape similar scrutiny.

36. Benardete interprets Odysseus's agenda differently. Discounting the possibility that Odysseus desires to spend time with his family, Benardete argues

instead that "once he kills the suitors, Odysseus becomes remarkably indifferent to the future." *Bow and Lyre*, 137.

37. For a discussion on the relative legitimacy of warfare, piracy, and trade in Homer and ancient Greece, see Souza, "Greek Piracy," in *The Greek World*, ed. Anton Powell (London: Routledge, 1995), 179–98.

38. As they eat in Dolios's home, the people of Ithaka learn of their dead sons and brothers and "with groaning and outcry" gather the bodies from Odysseus's house (24.412–19). They gather in an assembly, which results in more than half of them taking up arms and heading toward Odysseus (24.420–71).

39. "I will tell you how it is proper. Now that noble Odysseus has punished the suitors, let them make oaths of faith and friendship, and let him be king always; and let us make them forget the death of their brothers and sons, and let them be friends with each other, as in times past, and let them have prosperity and peace in abundance."

40. Ahrensdorf, *Homer on the Gods*, 204, 252.

41. Odysseus's preference to depart or stay and his subsequent prospects for a peaceful old age in Ithaka are debated issues. Throughout his interpretation, Benardete focuses on the brevity of Odysseus's stay in Ithaka and implies—though he does not quite say so much—that Odysseus (having no real desire to be with his family in Ithaka) wishes to leave again as soon as possible and be gone as long as possible. *Bow and Lyre*, 113, 146, 152. At the other end of the spectrum of possible interpretations lies Brann's sanguine assessment of Odysseus's future in Ithaka: "We know that Odysseus has one more trip to make. . . . And then peace, plenty, mutual love, and a long life do indeed ensue. . . . The Homeric Odysseus comes home for good to rule his island, guide its promising crown prince, and live to a ripe old age with his peerless wife, his partner." *Homeric Moments*, 114; see also Stanford, *Ulysses Theme*, 41; Saïd, *Homer and the "Odyssey,"* 365; Purves, "Unmarked Space: Odysseus and the Inland Journey," *Arethusa* 39, no. (Winter 2006): 1–20.

42. Odysseus has good reason to believe Teiresias's prophecy, as everything else that the prophet predicted about his journey home and the condition of his household when he arrived has been fulfilled.

Conclusion

1. Arendt, *Human Condition*, 23–25.
2. Arendt, *Human Condition*, 13, 30–32, 101, 176.
3. Arendt, *Human Condition*, 38–39.
4. Concurring in the comparison of the *Odyssey* to a novel, Brann argues that Odysseus's "relationships with women could not be more complex were

they an invention of a contemporary novelist, and his wife is his one and only mortal equal." *Homeric Moments*, 25.

5. Arendt, *Human Condition*, 41.

6. Arendt, *Human Condition*, 49. Arendt repeats her claim that an exclusively private life and humanity are not mutually possible. *Human Condition*, 64. Aristotle, on the other hand, not only defines slaves as human but explicitly addresses the possibility of virtuous slaves.

7. Arendt, *Human Condition*, 188, 201.

8. Arendt, *Human Condition*, 112.

9. Arendt, *Human Condition*, 52.

10. Arendt, *Human Condition*, 193.

11. Arendt, *Human Condition*, 194.

12. Indeed, Odysseus forgoes presence at home for the sake of the wealth of his home. Nor is he ashamed or unaware of this. He justifies his twenty-year absence to Penelope on the basis of the wealth with which he returns.

13. Clearly, this is a longstanding character trait. During the Trojan War Odysseus steals information and horses, acting as a thief in support of the war. His thieving and raiding continue during the voyage home.

14. When she meets him in Ithaka, Athena draws attention to this characteristic. She tells Odysseus by way of praise, "You wretch, so devious, never weary of tricks, then you would not even in your own country give over your ways of deceiving and your thievish tales. They are near to your nature" (13.293–95).

15. Stanford praises Odysseus's moderation, arguing that the value of moderation is Homer's overarching lesson: "In so far as Homer has any moral message in the *Iliad* and the *Odyssey* it comes to this: only by [Odysseus's] self-control and moderation can men achieve victory in life." *Ulysses Theme*, 34.

16. The suitors are cruel and threatening to Odysseus when he is disguised as a beggar. They receive Telemachos's guest—who is doubly due respect as a guest and a prophet—with insolence. Moreover, their table manners are atrocious in a manner that indicates not only a lack of civility but also impiety.

17. Odysseus's violence should also be considered in light of his future need to depart in order to fulfill Teiresias's prophecy and thereby once again render his family, household, and kingdom vulnerable. Given this, self-defense, albeit very broadly understood, joins Athena's command as a justification of Odysseus's actions.

18. Odysseus promises Eumaios and his loyal oxherd, Philoitios, their own land, homes, and wives and to treat them as brothers of Telemachos if they are successful in their battle with the suitors (20.209–16). Eumaios was born the son of a king but came to be Odysseus's servant after he was captured and sold into slavery as a small child. Philoitios's origins are not provided.

19. Deneen eloquently frames the issue presented by the juxtaposition of the epics: "The *Iliad*'s true counterpart remains: the *Odyssey* represents not only

an alternative to the *Iliad*'s vision, but also the first full-length commentary on and critique of the heroism of Achilles. . . . But the larger argument is, in fact, captured in the very epics about the two respective heroes and the question they pose: which of their lives, as captured and interpreted through song, constitutes the greatest *kleos* and makes one or the other finally the best of the Achaians?" *Odyssey of Political Theory*, 55–56.

20. Stanford, I believe, overstates the case and yet points to an important distinction when, after reviewing the limitations of various Achaian heroes, he argues that the "only kind of man that one can trust to bring a complex crisis to a safe conclusion is a man like Odysseus. Passionate heroism, glorious as it is, disrupts society and causes senseless destruction." *Ulysses Theme*, 40. Although this assessment ignores his faults, it does reflect Odysseus's efficacy within the Achaian army as a whole.

21. I rely upon and quote Peter L. Phillips Simpson's translation of *The Politics of Aristotle* throughout.

22. Ann Ward, "Friendship and Politics in Aristotle's *Nicomachean Ethics*," *European Journal of Political Theory* 10, no. 4 (2011): 443–62; Ann Ward, "Mothering and the Sacrifice of Self: Women and Friendship in Aristotle's *Nicomachean Ethics*," *Thirdspace* 7, no. 2 (2008): 32–57.

23. The virtues of children, on the other hand, are "incomplete" (1260a2–24).

24. "For since any household is part of a city and these are parts of a household, and since the virtues of a part must look to the virtue of the whole, the education of children and women must be undertaken with an eye to the regime, at least so it must be if having children and women who are serious makes a difference to having a serious city. But it must make a difference, for women are half the free and from children come those who share in the regime."

25. Swanson, *Public and Private*, 28, 45–68; see also Nichols, *Citizens and Statesmen: A Study of Aristotle's "Politics"* (Lanham: Rowman & Littlefield, 1992), 13–14, 29–33.

26. Salkever, "Women, Soldiers, Citizens," 240; Salkever, *Finding the Mean*, 174.

27. Nor does household life or even slavery preclude honor. As Aristotle explains, "Work differs from work, with some enjoying more honor and others being more necessary; as the proverb has it: 'slave before slave and master before master'" (1255b20).

28. I thus disagree with MacIntyre, who argues that for Homer the warrior stands alone as the "paradigm of excellence." *After Virtue*, 182; see also 122–30. MacIntyre's understanding of this warrior excellence rests on the conception of the warrior as striving for glory and public recognition. My conclusion—though I focus on the underlying loves rather than on the virtues they produce—is closer to that of Clay, who sees Odysseus as presenting an alternative to the

warrior's life and excellence: "According to the *Odyssey*, the best of the Greeks are necessarily Achilles and Odysseus. The definition of 'best' no longer centers on rank, power, and strength, as it did in the dispute between Agamemnon and Achilles, but rather on two modes of existence, two conceptions of the world and man's relation to it, embodied in Achilles and Odysseus, and summed up in part in the contrast between *bie* and *metis*." *Wrath of Athena*, 105.

Bibliography

Adkins, Arthur W. H. *Merit and Responsibility: A Study in Greek Values*. London: Oxford University Press, 1960.

Ahrensdorf, Peter J. *Homer on the Gods and Human Virtue: Creating the Foundations of Classical Civilization*. New York: Cambridge University Press, 2014.

Arendt, Hannah. *The Human Condition*. Chicago: University of Chicago Press, 1998.

Aristotle. *The Politics of Aristotle*. Translated by Peter L. Phillips Simpson. Chapel Hill: University of North Carolina Press, 1997.

Arthur, Maryline B. "Early Greece: The Origins of the Western Attitude towards Women." In *Women in the Ancient World: The Arethusa Papers*, edited by John Peradotto and J. P. Sullivan, 7–58. Albany: State University of New York Press, 1984.

Austin, Norman. *Archery at the Dark of the Moon*. Berkeley: University of California Press, 1975.

Balot, Ryan K., ed. *A Companion to Greek and Roman Political Thought*. Chichester: Wiley-Blackwell, 2013.

Benardete, Seth. *Achilles and Hector: The Homeric Hero*. South Bend: St. Augustine Press, 2005.

———. *The Bow and the Lyre: A Platonic Reading of the "Odyssey."* Lanham: Rowman & Littlefield, 2008.

Benhabib, Seyla. "Feminist Theory and Hannah Arendt's Concept of Public Space." *History of the Human Sciences* 6, no. 2 (1993): 97–114.

———. "The Pariah and Her Shadow: Hannah Arendt's Biography of Rachel Varnhagen." In *Feminist Interpretations of Hannah Arendt*, edited by Bonnie Honig, 83–104. University Park: Pennsylvania State University Press, 1995.

Bickford, Susan. "Constructing Inequality: City Spaces and the Architecture of Citizenship." *Political Theory* 28, no. 3 (2000): 355–76.

Block, Ernst. "Odysseus Did Not Die in Ithaka." In *Homer: A Collection of Critical Essays*, edited by George Steiner and Robert Fagles, 81–85. Englewood Cliffs: Prentice-Hall, 1962.

Bolotin, David. "The Concerns of Odysseus: An Introduction to the *Odyssey*." *Interpretation* 17, no. 1 (1989): 41–58.
Brann, Eva. *Homeric Moments: Clues to Delight in Reading the "Odyssey."* Philadelphia: Paul Dry Books, 2001.
Burkert, Walter. *Structure and History in Greek Mythology and Ritual*. Los Angeles: University of California Press, 1979.
Butler, Samuel. *The Authoress of the "Odyssey."* Chicago: University of Chicago Press, 1967.
Cain, Patrick N., and Mary P. Nichols. "Aristotle's Nod to Homer." In *Socrates and Dionysus: Philosophy and Art in Dialogue*, edited by Ann Ward, 54–73. Newcastle, UK: Cambridge Scholars Publishing, 2013.
Cairns, Douglas. *Aidos: The Psychology and Ethics of Honour and Shame in Ancient Greek Literature*. Oxford: Clarendon Press, 1993.
Calhoun, Craig, and John McGowan, eds. *Hannah Arendt and the Meaning of Politics*. Minneapolis: University of Minnesota Press, 1997.
Clay, Jenny Strauss. *Homer's Trojan Theater: Space, Vision, and Memory in the "Iliad."* Cambridge: Cambridge University Press, 2011.
———. *The Wrath of Athena: Gods and Men in the "Odyssey."* Princeton: Princeton University Press, 1983.
Cohen, Beth, ed. *The Distaff Side: Representing the Female in Homer's "Odyssey."* New York: Oxford University Press, 1995.
Crotty, Kevin. *The Poetics of Supplication: Homer's "Iliad" and "Odyssey."* Ithaca: Cornell University Press, 1994.
Deneen, Patrick J. *The Odyssey of Political Theory: The Politics of Departure and Return*. Lanham: Rowman & Littlefield, 2003.
Detienne, Marcel, and Jean-Pierre Vernant. *Les ruses de l'intelligence: La* mètis *des Grecs*. Paris: Flammarion, 1974.
Dietz, Mary G. *Turning Operations: Feminism, Arendt, and Politics*. New York: Routledge, 2002.
Dobbs, Darrell. "Reckless Rationalism and Heroic Reverence in Homer's *Odyssey*." *American Political Science Review* 81, no. 2 (1987): 491–508.
Donlan, Walter. "Character Structure in Homer's *Iliad*." *Journal of General Education* 21, no. 4 (1970): 259–69.
———. "Homer's Agamemnon." *Classical World* 65, no. 4 (1971): 109–15.
———. "Kin-Groups in the Homeric Epics." *Classical World* 101, no. 1 (2007): 29–39.
———. "Reciprocities in Homer." *Classical World* 75, no. 3 (1982): 137–75.
———. "The Unequal Exchange between Glaucus and Diomedes in Light of the Homeric Gift-Economy." *Phoenix* 43, no. 1 (1989): 1–15.
Doody, Margaret Anne. *The True Story of the Novel*. New Brunswick: Rutgers University Press, 1997.

Drews, Robert. *Basileus: The Evidence for Kingship in Geometric Greece*. New Haven: Yale University Press, 1983.
Eco, Umberto. *The Limits of Interpretation*. Indianapolis: Indiana University Press, 1990.
Elmer, David. "Helen Epigrammatopoios." *Classical Antiquity* 24, no. 1 (2005): 1–39.
———. "*Kita* and *Kosmos*: The Poetics of Ornamentation in Bosniac and Homeric Epic." *Journal of American Folklore* 123, no. 489 (2010): 276–303.
———. *Poetics of Consent: Collective Decision Making and the "Iliad."* Baltimore: Johns Hopkins University Press, 2013.
Elshtain, Jean Bethke. "The Mothers of the Disappeared: An Encounter with Antigone's Daughters." In *Finding a New Feminism: Rethinking the Woman Question for Liberal Democracy*, edited by Pamela Grande Jansen, 129–48. Lanham: Rowman & Littlefield, 1996.
———. "Political Children: Reflections on Hannah Arendt's Distinction between Public and Private Life." In *Reconstructing Political Theory: Feminist Perspectives*, edited by Mary Lyndon Shanley and Narayan Uma, 109–43. University Park: Pennsylvania State University Press, 1997.
———. *Public Man, Private Woman: Women in Social and Political Thought*. Princeton: Princeton University Press, 1981.
Euben, J. Peter. "Arendt's Hellenism." In *The Cambridge Companion to Hannah Arendt*, edited by Dana Villa, 151–64. Cambridge: Cambridge University Press, 2000.
———. "Justice and the Oresteia." *American Political Science Review* 76, no. 1 (1982): 22–33.
Falkner, Thomas, Nancy Felson, and David Konstan, eds. *Contextualizing Classics: Ideology, Performance, Dialogue—Essays in Honor of John J. Peradotto*, Lanham: Rowman & Littlefield, 1999.
Finley, M. I. *The World of Odysseus*. New York: New York Review of Books, 1954.
Fisher, Nick. "Hybris, Status, and Slavery." In *The Greek World*, edited by Anton Powell, 44–84. London: Routledge, 1995.
Flaumenhaft, Mera J. "The Undercover Hero: Odysseus from Dark to Daylight." *Interpretation* 10, no. 1 (1982): 9–42.
Foley, Helen P. "Penelope as Moral Agent." In *The Distaff Side: Representing the Female in Homer's "Odyssey,"* edited by Beth Cohen, 93–116. New York: Oxford University Press, 1995.
———. "'Reverse Similes' and Sex Roles in the *Odyssey*." In *Women in the Ancient World: The Arethusa Papers*, edited by John Peradotto and J. P. Sullivan, 59–78. Albany: State University of New York Press, 1984.
Foley, John. "Guslar and Aoidos: Traditional Register in South Slavic and Homeric Epic." *Transactions of the American Philological Association* 126 (1996): 11–41.

———. *Homer's Traditional Art*. University Park: Pennsylvania State University Press, 1999.

———. "'Reading' Homer through Oral Tradition." *College Literature* 34, no. 2 (2007): 1–28.

———. "Signs, Texts, and Oral Tradition." *Journal of Folklore Research* 33, no. 1 (1996): 21–29.

Friedrich, Paul, and James Redfield. "Contra Messing." *Language* 57, no. 4 (1981): 901–3.

Gilligan, Carol. *In a Different Voice: Psychological Theory and Women's Development*. Cambridge: Harvard University Press, 1982.

Graves, Robert. *Homer's Daughter*. New York: Doubleday, 1955.

Graziosi, Barbara. *Homer*. Oxford: Oxford University Press, 2016.

Graziosi, Barbara, and Johannes Haubold. *Homer Iliad Book VI*. Cambridge: Cambridge University Press, 2010.

———. "Homeric Masculinity: ἠνορέη and αγηνορίη." *Journal of Hellenic Studies* 123 (2003): 60–76.

Griffin, Jasper. "The Speeches." In *The Cambridge Companion to Homer*, edited by Robert Fowler, 156–70. New York: Cambridge University Press, 2004.

Hamilton, Alexander, John Jay, and James Madison. *The Federalist*. Gideon ed. Indianapolis: Liberty Fund, 2001.

Hammer, Dean. "Achilles as Vagabond: The Culture of Autonomy in the *Iliad*." *Classical World* 90, no. 5 (1997): 341–66.

———. *The "Iliad" as Politics: The Performance of Political Thought*. Norman: University of Oklahoma Press, 2002.

———. "Plebiscitary Politics in Archaic Greece." *Historia: Zeitschrift für Alte Geschichte* 54, no. 2 (2005): 107–31.

———. "The Politics of the *Iliad*." *Classical Journal* 94, no. 1 (1998): 1–30.

———. "'Who Shall Readily Obey?' Authority and Politics in the *Iliad*." *Phoenix* 51, no. 1 (1997): 1–24.

Hansen, Phillip. *Hannah Arendt: Politics, History, and Citizenship*. Stanford: Stanford University Press, 1993.

Haubold, Johannes. *Homer's People: Epic Poetry and Social Formation*. Cambridge: Cambridge University Press, 2000.

Heitman, Richard. *Taking Her Seriously*. Ann Arbor: University of Michigan Press, 2008.

Held, David. *Introduction to Critical Theory: Horkheimer to Habermas*. Berkeley: University of California Press, 1980.

Herodotus. *The Landmark Herodotus: The Histories*. Edited by Robert B. Strassler. Translated by Andrea L. Purvis. New York: Anchor Books, 2009.

Herzog, Don. *Cunning*. Princeton: Princeton University Press, 2006.

Hirsch, David H. "Penelope's Web." *Sewanee Review* 90, no. 1 (1982): 119–31.

Hobbs, Angela. *Plato and the Hero: Courage, Manliness and the Impersonal Good*. Cambridge: Cambridge University Press, 2000.
Holway, Richard. "Achilles, Socrates, and Democracy." *Political Theory* 22, no. 4 (1994): 561–90.
Homer. *Homeri Opera*. Edited by David B. Munro and Thomas W. Allen. Vols. 1–2. Oxford: Oxford University Press, 1920.
———. *Homeri Opera*. Edited by Thomas W. Allen. Vols. 3–4. Oxford: Oxford University Press, 1922.
———. *The Iliad*. Translated by Robert Fagles. London: Penguin Books, 1998.
———. *The Iliad*. Translated by Richmond Lattimore. Chicago: University of Chicago Press, 1961.
———. *The Odyssey of Homer*. Translated by Richmond Lattimore. New York: Harper Perennial Modern Classics, 2007.
Honig, Bonnie, ed. *Feminist Interpretations of Hannah Arendt*. University Park: Pennsylvania State University Press, 1995.
Horkheimer, Max, and Theodor Adorno. *Dialectic of Enlightenment: Philosophical Fragments*. Stanford: Stanford University Press, 2002.
Howland, Jacob. *The Republic: The Odyssey of Philosophy*. Philadelphia: Paul Dry Books, 2004.
Hyvonen, Ari-Elmeri. "Tentative Lessons of Experience: Arendt, Essayism, and 'The Social' Reconsidered." *Political Theory* 42, no. 5 (2014): 567–89.
Jansen, Pamela Grande, ed. *Finding a New Feminism: Rethinking the Woman Question for Liberal Democracy*. Lanham: Rowman & Littlefield, 1996.
Kateb, George. *Hannah Arendt: Politics, Conscience, Evil*. Totowa: Rowman & Allanheld, 1984.
———. "Political Action: Its Nature and Advantages." In *The Cambridge Companion to Hannah Arendt*, edited by Dana Villa, 130–50. Cambridge: Cambridge University Press, 2000.
Katz, Marylin A. *Penelope's Renown: Meaning and Indeterminacy*. Princeton: Princeton University Press, 1991.
———. "Women and Democracy in Ancient Greece." In *Contextualizing Classics: Ideology, Performance, Dialogue—Essays in Honor of John J. Peradotto*, edited by Thomas Falkner, Nancy Felson, and David Konstan, 41–68. Lanham: Rowman & Littlefield, 1999.
Kearns, Emily. "The Gods in the Homeric Epics." In *The Cambridge Companion to Homer*, edited by Robert Fowler, 59–73. New York: Cambridge University Press, 2004.
Klausen, Jimmy. "Hannah Arendt's Antiprimitivism." *Political Theory* 38, no. 3 (2010): 394–423.
Knox, Bernard. Introduction. In *The Iliad*. Translated by Robert Fagles. Penguin Classics Deluxe ed. London: Penguin Books, 1998, 3–64.

Kohn, Jerome. "Freedom: The Priority of the Political." In *The Cambridge Companion to Hannah Arendt*, edited by Dana Villa, 113–29. Cambridge: Cambridge University Press, 2000.

Konstan, David. *Sexual Symmetry. Love in the Ancient Novel and Related Genres*. Princeton: Princeton University Press, 1994.

Kundmueller, Michelle. "On the Importance of Penelope: Transcending Gender-Based Models of Private Virtue and Political Efficacy." *Polity* 50, no. 1 (2018): 43–71.

Lardinois, Andre, and Laura McClure, eds. *Making Silence Speak: Women's Voices in Greek Literature and Society*. Princeton: Princeton University Press, 2001.

Levy, Harold L. "Does Aristotle Exclude Women from Politics?" *Review of Politics* 52, no. 3 (1990): 397–416.

Locke, Jill. "Little Rock's Social Question: Reading Arendt on School Desegregation and Social Climbing." *Political Theory* 41, no. 4 (2013): 533–61.

Lutz, Mark J. "Wrath and Justice in Homer's Achilles." *Interpretation* 33, no. 2 (2006): 111–31.

MacIntyre, Alasdair. *After Virtue: A Study in Moral Theory*. 3rd ed. Notre Dame: University of Notre Dame Press, 2007.

MacLeod, Colin. *Collected Essays*. Oxford: Clarendon Press, 1983.

———. *Homer Iliad Book XXIV*. New York: Cambridge University Press, 1982.

Marso, Lori. "Simone de Beauvoir and Hannah Arendt: Judgments in Dark Times." *Political Theory* 40, no. 2 (2012): 165–93.

McClure, Laura. Introduction. In *Making Silence Speak: Women's Voices in Greek Literature and Society*, edited by Andre Lardinois and Laura McClure, 3–16. Princeton: Princeton University Press, 2001.

Murnagham, Sheila. *Disguise and Recognition in the "Odyssey."* Lanham: Rowman & Littlefield, 2011.

Nagler, Michael N. "Penelope's Male Hand: Gender and Violence in the *Odyssey*." *Colby Quarterly* 29, no. 3 (1993): 241–57.

Nagy, Gregory. *The Best of the Achaeans: Concepts of the Hero in Archaic Greek Poetry*. Rev. ed. Baltimore: Johns Hopkins University Press, 1999.

Nichols, Mary P. *Citizens and Statesmen: A Study of Aristotle's "Politics."* Lanham: Rowman & Littlefield, 1992.

———. "Toward a New—and Old—Feminism for Liberal Democracy." In *Finding a New Feminism: Rethinking the Woman Question for Liberal Democracy*, edited by Pamela Grande Jansen, 171–92. Lanham: Rowman & Littlefield, 1996.

O'Gorman, Ellen. "A Woman's History of Warfare." In *Laughing with Medusa: Classical Myth and Feminist Thought*, edited by Vanda Zajko and Miriam Leonard, 189–207. Oxford: Oxford University Press, 2006.

Okin, Susan Moller. "Philosopher Queens and Private Wives: Plato on Women and the Family." *Philosophy and Public Affairs* 6, no. 4 (1977): 345–69.

Oswald, Alice. *Memorial: A Version of Homer's "Iliad."* New York: W. W. Norton, 2013.
Peradotto, John, and J. P. Sullivan, eds. *Women in the Ancient World: The Arethusa Papers*. Albany: State University of New York Press, 1984.
Plato. *The Republic of Plato*. Edited and translated by James Adam. 2 vols. Cambridge: Cambridge University Press, 2009.
———. *The Republic of Plato*. Translated by Allan Bloom. 2nd ed. New York: Basic Books, 1991.
Platonis. *Respublica*. Edited by S. R. Slings. Oxford: Oxford University Press, 2003.
Pomeroy, Sarah H. *Goddesses, Whores, Wives, and Slaves: Women in Classical Antiquity*. New York: Schocken Books, 1975.
Powell, Anton, ed. *The Greek World*. London: Routledge, 1995.
Purves, Alex. "Unmarked Space: Odysseus and the Inland Journey." *Arethusa* 39, no. 1 (Winter 2006): 1–20.
Raaflaub, Kurt. "Conceptualizing and Theorizing Peace in Ancient Greece." *Transactions of the American Philological Association* 139, no. 2 (2009): 225–50.
———. *The Discovery of Freedom in Ancient Greece*. Chicago: University of Chicago Press, 1985.
———. "Homer, the Trojan War, and History." *Classical World* 91, no. 5 (1998): 386–403.
Redfield, James. *Nature and Culture in the "Iliad": The Tragedy of Hector*. Durham: Duke University Press, 1994.
———. "The Proem of the *Iliad*: Homer's Art." *Classical Philology* 74, no. 2 (1979): 95–110.
Redfield, James, and Paul Friedrich. "Speech as a Personality Symbol: The Case of Achilles." *Language* 54, no. 2 (1978): 263–88.
Reeve, C. D. C. *Blindness and Reorientation: Problems in Plato's "Republic."* Oxford: Oxford University Press, 2013.
Ruderman, Richard S. "Odysseus and the Possibility of Enlightenment." *American Journal of Political Science* 43, no. 1 (1999): 138–61.
Saïd, Suzanne. *Homer and the "Odyssey."* Oxford: Oxford University Press, 2011.
Salkever, Stephen. *Finding the Mean: Theory and Practice in Aristotelian Political Philosophy*. Princeton: Princeton University Press, 1990.
———. "Women, Soldiers, Citizens: Plato and Aristotle on the Politics of Virility." *Polity* 19, no. 2 (1986): 232–53.
Saxonhouse, Arlene W. "Political Women: Ancient Comedies and Modern Dilemmas." In *Finding a New Feminism: Rethinking the Woman Question for Liberal Democracy*, edited by Pamela Grande Jansen, 149–70. Lanham: Rowman & Littlefield, 1996.
———. "Thymos, Justice, and Moderation of Anger in the Story of Achilles." In *Understanding the Political Spirit: Philosophical Investigations from Socrates*

to *Nietzsche*, edited by Catherine H. Zuckert. New Haven: Yale University Press, 1988.

———. *Women in the History of Political Thought: Ancient Greece to Machiavelli*. Westport: Praeger, 1985.

Schein, Seth L. "Female Representations and Interpreting the *Odyssey*." In *The Distaff Side: Representing the Female in Homer's "Odyssey,"* edited by Beth Cohen, 17–28. New York: Oxford University Press, 1995.

———. *The Mortal Hero: An Introduction to Homer's "Iliad."* Berkeley: University of California Press, 1984.

———, ed. *Reading the "Odyssey."* Princeton: Princeton University Press, 1996.

Scully, Stephen. *Homer and the Sacred City*. Ithaca: Cornell University Press, 1990.

Segal, Charles Paul. "*Kleos* and Its Ironies in the *Odyssey*." In *Reading the "Odyssey"*: Selected Interpretive Essays, edited by Seth L. Schein, 201–22. Princeton: Princeton University Press, 1996.

———. "The Phaecians and the Symbolism of Odysseus's Return." *Arion* 1, no. 4 (1962): 17–64.

Shanley, Mary Lyndon, and Narayan Uma, eds. *Reconstructing Political Theory: Feminist Perspectives*. University Park: Pennsylvania State University Press, 1997.

Shay, Jonathan. *Achilles in Vietnam: Combat Trauma and the Undoing of Character*. New York: Scribner, 1994.

Simonsuuri, Kristi. "Simone Weil's Interpretation of Homer." *French Studies* 39, no. 2 (1895): 166–77.

Slatkin, Laura M. "Composition by Theme and the *Mētis* of the *Odyssey*." In *Reading the "Odyssey,"* edited by Seth L. Schein, 223–38. Princeton: Princeton University Press, 1996.

Souza, Philip de. "Greek Piracy." In *The Greek World*, edited by Anton Powell, 179–98. London: Routledge, 1995.

Stanford, W. B. *The Ulysses Theme*. Dallas: Spring Publications, 1963.

Steiner, George, and Robert Fagles, eds. *Homer: A Collection of Critical Essays*. Englewood Cliffs: Prentice-Hall, 1962.

Stoneman, Richard. "The 'Theban Eagle.'" *Classical Quarterly* 26, no. 2 (1976): 188–97.

Swanson, Judith. *The Public and the Private in Aristotle's Political Philosophy*. Ithaca: Cornell University Press, 1992.

Thompson, Martyn P. "Reception Theory and Interpretation of Historical Meaning." *History and Theory* 32, no. 3 (1993): 248–72.

Thucydides. *The Landmark Thucydides: A Comprehensive Guide to "The Peloponnesian War."* Edited by Robert B. Strassler. Translated by Richard Crawley. New York: Simon & Schuster, 1998.

Tocqueville, Alexis de. *Democracy in America*. Translated by Phillips Bradley and Francis Bowen. New York: Alfred A. Knopf, 1994.

Topper, Keith. "Arendt and Bourdieu between Word and Deed." *Political Theory* 39, no. 3 (2011): 352–77.
Tronto, Joan C. *Moral Boundaries: A Political Argument for an Ethic of Care*. New York: Routledge, 1993.
Vermeule, Cornelius. "Greek Funerary Animals." *American Journal of Archaeology* 76, no. 1 (1972): 49–59.
Vernant, Jean-Pierre. "The Refusal of Odysseus." In *Reading the "Odyssey": Selected Interpretive Essays*, edited by Seth L. Schein, 185–91. Princeton: Princeton University Press, 1996.
Vetter, Lisa Pace. *"Women's Work" as Political Art*. Lanham: Lexington Books, 2005.
Villa, Dana., ed. *The Cambridge Companion to Hannah Arendt*. Cambridge: Cambridge University Press, 2000.
Ward, Ann. "Friendship and Politics in Aristotle's *Nicomachean Ethics*." *European Journal of Political Theory* 10, no. 4 (2011): 443–62.
―――. "Mothering and the Sacrifice of Self: Women and Friendship in Aristotle's *Nicomachean Ethics*." *Thirdspace* 7, no. 2 (2008): 32–57.
―――, ed. *Socrates and Dionysus: Philosophy and Art in Dialogue*. Newcastle, UK: Cambridge Scholars Publishing, 2013.
Ward, Ian. "Helping the Dead Speak: Leo Strauss, Quentin Skinner and the Arts of Interpretation in Political Thought." *Polity* 41, no. 2 (2009): 235–55.
Weil, Simone. *The "Iliad" or the Poem of Force*. Edited by James P. Holoka. New York: Peter Lang, 2003.
Weil, Simone, and Rachel Bespaloff. *War and the "Iliad."* New York: New York Review of Books, 2005.
Winkler, John J. *The Constraints of Desire: The Anthropology of Sex and Gender in Ancient Greece*. New York: Routledge, 1990.
Winn, James Anderson. *The Poetry of War*. New York: Cambridge University Press, 2008.
Wolin, Sheldon S. "On Hannah Arendt: Democracy and the Political." *Salmagundi* 60 (1983): 3–19.
Woodford, Susan. "Palamedes Seeks Revenge." *Journal of Hellenic Studies* 114 (1994): 164–69.
Worman, Nancy. "This Voice Which Is Not One: Helen's Verbal Guises in Homeric Epic." In *Making Silence Speak: Women's Voices in Greek Literature and Society*, edited by Andre Lardinois and Laura McClure, 19–37. Princeton: Princeton University Press, 2001.
Zajko, Vanda, and Miriam Leonard, eds. *Laughing with Medusa: Classical Myth and Feminist Thought*. Oxford: Oxford University Press, 2006.
Zanker, Graham. *The Heart of Achilles: Characterization and Personal Ethics in the "Iliad."* Ann Arbor: University of Michigan Press, 1996.
Zaretsky, Eli. "Hannah Arendt and the Meaning of the Public/Private Distinction." In *Hannah Arendt and the Meaning of Politics*, edited by Craig

Calhoun and John McGowan, 207–31. Minneapolis: University of Minnesota Press, 1997.

Zeitlin, Froma I. "Figuring Fidelity in Homer's *Odyssey*." In *The Distaff Side: Representing the Female in Homer's "Odyssey,"* edited by Beth Cohen, 117–54. New York: Oxford University Press, 1995.

Zuckert, Catherine H., ed. *Understanding the Political Spirit: Philosophical Investigations from Socrates to Nietzsche*. New Haven: Yale University Press, 1988.

Index

Achilles
    Arendt's view of, 7, 49, 51
    battlefield excellence of, 26, 33
    disinterest in own burial and, 55
    friendship susceptibility and, 53
    "fury" of as theme, 55–56
    future plans for returning home, 52
    honor not at forefront of desires, 14–15, 50, 51–52, 55, 57
    opening quarrel with Agamemnon, 51
    plea for return by Odysseus fails, 74–75
    postmortem glimpse of Achilles, 56
    reconciliation with Agamemnon, 54
    sorrowing over loss of Briseis, 51
    "straining to win glory" in battle, 54–55
    weeping for father's death, 69
    See also Patroklos
Adorno, Theodor, on Odysseus as "traitor to truth," 15, 117
After Virtue (MacIntyre), 2
Agamemnon
    absence of love for wife, 34–35
    Briseis taken by, 36, 51, 180
    claim of supremacy in Achilles' absence, 39–40
    death for prisoners rather than capture, 44
    discontinuing war suggested twice by, 38, 39, 47, 179–180
    efforts made to motivate men in battle, 41–42
    fate of family inconsequential to, 43, 44–45
    honor comes from leadership, 33–34, 35–36
    Klytaimestra's betrayal and, 137, 138
    lion, 37–41
    lord of men, 33–37
    love for Menelaus and, 40–41
    love of honor after death, 44–45
    love of honor contrasted to Ajax's, 36–37, 46
    "madness" as explanation for behavior, 39
    motivations of, 37–38
    Myth of Er and, 11, 15, 44, 95
    Odysseus's response to plan of, 38–39
    own daughter offered to Achilles, 43
    personal goals, 44
    shade of, 44–45
    shepherd of the people, 41–44

Agamemnon *(continued)*
  refusal to give up Chryseis, 34–36, 180
  risk-taking warrior, 37
  single-minded love of honor and, 15, 46, 179, 180
  speech from Hades in the *Odyssey*, 45
  on Trojan women, 43
  See also Klytaimestra; Odysseus
Ahrensdorf, Peter J., on Odysseus, 15, 117, 158
Ajax
  courage and commitment of, 26, 28–29, 32, 33, 46
  exemplifies love of honor, 197
  friendship and, 52–53
  love of honor and, 15, 27–28, 32–33, 46, 179
  man of few words, 27–28
  Myth of Er and, 11–12, 33, 46
  physical advantages of, 26
  praise by Homer, 26–27
  teamwork and, 29–32
  women and, 32–33
Andromache
  faithfulness of, 13
  Hektor's death mourned by, 67–68
  Hektor's devotion to, 49, 51, 61–66, 94
  as prize to mark honor of men, 180
  suffering of, 69–70, 180
  See also Hektor
animal, 4–5, 7–8, 10, 12, 25, 46, 89, 134, 175–176, 192
Antinoos (suitor of Penelope), 143, 147, 159–160, 166
Arendt, Hannah
  on Achilles, 7, 49, 51
  Christianity and, 10
  complexity of Homeric heroes overlooked by, 49, 50
  distinction between public and private life, 6, 8–9
  Homer's Odysseus is antithesis of summation of "human essence" by, 176, 188
  on Homer's *Odyssey*, 175
  Human Condition, The, 3
  influence of, 9–10
  on intimacy lacking in ancient Greece, 183, 185
  on lack of relevance of Homeric heroes, 2, 3
  Myth of Er and, 12–13
  on Penelope's virtue, 134
  on private life as futile, 5–6, 8, 10, 183
  on public pursuit of honor, 3
  on speech and the public stage, 6–7
  See also Aristotle
Aristotle
  Arendt's distinction between public and private challenged, 9–10
  Arendt's view on excellence in public pursuit of honor and, 4–5, 183
  Homer challenges virtues of glory, 46
  household defined by, 192–93
  Politics, 177, 192–94
Athena
  commands made to Odysseus upon his homecoming, 161–62
  compliments Odysseus on skillful use of speech, 195
  disguised as Mentor incites battle, 173
  flight of army stopped early in *Iliad*, 92
  praise for self-control, 195
  Odysseus plans fulfilling command of, 172

Odysseus's response to, 162–63
Odysseus urged not to regret
    violence, 191
on Penelope's mind, 138
punishment of suitors desired by,
    165, 171
unimpressed with Odysseus's
    execution of her commands, 169
warning to Odysseus to stop for
    fear of Zeus, 173–74
Wrath of Athena, The, 16
Atlanta, Myth of Er and, 11–12, 176

basileus, defined, 158, 159
bed, 2, 35, 68, 77, 112–113, 121,
    139, 145, 147, 150, 153–154,
    164, 181, 184, 187
Benardete, Seth
    Bow and the Lyre, The, 15–16
    on Odysseus's desire for knowledge,
        100–101
Briseis, 70, 78–79, 180
    Achilles's longing for Briseis, his
        "dear" prize, 51–52
    Agamemnon's assessment of, 43
    prize taken from Achilles by
        Agamemnon, 35–36
    returning of to Achilles, 39, 54
    See also Chryseis

Chryseis, 70, 73, 79
    capture of, 34–36
    as prize to mark honor of men,
        180
    value of according to Agamemnon,
        43, 44
    See also Briseis
Clay, Jenny Strauss
    on Odysseus's love of private life,
        101, 114–15
    Wrath of Athena, The, 16
courage, 2, 5–6, 8, 12, 15, 17, 19, 193

Agamemnon and, 37–38, 41–42,
    46, 50, 57–58, 60–64, 66
Ajax and, 25–26, 28–29, 32, 33,
    46
Hektor and, 58, 60, 64, 66
Odysseus and, 71–73, 84–85,
    89–90, 96, 99, 115, 134, 159,
    162, 176, 181, 183, 195
Penelope and, 46–48, 134, 139,
    141–142, 146–148, 151, 155–156
cowardice, 20, 29
    Agamemnon and, 37–38, 41
    Odysseus and, 80, 83–84, 91–92,
        99
cunning, 47, 91, 99, 110, 134, 155

Deneen, Patrick
    on Odysseus's desire for
        transcendence, 101, 114
    Odyssey of Political Theory, The, 15
Dialectic of Enlightenment (Hockheimer
    and Adorno), 15, 117
Diomedes
    Agamemnon accused of cowardice
        by, 38
    on Agamemnon's situation, 37
    domestic scene after raid, 89
    immortal honor awarded to, 179
    new battle plan proposed by, 38
    Odysseus failure to pay heed to,
        83, 181
    praise for Odysseus, 87
    takes lead during raid, 88
    See also Night Raid
dog, 2, 5, 152, 164–165, 167–168,
    175, 186
Donlan, Walter, 17, 78, 159

Elmer, David, 73
Eumaios
    Arendt's understanding of
        "excellence" and, 5

Eumaios *(continued)*
  disobedience and cruelty of, 171
  on enslavement, 5
  excellence and value of private life, 185, 191
  Odysseus's decision to free, 193
  Odysseus's reliance on, 163–65
Eurypylos, Ajax and, 31

family, 2, 5, 7–8, 14, 26, 31–32, 35, 43, 45, 50, 53, 58–60, 64–67, 70–71, 92, 94–96, 100–102, 118–120, 125–129, 133, 143, 152, 157–159, 161, 165, 167, 171–175, 181–184, 186–189, 192–193, 195–196, 198
female characters in Homer
  humanity of, 180
  pivotal, 135–36
  virtues celebrated, 17, 18, 192–93
  See also Trojan women
friendship, 2, 9, 13, 14–18, 20–21, 40, 44, 50, 52–53, 57, 63–64, 67, 69, 74, 133–135, 145, 155, 174, 181, 187, 191,193, 198
fury, 28, 36, 55, 71, 75, 84–85

glory, love of
  Achilles and, 54–55, 67–70
  Aristotle on, 46
  Hektor and, 64–65
  human price of, 67–70, 180
  Odysseus and, 80, 175, 186, 188
grief, 15, 20–21, 40, 51, 62, 67–70, 127–128, 146, 148, 162, 166, 184

Hammer, Dean, on politics in Homer, 9
happiness / happy / unhappy, 1, 8, 11, 14, 16–17, 21, 27–28, 40, 52, 54, 56, 59–60, 68, 75–76, 82, 88, 96, 107, 118, 121–122, 125, 128–129, 135, 143, 153–154, 156–159, 161–163, 165, 168, 173–175, 181–182, 186–188, 190–191, 197–198
Hektor
  burial statement of, 69
  conflicting desires of, 58–59, 65
  contrast to Achilles on price of glory, 65
  courage of, 66
  death of, 65–66
  desire for Alexandros' death (to end war), 59–60
  desire for glory and, 64–65
  example of tension between love and public honor, 67
  fear of shame and, 64, 65
  love for wife and family, 61–62, 63, 64, 66–67
  most feared of Trojans, 57
  protection of wives and children emphasized by, 60
  tribute after death of, 66
  tricked by gods, 65–66
  Trojan women urged to ask for Athena's help, 61
  uncertainties faced by, 58
  urged by Sarpedon to fight for family, 60–61
  vision of a fallen Troy and his family's fate, 62–63
  war opposed by, 59, 60
  Zeus's decree and, 57–58
  See also Andromache
Helen, 40, 59–62, 64, 80
  Penelope and, 134, 137, 139–140, 148, 150
  recovery of, 73, 94, 99, 103, 124
  return of possessions by Priam, 59–60
homecoming eve for Odysseus
  identity and story revealed to hosts, 126

initial meeting with Nausika, 128
love of home dominates story,
  126–27, 129–130
mother, Antikleia, explains
  presence in Hades, 127–28
yearning for Penelope, 128–29, 130
homecoming: Odysseus reclaims
  Ithaca
  Athena calls halt to battle, 173–74
  Athena's commands upon arrival
    in Ithaka, 161–62
  Athena unimpressed with
    execution of commands, 169
  building relationship with
    Telemachos, 163–64
  cruelty shown in punishing
    servants, 167–68
  decision to torture Melanthios, 171
  emotional turmoil over desire to
    proclaim his return, 165–67
  family reunion after suitors' deaths,
    171–72
  identity proclaimed for first time,
    168–69
  love of honor overcome in favor of
    private life, 175–76
  Odysseus after slaughter of last
    suitor, 169–171
  on Odysseus's love of private life,
    176–77
  peace settlement ends *Odyssey*, 174
  plan to restore wealth by raiding
    the neighboring islands, 172–75,
    181, 189, 190
  rage growing within him to reclaim
    home, 167
  response to Athena's commands,
    161–63
  retribution against disloyal
    servants, 170–71
  reunion with his father, 173
  suitors attacked in controlled
    manner, 167–68

Teiresias's prophecy and, 174
unsure that suitors should be
  punished, 165
visit to swineherd and, 163
warning to son to be strong in
  coming battle, 173
See also Teiresias
homecoming: Odysseus seeking
  ambiguity of desire for home, 117
  Demodokos tells story of wooden
    horse at feast, 124
  on eve of homecoming identity
    and story revealed, 126
  focus on homecoming despite lure
    of honor in games, 123
  Ithaka described and desire to
    return acknowledged to King
    Alkinoos, 125–26
  Nausikaa and steadfast goal of
    home, 121–22, 190
  Phaiakia temptations offered, 121,
    130
  return to Ithaka after 10 years of
    wandering, 117
  self-restraint shown, 124, 159, 182,
    195
  victory at discus throw, 124
  wariness of threat of pleasures and,
    122
  weeping by Odysseus upon hearing
    own story, 124–25
  See also Kalypso
honesty / dishonesty 100, 103–4, 141
honor, love of
  Achilles and, 14–15, 50, 51–52,
    55, 57
  Agamemnon and, 15, 33–37,
    44–46, 75–77, 179, 180
  Ajax and, 15, 17–28, 32–33, 46,
    179, 197
  Arendt on, 3, 4–5, 183
  Iliad and, 18, 19–20, 46, 129, 182
  prioritized by leaders, 197–98

honor, love of *(continued)*
  vs. love of private life, 10, 12, 123, 175–76, 197–98
  Odysseus and, 73, 74, 88, 110, 111, 114, 129
Horkheimer, Max, 15, 117
household, 2, 5, 6–8, 14, 16, 21, 63, 68, 111, 122, 127–128, 133–134, 136, 147, 152, 154, 156–158, 162–163, 165–166, 168, 170–171, 175–177, 181–183, 184–194, 196, 198
Howland, Jacob, *Republic: Odyssey of Philosophy, The*, 16
Human Condition, The (Arendt), 3, 15

impulse, 2, 36–37, 108, 115, 124, 129, 140–141, 148–149, 159, 162, 166–167, 173, 174–176, 181, 195
intimacy, 8, 183–184, 196
intellect / intelligence, 2, 17, 19, 47, 63, 71–73, 79, 89, 91, 94–95, 99, 115, 121, 131, 134, 138–142, 146–147, 151–152, 155–156, 159, 167, 176, 181, 183, 185, 195

justice, 1, 11, 13, 15, 17–18, 20, 51, 117, 176–177, 180, 182, 188–196

Kalypso, 103, 105
  beauty and charm compared to Penelope, 126, 130
  desire for Odysseus to be her husband, 104
  Odysseus' desire to leave and return home, 117–121
  Odysseus' "entrapment" by, 106–7, 120
  offer of immortality to Odysseus, 101

"king" in Ithaka
  "being foremost among an elite group," 161
  meaning of, 159–160
  Odysseus's role unclear, 160–61, 175
  See also *basileus*; Telemachos
Klytaimestra
  Agamemnon's disdain for, 34–35, 43, 44, 137–38
  in backdrop of the *Odyssey*, 137–38
  Penelope compared to, 134, 137, 138–39, 140
  See also Agamemnon

love of glory. *See* glory, love of
love of honor. *See* honor, love of
love of private life. *See* private life, love of

MacIntyre, Alasdair
  After Virtue, 2
  on irrelevance of emotions in Homeric characters, 13–14
  on lack of relevance of Homeric heroes, 2, 3
  passion discounted by, 25
  on Penelope's virtue, 134
marriage, 5, 16, 52, 63, 117–118, 121, 128–130, 133–135, 137–138, 141–142, 144, 146–147, 155–157, 180–181, 184, 187, 190, 193, 196
Memorial (Oswald), 51
Menelaus
  Agamemnon's affection for, 35, 40–41, 44, 60
  Ajax and, 29–31
  duel between Alexandros and, 57
  Odysseus defended by, 86
  recovery of Helen and, 94, 99, 103
moderate / moderation, 2, 12, 14, 17, 19, 21, 36–37, 46–47, 57,

84, 95–96, 99, 111, 115, 123, 140–141, 148, 159, 165, 167, 170–171, 176, 179–181, 188–193, 193, 195, 198
Myth of Er
  content of, 10–12
  contrast between Arendt and, 12–13
  on Odysseus's love of private life, 95–96, 161, 176
  pursuit of happiness and, 14
  pursuit of public honor and, 15, 36, 46
  See also Arendt, Hannah; MacIntyre, Alasdair

Nausikaa, 117, 121–22, 128, 190
Night Raid
  bath of Odysseus concludes book, 89, 91
  capture and decapitating of Dolon, 88
  central role in both epics, 86–87
  description of mission, 86–88
  Odysseus not bathed in public honor by, 90, 95
  patience of Odysseus as he sets forth plan, 88, 91, 95, 195
  See also Diomedes; Odysseus: battlefield behavior

Odysseus
  accused of cowardice (book VIII), 83, 91, 99
  ambiguity of failure to pay heed to Diomedes, 83
  appeal to Agamemnon's love of honor, 75–77
  characterization complexities of, 14–16, 71–72, 94–96, 117, 158
  as distinguished from Achilles and Hektor, 96
  excellence shown in public competitions, 90–91, 131
  fight with Lykians and, 82–83
  gifted in intelligence and speech, 91, 95
  hanging back in battle challenged by Agamemnon, 81
  honored among peers, 73, 74
  leadership failure to bring army safely home, 181
  lesser love of honor explains battle performance, 91, 95, 181–82
  loving father of Telemachos, 90–94, 181, 186
  moment of prominence in battle, 81–82
  Myth of Er and, 11–12, 95–96, 161, 176
  patient, 86–90
  physical description of on field, 80
  plea for Achilles' return fails, 74–75
  private life as preference, 12, 92, 101, 114–15, 130–31, 157–58, 176–77
  scene in book XI: final battle, 84–86
  skill at restoring social order, 73–74
  speech facilitating reconciliation of Achilles and Agamemnon, 77–80, 95
  speech to Agamemnon about leaving Troy, 92–93
  strategic in pursuit of honor, 80, 129
  trustworthiness of speeches, 72
  undistinguished as a warrior, 83–84, 90, 95, 99, 181
  See also Night Raid; Penelope; entries beginning with homecoming
Odyssey of Political Theory, The (Deneen), on Odysseus, 16
Oswald, Alice, Memorial, 51

philosophy, 9, 11, 16, 193, 197

Patroklos
  Achilles's love for, 50, 54, 57, 69, 182
  death of mourned by Achilles, 49, 51, 54, 56
  plea for Achilles to return to battle, 53
Penelope
  ambiguity of political role in Ithaka, 133, 136–37
  courage of, 146–48
  excellence of character and, 134, 137, 138, 140–41, 155
  fear of being tricked by man or god, 139–140
  on fending off suiters and remarriage, 138–39
  intelligence of, 138, 141–46
  marriage at center of homecoming, 16, 133, 134–35, 138, 156, 181
  Odysseus' longing for, 93–94, 95, 156
  relationship with husband, 13, 16–17, 151–55
  self-restraint of, 148–151, 183–84
  virtues compared with those of other female characters, 133–34, 136, 137, 138–39, 140
  virtues correspond to those of husband, 141–42
Plato, 10, 15, 18, 46, 183
politics / political, 1–10, 12, 14–17, 29, 25–26, 36, 46, 49, 59–60, 70, 72–73, 93, 95, 102, 120, 129, 133–142, 153, 158, 160–161, 171, 174–177, 179, 181–185, 188–189, 191–198
Politics (Aristotle), 177, 192
Priam, 140
  Hektor's body returned to, 56
  Odysseus described by, 80
  offer to return Helen's possessions, 59–60
  open grief for Hektor and others, 69, 184
private life, love of
  Arendt's view of, 6, 8–9, 10, 183
  Odysseus and, 101, 114–15, 175–77
  prioritization of, 12, 92, 185, 191, 196, 198
  Socrates on, 9–10, 158, 176
  as theme of *Odyssey*, 19–20, 100, 157–59
  vs. love of honor, 197
prudence / prudent, 71–73, 121, 129, 148, 162, 165–166, 175, 180, 191, 194

quarrel, 33, 39, 44, 46, 51, 69, 75, 79, 195

Raaflaub, Kurt, on meaning of *basileus*, 159
reading Homer, 17–21
  complexity of epics, 19
  Iliad: historical accuracy of, 17–18, 182
  Iliad: love of honor dominates, 18, 19–20, 46, 129, 182
  Odyssey: complex structure of, 100
  Odyssey: desire for private life dominates, 19–20, 100, 157–59
  Odyssey: as first novel, 184–85
  Odyssey: historical accuracy of, 17–18
  Odyssey: a poem of homecoming, 20, 21, 100–101, 102, 181
  literary approach to, 18
  reasons for study, 17
Redfield, James, 18, 72

Index

Republic (Plato)
  on Socrates implications about justice, 189–190
  tension between honor and private life and, 10, 12
Republic: Odyssey of Philosophy, The (Howland), 16

Salkever, Stephen, 46, 192–93
Sarpedon, 57, 60–61
self-restraint
  Odysseus and, 2, 11–12, 71, 89, 91, 101, 114–115, 121, 123–124, 130–132, 158–159, 182, 195
  Penelope and, 134, 140–141, 148–151, 155–156, 166–167, 181–184, 188
  speech, 2, 5–7, 10, 12, 17, 20, 27, 35, 37, 40–41, 43–45, 52, 54, 56–57, 60, 66, 68, 71–79, 86, 91, 93–94, 103–104, 123, 128, 134, 143, 155–157, 169–176, 181–184, 191–192, 195
Socrates
  justice defined by, 189–190
  Myth of Er and, 10–11, 15, 25, 33, 96, 156
  on Odysseus's love of private life, 158, 161, 176
  on preference for private life, 9–10, 183
  See also MacIntyre, Alasdair
Swanson, Judith, 9

Teiresias
  fulfillment of prophecy, 174, 183, 196
  Odysseus and Circe visit, 133
  Odysseus's homecoming prophesized by, 126–27, 154
  prophet of *Odyssey*, 103

Telemachos
  claim to throne unclear, 159–160, 161, 164, 175, 183
  relationship with father, 90–94, 162–64, 181, 186
  warned by father to succeed in coming battle, 173
Teukros, 30, 32, 43, 90
Trojan women, 43, 61, 62
  See also female characters in Homer
trustworthiness of *Odyssey*'s adventures, 106–107
tyranny / tyranny, 11–12, 147, 176

virtue, celebration of in Homer, 17, 18, 192–93

weep, 53, 68–69, 119, 124–125, 128, 136, 140, 144, 150–153, 163, 170, 173, 185
Weil, Simone, 50–51
wiles / wily, 17, 138, 141–142, 144, 187
wisdom, 12, 36, 78, 165
wooden horse ruse, 11, 86, 90, 94, 99, 124
wrath
  Achilles and, 32, 34, 50–51, 173, 182, 185
  Athena and, 16, 165
  nurturing of in *Iliad*, 179–180
  Odysseus and, 148, 169, 171
  Zeus and, 174
Wrath of Athena, The (Clay), 16

Zeus, 17, 30, 38, 45, 54, 57, 64, 73, 82–83, 92, 94, 103–104, 118, 146–147, 165, 168, 171, 173–174, 191, 195